Windows® 2000 Professional

Other Books by New Riders Publishing

Planning for Windows 2000
Eric Cone, Jon Boggs, & Sergio Perez
ISBN: 0-7357-0048-6

Windows NT DNS
Michael Masterson, Herman Kneif,
Scott Vinick, & Eric Roul
ISBN: 1-56205-943-2

Windows NT Network Management:
Reducing Total Cost of Ownership
Anil Desai
ISBN: 1-56205-946-7

Windows NT Performance Monitoring,
Benchmarking & Tuning
Mark Edmead & Paul Hinsburg
ISBN: 1-56205-942-4

Windows NT Registry
Sandra Osborne
ISBN: 1-56205-941-6

Windows NT TCP/IP
Karanjit Siyan
ISBN: 1-56205-887-8

Windows NT Terminal Server
& Citrix MetaFrame
Ted Harwood
ISBN: 1-56205-931-9

Cisco Router Configuration &
Troubleshooting
Mark Tripod
ISBN: 1-56205-944-0

Exchange System Administration
Janice Rice Howd
ISBN: 0-7357-0081-8

Implementing Exchange Server
Doug Hauger, Marywynne Leon
& William C. Wade III
ISBN: 0-7357-0024-9

Network Intrusion Detection:
An Analyst's Handbook
Stephen Northcutt
ISBN: 0-7357-0868-1

Understanding Data Communications,
Sixth Ed.
Gilbert Held
ISBN: 0-7357-0036-2

Windows 2000 Deployment &
Desktop Management
Jeffrey Ferris
ISBN: 0-7357-0975-0

Windows® 2000 Professional

New
Riders

201 West 103rd Street,
Indianapolis, Indiana 46290

Jerry Honeycutt

Windows® 2000 Professional

International Standard Book Number: 0-7357-0950-5

Library of Congress Catalog Card Number: 00-100401

04 03 02 01 00   7 6 5 4 3 2

Interpretation of the printing code: The rightmost double-digit number is the year of the book's printing; the rightmost single-digit number is the number of the book's printing. For example, the printing code 00-1 shows that the first printing of the book occurred in 2000.

Printed in the United States of America

Trademarks

Warning and Disclaimer

Publisher
David Dwyer

Associate Publisher
Brad Koch

Executive Editor
Al Valvano

Managing Editor
Gina Brown

Product Marketing Manager
Stephanie Layton

Acquisitions Editor
Theresa Gheen

Editor
Nancy Sixsmith

Technical Editors
Louis Columbus
Ross Yeatman

Indexers
Cheryl Lenser
Miriam R. Lowe

Manufacturing Coordinator
Chris Moos

Book Designer
Louisa Klucznik

Cover Designer
Aren Howell

Composition
Scan Communications Group, Inc.
Amy Parker

Contents

About the Author

Jerry Honeycutt empowers people to work and play better by helping them use popular technologies, such as the Internet and the Windows product family. Jerry graduated from the University of Texas at Dallas in 1992 with a B.S. degree in computer science. Prior to attending UTD, he spent three years at Texas Tech University in Lubbock, TX. In his spare time, Jerry plays golf, dabbles with photography, and travels.

About the Technical Reviewers

Louis Columbus has more than 17 years of product management, sales, and market analysis and planning experience, and has been actively involved with electronic commerce for the last five years. As Director of Market Research for ZLand.com, he leads business-to-business electronic commerce initiatives, including the definition of target markets, business development in the small business arena, competitive analysis, and investment analysis. Louis also teaches electronic commerce and the fundamentals of networking operating systems at California State University, Fullerton, and has taught at the University of California, Irvine. He serves as a contributing editor to *Desktop Engineering Magazine*, writing on topics of interest to technical professionals. Louis has published 11 books on a variety of operating system, hardware, and electronic commerce topics. He majored in marketing and information systems design at the University of Arizona and has an MBA from Pepperdine University.

Ross Yeatman has worked in the computer industry for more than six years. He is currently Assistant Director of Computing Services at the University of Arkansas, Fayetteville. One of his primary responsibilities is planning, implementing, and managing Microsoft Networking resources on the campus network. Ross has a degree in business administration with an emphasis on information systems and is a Microsoft Certified Systems Engineer.

For Travis Honeycutt, my brother
—Jerry Honeycutt

Acknowledgments

So many people worked to make a book happen, and I hope I don't leave anyone out in these acknowledgments. First, I have to thank Al Valvano, a tireless individual who knows what he is doing. Also, Theresa Gheen deserves a special nod for the amazing patience she demonstrated throughout this project.

Nancy Sixsmith, with whom I've previously had the distinct pleasure of working, did an outstanding and enviable job of coordinating, developing, and editing this book. Thank you for all your hard work. Our technical editors also did their bit of magic by checking the details: Ross Yeatman and Louis Columbus. Thanks.

Tell Us What You Think

As the reader of this book, you are the most important critic and commentator. We value your opinion and want to know what we're doing right, what we could do better, what areas you'd like to see us publish in, and any other words of wisdom you're willing to pass our way.

As the Executive Editor for the Networking team at New Riders Publishing, I welcome your comments. You can fax, email, or write me directly to let me know what you did or didn't like about this book—as well as what we can do to make our books stronger.

Please note that I cannot help you with technical problems related to the topic of this book, and that due to the high volume of mail I receive, I might not be able to reply to every message.

When you write, please be sure to include this book's title and author as well as your name and phone or fax number. I will carefully review your comments and share them with the author and editors who worked on the book.

Fax: 317-581-4663
Email: nrfeedback@newriders.com
Mail: Al Valvano
        Executive Editor
        New Riders Publishing
        201 West 103rd Street
        Indianapolis, IN 46290 USA

Introduction

Although Microsoft Windows 98 is certainly easy to use, it doesn't provide the big three *capabilities*: reliability, security, and manageability. These shortcomings made Windows 98 a less-than-ideal desktop operating system for businesses of any size. Although these *were* features of Microsoft Windows NT Workstation 4.0, it never caught up with Windows 98. It wasn't as easy to use. Plug and Play was absent. Support for mobile users and power-management features for portable computers were missing. Microsoft didn't really have anything that helped businesses reduce the total cost of owning desktops.

Combining the best of both operating systems, Microsoft Windows 2000 Professional started life in September 1996. According to Jim Allchin, Senior Vice President at Microsoft Corporation, "The mission of the Windows 2000 Professional development team was to create a mainstream client operating system that goes beyond Windows 98 in simplicity; that goes beyond Windows NT 4.0 Workstation in terms of reliability, security, and power; and that reduces the costs associated with managing networks." Windows 2000 Professional succeeds. Not only does it expand the strengths of Windows NT Workstation 4.0 but it also includes the best of Windows 98. It supports Plug and Play. It supports mobile users with features that will make Windows 98 users weep, and it supports advanced power management on portable computers. Additionally, hundreds of enhancements that pervade every nook and cranny of Windows 2000 Professional will make you say, "Wow! That's cool!" on more than one occasion. In short, Microsoft's latest adds *usability* to the big three.

Businesses will realize their biggest savings by using Windows 2000 Professional on a heterogeneous Windows 2000 network. They can take advantage of Active Directory, Group Policy, IntelliMirror, and other unique features that make managing desktops easier. Still, Windows 2000 Professional plays well on other networks, too. It fully supports Microsoft Windows NT Server 4.0, Novell NetWare, and UNIX networks. For more information about upgrading your network, see *Inside Windows 2000 Server*, also by New Riders Publishing, ISBN: 1-56205-929-7.

Name Changes

On the 27th day of October 1998, Microsoft renamed *Windows NT Workstation 5.0* to *Windows 2000 Professional*. This might be a lot easier for authors to type, but it clouds minds. Users frequently think that Windows 2000 Professional is the next version of Windows 98, which is logical because both abuse years as version numbers. After writing *Introducing*

Microsoft Windows 2000 Professional (MS Press, 1999), for instance, I received many messages asking if this product was the next version of Windows 98. If you're wondering what the company is naming the follow-up version of Windows 98, it's *Windows Millennium*. Although that name ought to keep everyone straight, Microsoft added "Built on NT Technology" as a tagline to Windows 2000 Professional, just to make sure.

The name change didn't just affect Windows 2000 Professional. It also affected what the company once called Windows NT Server 5.0. Instead of a single product called Windows 2000 Server, however, the company has three:

- **Windows 2000 Server** is the traditional product. It supports two-way symmetric multiprocessing (SMP), and is appropriate for small-to-medium businesses when used for Web servers, resource servers, and so on.

- **Windows 2000 Advanced Server** is a more advanced server product that supports four-way SMP, more physical memory, clustering, and load balancing. It's appropriate for large database applications.

- **Windows 2000 Datacenter Server** is the most powerful server product that Microsoft offers. It supports 16-way SMP, 64 gigabytes of physical memory, clustering, and load balancing. It's appropriate for large data warehouses, and online transaction processes, server consolidation, and so on.

All told, the name change makes sense and folks will get used to it, if they haven't already. It falls in line with *Microsoft Office 2000*, and confusion with Windows 98 and Windows Millennium is a marketing issue—nothing more. Although there is a question about whether this means that Windows 98 will be orphaned, according to sources at Microsoft, it will thrive as a consumer operating system for many years to come. Microsoft's gain from the name change is worth any trouble it causes, too. First, it implies a major milestone in the product, which is true. Second, it removes the stigma associated with the word *workstation*, which people associate with high-powered workstations that are far beyond their capabilities. The name *Windows 2000 Professional* says it all: It's the professional's operating system for a new millennium.

Organization and Content

I wrote this book for intermediate and advanced users, who I affectionately refer to as *power users*. These power users include administrators, who must learn the ins-and-outs of any operating system that they deploy in their organizations. Thus, not only does this book include inside information about Microsoft's latest desktop operating system, it also includes information about how to best deploy and manage this system. *Windows 2000 Professional* has four parts, in which you find the following information:

- Part I, "Introducing Windows 2000 Professional," shows you how to install the operating system on an individual computer and how to get it up and running quickly. You learn how to configure the computer's hardware and troubleshoot problems.

- Part II, "Using Windows 2000 Professional," digs into many of the operating system's new features. These chapters shy away from step-by-step instructions, unless necessary, but give you information that you won't find in the operating system's already excellent Help (or information that's not obvious in Help).

- Part III, "Networking Windows 2000 Professional," shows you the operating system's new networking features and helps you get them working on your network as quickly as possible. You learn how to use these features with Windows NT Server 4.0, as well as Windows 2000 Server.

- Part IV, "Appendixes." In the back of this book, you find a handful of useful appendixes. Appendix A is a glossary that contains terms you might not know, particularly if you're upgrading from Windows 98. Appendix B, "Quick Start for Windows 98 Users," and Appendix C, "Quick Start for Windows NT Workstation 4.0 Users," give explicit instructions for upgrading to Windows 2000 and show you where to find familiar features that are in different places. For example, Device Manager isn't in the same location as Windows 98 users expect. Appendix D, "Frequently Asked Questions" contains a list of frequently asked questions, which I've culled from beta newsgroups, messages I've received, and other sources.

Features and Conventions

Windows 2000 Professional has better Help than any of its predecessors. Because Help is so much better, it actually makes buying many books about this operating system a waste of time and money because they duplicate information that's already at your fingertips. To make sure this book is valuable to you, I don't duplicate information that's in Help, unless doing so is necessary for clarity. I've designed this book's content to supplement Help by giving you information that's not easily accessible. You don't just learn how to use history lists, for example—you learn where the operating system stores them in the Registry. You don't just learn how to run applications— you learn about the most common application failures and what to do about them.

This book uses a variety of elements to communicate more clearly. Notes, Tips, Cautions, and Sidebars provide information that's useful and applies to the passage you're reading. Tips provide hints and tricks that help you work smarter and faster. Notes contain useful information that's not essential, but is nonetheless interesting. Don't ignore cautions, which warn about actions that can damage the computer's configuration. Sidebars are detours. They give background, historical, or otherwise useful information that is relevant but not essential. I frequently use sidebars as tutorials when providing the same information in the text would hinder advanced users who already understand the information.

Keyboard Conventions

Keyboard conventions help you better understand the steps in instructions:

Hotkeys	Underlined characters are hotkeys. For example, the *V* in **View** is a hotkey. To use a hotkey, press Alt and the underlined letter.
Key combinations	A plus sign separates key combinations. For example, Ctrl+Alt+Delete means hold down Ctrl, hold down Alt, and then press and release Delete.
Dialog boxes	Instructions won't tell you to click **OK** to close a dialog box, saving your changes. All other instructions are explicit: "In the **Scheme** list, click **Windows Standard**."
Menu commands	Instructions for menus are explicit. "On the **Edit** menu, click **Copy**" is an example. So is "On the **Start** menu, click **Programs**, point to **Accessories**, and then click **Wordpad**." When instructions tell you to point to a submenu, pointing the mouse at it is enough to open it.

tip

Note that Windows 2000 has an option to disable the underlined character in hotkeys until you press Alt or Shift+F10 to display a menu. To enable hotkeys full-time, click the **Effects** tab on the **Display Properties** dialog box, and select the **H**ide keyboard navigation indicators until I use the Alt key check box.

tip

This book refers to special-purpose keys by the text that actually appears on a standard 101-key keyboard. For example, you'll see "Press Esc," "Press Delete," or "Press Enter." However, some keys on your keyboard don't have words on them. Here are the conventions used for those keys:

Backspace key

Up-, down-, left-, or right-arrow key

Mouse Conventions

The following terms describe how to operate the mouse:

Click	Click the left mouse button one time.
Double-click	Click the left mouse button twice on the same spot, quickly. With Windows 2000 Professional's single-click feature, pointing at an icon in Microsoft Windows Explorer and then clicking it does the same thing as double-clicking it.
Drag	Click an item and, while continuing to hold down the left mouse button, drag it.
Drop	Release the left mouse button to drop an item that you're dragging.
Point	Position the mouse pointer over an item. Pointing at most submenus opens them automatically after a small delay.

Typeface Conventions

This book's typeface conventions make it easier to read:

Italic	*Italic* indicates new terms. It also indicates placeholders in commands, addresses, and code. You replace the placeholder with suitable text. On occasion, I use italic for emphasis.
Bold	**Bold** represents the text you type.
`Monospace`	`Monospace` generally indicates code, but it is also the way I format registry keys and values, as well as Internet addresses.

Special Directories

Inspired by Windows 2000 Professional's environment variables, I use the following placeholders:

UserProfile	Represents the directory in which Windows 2000 Professional stores user profiles. This is C:\Documents and Settings, but administrators change the location in setup scripts.

SystemDrive	Represents the drive on which you installed Windows 2000 Professional—usually C.
SystemRoot	Represents the drive and directory in which you installed Windows 2000 professional—usually C:\Winnt.
WinDir	Same as *SystemRoot*, but I seldom use it in this book.

Registry Keys

The registry is a key part of Windows 2000 Professional's configuration. I liken it to the heart and soul of the operating system. As such, you find many references to subkeys and values in the registry, particularly when the information helps you customize the operating system or better understand how it works. To make these references easier to ready, I use the following abbreviations for the root keys:

HKCR	HKEY_CLASSES_ROOT
HKCU	HKEY_CURRENT_USER
HKLM	HKEY_LOCAL_MACHINE
HKU	HKEY_USERS
HKCC	HKEY_CURRENT_CONFIG

I

Introducing Windows 2000 Professional

1

Installing Windows

Depending on who you ask, installing Microsoft Windows 2000 Professional is or isn't easier than installing its predecessor, Microsoft Windows NT Workstation 4.0. Users with typical configurations and hardware that's on are on Microsoft's official list of compatible hardware, the infamous *hardware compatibility list*, have no problem (the hardware compatibility list is available at http://www.microsoft.com/hcl). Set up and go—those are the users posting messages to the beta newsgroups with subject lines such as "Wow" and "Smooth install." Users with atypical configurations or hardware that treads slightly outside of the hardware compatibility list report horror stories, though. These reports run the gamut between crippled devices and lost data files. Fortunately, most users won't run into any of these problems because the users on the beta newsgroups aren't representative of typical users.

Part of the problem doesn't have anything to do with Windows 2000 Professional as much as with users' expectations for the operating system's Plug and Play features. Just because it's a Plug and Play operating system doesn't mean that it provides Windows 98-level flexibility and hardware compati-bility. Dropping a no–name sound card into the computer and expecting Windows 2000 Professional to properly configure it doesn't make sense. That dog don't hunt, so you might as well get used to checking the hardware compatibility list before buying hardware. What you get out of the bargain is a real, industrial-strength operating system versus a mere toy for home users.

Installing Windows 2000 Professional is definitely easier than installing its predecessor. The early text-based part of the setup program is almost identical. The later graphics-based part of the setup program is new and much easier due to improvements in the user interface and the operating system's capabilities. Configuring a network connection while installing the operating system is much easier, for example, assuming that your network adapter is on the hardware compatibility list. The setup program asks fewer questions now, and it asks all the questions at one time so that users can wander off to a long coffee break while the process completes. Users who want the ultimate, a trip to a local espresso bar while the setup program does its thing, can create a simple script that answers all the questions while they're skimming the froth off the top of a large cappuccino.

So early in the book, and already I told you that installing Windows 2000 Professional can be a pain in the disk, but the setup program is easier to use. Both are true. This chapter helps you install Windows 2000 Professional successfully, however, the first time you rip the Windows 2000 Professional CD-ROM out of the jewel case. It gives you advice on how to prepare for the setup process, rather than installing the operating system willy-nilly. It contains step-by-step guides to installing the operating system in the three most common scenarios: upgrading an earlier version of Microsoft Windows, installing a clean copy of Windows 2000 Professional (a process I call *wipe-and-load*), or dual-booting the operating system with another version of Windows. Toward the end of this chapter, you learn assorted advanced techniques, such as using a script to automate the setup process.

Requirements

In general, Windows 2000's setup program is good about reporting incompatible hardware and software before it gets very far in the process. This is primarily true when upgrading from an earlier version of Windows, not necessarily when doing a wipe-and-load. Although Microsoft does provide you with the tools necessary to ensure that Windows 2000 professional works properly on your computer, you have to know where to look. That, of course, is the point of this section.

Make sure that you double-check the documentation on the Windows 2000 Professional CD-ROM. It has several text files that contain late-breaking information that isn't in this book or Microsoft's documentation. If nothing else, browse the Read1st.txt file that's in the root directory of the CD-ROM, but also look at these:

- **Read1st.txt**   Contains last-minute information that's not in Windows 2000 Professional's documentation.
- **Relnotes.doc**   Contains comprehensive bits of information about Windows 2000 Professional's new features.
- **Setuptxt\Pro1.txt**   Contains instructions for installing Windows 2000 Professional on a single computer.
- **Setuptxt\Pro2.txt**   Contains instructions for using advanced options such as choosing a file system.

Software

First and foremost, forget about your 16-bit device drivers; they don't work in Windows 2000 Professional. If you rely on 16-bit device drivers for your CD-ROM, scanner, or any other device, contact the vendor to get updated 32-bit device drivers. In most cases, you can get these device drivers from the vendor's Web site.

16-bit device drivers are a definite no-no, but software compatibility is a bit fuzzier. Most software works well if you install it after installing Windows 2000 Professional. I've found only one application that didn't work with the new operating system; but I don't play many games, either, which frequently choke. *Upgrade packs* help because they upgrade software so that it works properly, but many vendors are belligerently refusing to develop upgrade packs, opting to produce and charge for newer versions of their products that do indeed work in Windows 2000 Professional. Also, Microsoft has backed off on its commitment to put available upgrade packs on the Windows 2000 Professional CD-ROM, citing a lack of cooperation from software vendors. So you must check with each vendor to see whether you must use an upgrade pack. Also, search UseNet for information about using a particular program with Windows 2000 Professional, a task you can easily perform using DejaNews (`http://www.deja.com`).

Windows 2000 Professional's setup program can generate an upgrade report without putting you through the actual upgrade process. This report is applicable only when upgrading from an earlier version of Windows. It lists the software that will not work, as well as the software that requires upgrade packs in order to work properly. It also reports any 32-bit device drivers that won't work in Windows 2000 Professional, handy information if you're upgrading from Windows 98. At the MS-DOS command prompt or in the Run dialog box, type **winnt32 /checkupgradeonly** to generate an upgrade report. The result is a dialog box that looks similar to Figure 1.1.

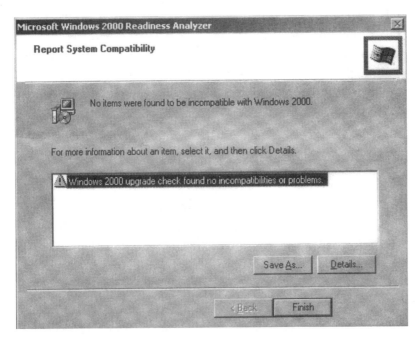

Figure 1.1   The setup program also saves a copy of this report in *SystemRoot*\Upgrade.txt.

After generating the report, do one of the following and then follow the report's instructions to upgrade your software:

- Click one of the items in the list and then click <u>D</u>etail to get more information about it.
- Click Save <u>A</u>s and then choose a file in which to save the report as a text file. Listing 1.1 shows what the report looks like.

Listing 1.1: Sample Upgrade Report

```
Upgrade Report
– – – – – –
This report describes known problems you might encounter after you
upgrade to Windows 2000. Read this report to determine the hardware
files and upgrade packs you need, then visit Microsoft on the
Internet at http://www.microsoft.com/windows/professional/, or
contact your hardware or software manufacturer.

Contents:
        General Information
```

```
General Information
— — — — — — — — —·
```

This section provides important information that you need to be aware
of before you upgrade.

```
Network Drives
```

Setup will not look for programs on the following network drives:

```
    h:\
```

```
Backup Files Found
```

> Setup found files on your computer that appear to be a backup of
> part of Windows 98. During the upgrade to Windows 2000, Setup
> removes Windows 98 from your computer, including any backups you
> may have on your hard disk. Protect your backup files by copying
> them to floppy disks, a network server, a compressed archive
> file, or other backup mechanism.

```
Windows Messaging Services
```

> Setup has detected a version of messaging (MAPI) that does not
> function on Windows 2000. Obtain an upgrade pack for your e-mail
> program, or reinstall it after upgrading to Windows 2000.

Hardware

Windows 2000 Professional's hardware requirements are bigger than those
for Windows NT Workstation 4, but not unreasonably so, considering the
amount of processing power available at very reasonable prices. Try telling
that to a company that owns 15,000 computers with 133 MHz (megahertz)
Intel Pentium processors in them. Oddly enough, home users are in a better
position to upgrade their equipment than most businesses are. The requirements? I'm going to present you with two different lists of hardware
requirements, side-by-side in the following table; the first column contains
Microsoft's official recommendations and the second contains my recommendations based upon experience:

Component	Microsoft Requirement	My Recommendation
Processor	166 MHz Pentium or compatible	300 MHz Pentium II or compatible
Memory	64 MB (megabytes)	96 MB

continues

Component	Microsoft Requirement	My Recommendation
Hard Disk	2 GB (gigabytes) with 650 MB free	2 GB with 650 MB free
Display	VGA or better display adapter and monitor	SVGA or better display adapter and 17-inch monitor
Input Devices	Keyboard and pointing device	Keyboard and wheel mouse

My recommendations might seem a bit extreme, but allow me to explain. Using Windows 2000 Professional on a computer containing a 233 MHz Pentium processor with 64 MB of memory was too painful for me to recommend to anyone. The user interface was sluggish, starting the computer took more time than I like, and running more than one program at a time stretched my patience about as far as it goes. The point at which I became satisfied with the operating system's performance was after installing it on a computer containing a 300 MHz Pentium II and 96 MB of memory. I recommend a 17-inch monitor strictly because a 15-inch monitor doesn't provide enough real estate to manage your desktop effectively. Nobody likes squinting at the monitor. Of course, use what you have to use, but if your computer just barely meets Microsoft recommendations, I recommend that you install Windows 98 and forget about Windows 2000 Professional until you can upgrade the hardware.

Windows 2000 Professional's setup program has additional requirements, beyond those of the operating system. They're different, depending on how you're installing the operating system:

- To install from the CD-ROM, the computer should have a 12X or faster CD-ROM drive. Also, if an operating system isn't installed on the computer or if you don't have access to the CD-ROM drive, you must have a 3.5-inch floppy drive in order to use the setup startup disks.

- To install from a network, the computer must contain a network adapter and have a connection to the network containing Windows 2000 Professional's source files. Also, the user must have access to the network share containing the source files.

Microsoft includes two tools to make sure that your computer not only meets the minimum requirements, but also contains hardware that's compatible with the operating system: the hardware compatibility list (HCL) and the Microsoft Compatibility Tool. The HCL, which you read about in the introduction of this chapter, describes the hardware that works with Windows 2000 Professional. You find this list on the Windows 2000 Professional CD-ROM in Support\Hcl.txt. Open it in any text editor, such as Microsoft Notepad, and even search it for brand names, devices, and so on. This list is current as of the day Microsoft shipped the operating system. The online version, `http://www.microsoft.com/hcl`, is more current and easier to search. Make it policy to always check the HCL before purchasing any new hardware but, keep in mind that just because a device isn't on the list, it doesn't mean it won't work. Before purchasing a device that's not on the list, check with the vendor to see if they provide drivers for Windows 2000 Professional.

Note

On September 2, 1999, Compaq Computer Corporation announced that it would no longer support products built on NT technology on Alpha systems. The company intends to deliver Service Pack 6 for Windows NT Workstation 4 and then cease development. No 64-bit version of Windows 2000 will ever see the light of day, much less a 32-bit version of Windows 2000 Professional for Alpha. For more information, see Compaq's Digital Web site, `http://www.windows.digital.com`.

Network

Software and hardware requirements make sense. Network requirements? You bet. If you're connecting a computer that's running Windows 2000 Professional to a network, particularly a homogeneous Microsoft network, make sure that the network is ready. Users who aren't connecting to a business network can skip the rest of this section, which I address to administrators who are installing Windows 2000 Professional for use on a Microsoft network.

First, if you're joining the computer to a domain, it must have a computer account on that domain. A *computer account* uniquely identifies the computer to the domain, just as your user name identifies you to the domain. If you're upgrading from Windows NT Workstation 4, the computer already has an account. If you're upgrading from Windows 98 or installing Windows 2000 Professional in a dual-boot combination with Windows NT Workstation 4, you must create a new computer account on the domain.

Adding computer accounts is a conundrum with no easy solution. Users must have access to credentials with administrative rights on the domain in order to add the computer account during the setup process. This opens a security hole so big that you can drive a Ford Expedition through it. One option is to create a temporary account that has just enough rights to add computer accounts to the domain. Then, after users finish installing the operating system, remove the account. If, as an administrator, you don't want to leave the fate of your promotion in the hands of users, create computer accounts in advance and make sure that users know which computer accounts they are to use when installing the operating system.

Using IntelliMirror, a combination of features that makes managing users' documents and settings far earlier than possible before, or even just roaming profiles, one key part of IntelliMirror requires that you enable roaming profiles on the network. Enabling roaming profiles also requires that you assign a home directory to each user. Instructions for assigning home directories and enabling roaming profiles differ, so consult your documentation.

Note

If you're upgrading from Windows 98 and want to use roaming profiles, make sure that the workgroup name is the same as the domain name before you start the setup program. Also, make sure that you create a new computer account and that the computer will have access to the domain during the setup process. Doing so prevents users from having to manually create their roaming profile after installing Windows 2000 Professional.

Setup Preparation

Before installing Windows 2000 Professional, you have preparations to make and decisions to make:

- Have you recorded your computer's configuration so you can manually configure devices, if necessary?
- Have you collected the settings necessary to connect to the network from the administrator?
- Have you backed up your computer so that you can restore it if something goes wrong?
- Do you want to upgrade your existing version of Windows or start over by formatting the disk?
- Do you want to use Windows 2000 Professional and another version of Windows on the same computer?
- If you want to format the disk and start over, do you want to repartition the disk to take advantage of the operating system's support for big disks?
- Do you want to convert an existing disk from FAT to NTFS, the file system I recommend you use with Windows 2000 Professional?

Although skipping these steps is tempting, spend a few moments collecting the information and performing the steps you learn about in the following sections. Those include recording your computer's current configuration, gathering network settings, and backing up your important files. In each section, I explain why the preparation is important to your success.

Record Configuration

I admit my mistakes when I make them; hopefully, you learn from them. After logging on to Windows 2000 Professional, I found that it couldn't figure out which resources my network adapter uses. Having converted the file system to NTFS, I was unable to install and run the adapter's diagnostics, the very program that I must use to query its resources. In order to unlock the mystery IRQ, I had to install the adapter on another computer, install and run the diagnostics, and then replace the adapter. This was an hour of work that I would have avoided had I recorded the computer's configuration.

Any operating system that you can upgrade to Windows 2000 Professional has an easy way to record your computer's configuration. In Windows 95 and Windows 98, use Device Manager to print the computer's configuration, including the resources that each device uses. In Windows NT Workstation 3.51 and Windows NT Workstation 4, use Windows NT Diagnostics to print similar information. Windows NT Diagnostics also prints the computer's network configuration, including the computer account, workgroup or domain name, WINS (Windows Internet Naming Service), and DNS (Domain Name System) server IP addresses, IP addresses, and other network settings.

Gather Network Settings

Gather the following network settings before starting Windows 2000 Professional's setup program:

- Computer name
- Domain or workgroup name
- IP address, if using static IP addresses
- WINS or DNS server IP address
- Other network settings, as required by your network administrator

If you're using Windows NT Workstation, these settings are available in the Network Properties dialog box. In Control Panel, double-click the Network icon and then record the settings on each tab. In Windows 98, these settings are also in the Network Properties dialog box, but they might not reflect the settings you must use to connect Windows 2000 Professional to the network. For example, although Windows 98 certainly does have a computer name, it might not reflect the name of the computer account that the administrator created for you. Checking these settings with the administrator before installing Windows 2000 Professional is a good idea.

Back Up Important Files

The most important thing you can do before installing Windows 2000 Professional is back up the computer. Do a full backup, if possible, so that you can easily restore the computer if something goes awry. As much as I'd like to tell you that installing the operating system is always successful, it just isn't so. On a number of occasions, I had to give up and restore the previous configuration because the hardware just wasn't compatible with the new operating system. *Just do it*:

- On Windows 95 or Windows 98's Start menu, choose <u>P</u>rograms, followed by Accessories and System Tools, and then click Backup.
- On Windows NT 3.51 or Windows NT 4's Start menu, choose <u>P</u>rograms, followed by Administrative Tools (Common), and then click Backup.

Other files deserve special attention, beyond including them in the full back up. These are files that you can quickly copy to a 3.5-inch disk and are handy immediately after installing Windows 2000 Professional:

- Batch files and scripts
- Scheduled jobs in Task Scheduler and AT command
- Registry customizations, exported to a REG file
- Application data in *UserProfile* and Profile files
- Other configuration files that make migrating to Windows 2000 Professional easier
- Documents and related files

A quick way to make sure that important files are accessible after installing Windows 2000 Professional is to copy your profile folder to the network ahead of time. Copy *SystemRoot*\Profiles*Name* if you're using Windows NT Workstation 3.51 or Windows NT Workstation 4. Do the same if profiles are enabled in Windows 95 or Windows 98; otherwise, copy Application Data, Desktop, Favorites, My Documents, and Local Settings. As an example, Application Data contains your Microsoft Outlook 2000 toolbar configuration, signatures, and stationery, which you'd surely miss if you didn't have a copy.

Choose an Install Type

Two methods you can use to install Windows 2000 Professional are to
upgrade from a previous version of Windows and install a new copy of the
operating system. Upgrade if an upgrade path from your current operating
system is available, if you want to replace your existing operating system with
Windows 2000 Professional, and if you want to keep your existing files and
preferences. Upgrade paths are available for all releases of Windows 95,
Windows 98, Windows NT Workstation 3.51, and Windows NT Workstation 4. Install a new copy of Windows 2000 Professional if you want to
format the disk and start over, if you're using an operating system for which
an upgrade path isn't available, if you don't want to keep existing files and
preferences, or if you want to dual-boot the operating system with an earlier
version of Windows. The differences between each method are distinct:

- **Upgrade**   The setup program installs Windows 2000 Professional in the
  same folder as the existing operating system, replacing its files but preserving as many of its settings as possible.
- **New Install**   The setup program installs Windows 2000 Professional in a
  new folder, doesn't replace the existing operating system's files, and doesn't
  use the existing operating system's settings. You must reinstall each application that you want to use in Windows 2000 Professional.

Installing a new copy of Windows 2000 Professional on a freshly formatted disk (wipe-and-load) is what I recommend to individual users when they
have the time and skill necessary to reconfigure the computer. Doing so
removes the months and years of *DLLs* (*dynamic link libraries*) and other drop-
pings left behind by programs users removed long ago. The result is a clean
system that has fewer problems in the long run.

Repartition the Disk

Windows 2000 Professional is welcomed by anyone who has struggled with
Windows NT Workstation 4's limitations. Although NTFS supports large
drives, the system partition was limited to 2 GB because a clean installation
of the operating system usually starts with a FAT16 partition, and the operating system doesn't support FAT32 at all (the next section describes the differences). Systems Internals (`http://www.sysinternals.com`) publishes a FAT32
file system driver for Windows NT Workstation 4, but that doesn't help
install the operating system on a partition bigger than 2 GB. Disk Manager
does not support increasing the size of the system partition, and most users
aren't aware that a few utilities can perform that feat, so many large disks
have a single 2 GB partition and a lot of unused space. Wow.

Windows 2000 Professional can reclaim that unused space. Because Windows 2000 Professional supports FAT32, you can create a system partition up to 2 TB (terabytes), but the practical limit is more like 32 GB. Before installing the operating system, use Fdisk (Fixed Disk Setup Program) to consolidate the disk's partitions into a single large partition. Enable support for large disks by pressing **Y** when it asks, "Do you wish to enable large disk support (Y/N)?" You can partition the disk into two or more smaller disks, but I do recommend that you stick with a single large partition so that you have room for profiles, enhancements, and other bloat-ware you want to install on the system partition. After partitioning the disk, restart the computer by using a bootable MS-DOS disk and then format the disk by typing **format c:** at the command prompt.

An alternative way to partition and reformat the disk is to use Windows 2000 Professional's Setup program. You are by no means stuck with Fdisk, which is a relief to users who find it cumbersome and confusing. The setup instructions you see later in this chapter show you how to repartition and format a disk as part of the setup process, but the process has a few caveats of which you should be aware:

- Start the Setup program using the Setup startup disks, and you don't have to have a hard disk on which the Setup program can put its swap file. That means that you can drop a new hard drive in the computer, start the computer with the Setup startup disks, and install Windows 2000 Professional on an unformatted disk.

- Start the Setup program from the MS-DOS command prompt, and you must have at least one hard disk on which the Setup program can put its swap file. You can't start the computer using a bootable MS-DOS disk, run the Setup program, and install Windows 2000 Professional on an unformatted disk. You can, during the setup process, repartition the disk as you see fit.

If you're going to run the Setup program from the MS-DOS command prompt and want to repartition the disk, do so before starting the Setup program. If you're going to start the Setup program by using the setup startup disks, you can wait to repartition the disk later.

Note

A brief explanation about the terms *FAT*, *FAT16*, and *FAT32* is in order. FAT is a generic term for all file systems that are based on a *file allocation table*. FAT16 is the original implementation, which supports disks up to 2 GB in size, introduced with early versions of MS-DOS. FAT32 is a new implementation of FAT that supports much bigger disks and uses space more efficiently.

Choose a File System

I strongly recommend that you use NTFS, particularly if Windows 2000 Professional is the only operating system you're installing on the computer. My thinking is that you should use the best file system available, given the limitations with which you're working. NTFS is the best. It has the same capabilities as the FAT file system. It secures files and has darned good file compression. It supports large disks, up to 2 TB, and performance is stable, no matter how big the disk. It's a winner and, if it sounds too good to be true, it could be if your situation doesn't allow you to use it.

You can't use NTFS on the boot partition if you're installing Windows 2000 Professional in a dual-boot configuration with another operating system that doesn't support it. You can leave the original operating system on the boot partition, however, and install Windows 2000 Professional on a separate partition that you format with NTFS. For example, put Windows 98 on a FAT32 boot partition, drive C; and put Windows 2000 Professional on separate NTFS partition, drive D. Keeping with my theory that you should use the best file system, format the boot partition using FAT32 if you're installing Windows 2000 Professional with Windows 95 OSR2 or Windows 98. Format the boot partition using FAT16 if you're installing the operating system with any other version of Windows, including the original release of Windows 95, or MS-DOS.

Table 1.1 compares file systems by showing their minimum and maximum partition sizes, maximum file size, and the operating systems that support them. Some items in this table require more explanation. First, MS-DOS, Windows 95 OSR 2, and Windows 98 limit FAT16 partitions to 2 GB; however, Windows NT 3.51 and Windows NT 4 format FAT16 partitions up to 4 GB. Second, the table tells you that FAT16 supports smaller disks than FAT32, but it doesn't tell you that FAT32 is far more efficient than FAT16 on 2-GB disks, but the reverse is true on small disks. It also doesn't tell you that Windows 2000 Professional formats only the first 32 GB of a FAT32 partition, even if it will recognize a previously formatted FAT32 partition of any size. Taking these notes into account, Windows 2000 Professional automatically formats any disk bigger than 2 GB using FAT32, even if you choose to format it FAT16.

The first time I differentiate between NTFS 4 and 5 is in Table 1.1. NTFS 5 is the latest version of NTFS and is the version in Windows 2000 Professional. It includes many new features, including data encryption, disk quotas, distributed link tracking, mount points, and more. For more information about NTFS 5, see Chapter 7, "Managing Disks and Files."

Windows NT Workstation 4 requires at least Service Pack 4 to read NTFS 5 partitions and even then, it fails on NTFS 5 partitions that use features unique to Windows 2000 Professional. For example, trying to access an encrypted file from within Windows NT Workstation 4 results in an error message that says "Access denied." Because of subtle differences between the two, don't install Windows NT Workstation 4 and Windows 2000 Professional in a dual-boot configuration on the same partition. Make sure that you install each on separate partitions.

Table 1.1 **File Systems**

	Minimum Partition Size	**Maximum Partition Size**	**Maximum File Size**	**OS**
FAT16	N/A	2 GB	2 GB	Windows 3.1
				Windows 95
				Windows 98
				Windows NT 3.1
				Windows NT 3.5
				Windows NT 3.51
				Windows NT 4
				Windows 2000
FAT32	512 MB	2 TB	4 GB	Windows 95 OSR2
				Windows 98
				Windows 2000
NTFS 4	20 MB	15 EB (exabytes)	N/A	Windows NT 3.1
				Windows NT 3.5
				Windows NT 3.51
				Windows NT 4
				Windows 2000
NTFS 5	20 MB	15 EB	N/A	Windows NT 4
				Windows 2000

Note

From this point forward, I won't distinguish between NTFS 4 and 5, unless necessary. If you don't see a version number, assume that I'm referring to the version of NTFS that comes with Windows 2000 Professional: version 5.

Upgrading to Windows 2000 Professional

Just prior to starting Windows 2000 Professional's Setup program, clean up the computer to make sure that the Setup program doesn't fail. On more than one occasion, I had to restart the Setup program because I forgot the items on this list:

- Decompress your disks. You can't install Windows 2000 Professional on a compressed disk because the operating system doesn't support any compression technologies other than its own.

- Break any disk mirrors in Windows NT Workstation 4 because they don't work properly in Windows 2000 Professional. Chapter 7, "Managing Disks and Files," shows you how to mirror disks after you install the operating system.

- Disconnect the UPS (uninterruptible power supply) from the computer's serial port. The Setup program's hardware-detection process probes each serial port. Not only does this start the UPS beeping like a smoke detector on a low battery, it confuses the operating system by incorrectly reporting information about the serial port.

- Disable BIOS virus protection, and shut down any virus scanners such as Norton Antivirus. Both prevent the setup program from working properly, and virus scanners that vendors designed for earlier versions of Windows will not work in Windows 2000 Professional.

- Disable third-party network clients and services, particularly those that might interfere with the setup program. The exception is network clients and services required to install Windows 2000 Professional from the network, of course.

- Shut down applications that are not essential to run the Setup program. These include Microsoft Windows Explorer or any other program that might interfere with the Setup program.

After cleaning the computer by minimizing the trouble spots, double-check the computer's settings, making sure that everything works properly. Check everything. In Windows 98's Device Manager, make sure that you don't see any little yellow or red icons; if you do, fix the problem. Make sure that your network connections are working properly and that you have access to the resources that you expect. Windows 2000 Professional's setup program migrates your settings from the operating system you're upgrading. By getting these settings right in an environment with which you are already familiar, you don't have to struggle to fix problems in a somewhat alien environment. In other words, pay a little now or a lot later.

To start the Setup program, you need either the Windows 2000 Professional CD-ROM or access to a network share that contains the source files. If you have or the administrator wants you to use an answer file to automate the setup process, make sure that you have access to it. Insert the CD-ROM in the drive, close the drive door, and the Setup program should start automatically. If not, start the Setup program by typing at the MS-DOS command prompt *d:\i386\winnt32.exe*, where *d* is the drive containing the CD-ROM. When the Setup program asks whether you want to upgrade or install a new copy of the operating system, click Upgrade to Windows 2000 (Recommended). A number of command-line options are available, too, which you can add to the command to control how the Setup program installs Windows 2000 Professional. This list describes those options in the Setup program's own words:

```
winnt32          [/s:sourcepath]
                 [/tempdrive:drive_letter]
                 [/unattend[num]:[answer_file]]
                 [/copydir:folder_name]
                 [/copysource:folder_name]
                 [/cmd:command_line]
                 [/debug[level]:[filename]]
                 [/udf:id[,UDF_file]]
                 [/syspart:drive_letter]
                 [/checkupgradeonly] [/cmdcons]
                 [/m:folder_name] [/makelocalsource]
                 [/noreboot]
```

`/s:sourcepath`
Specifies the source location of the Windows 2000 files. To simultaneously copy files from multiple servers, specify multiple /s sources. If you use multiple /s switches, the first specified server must be available or Setup will fail.

`/tempdrive:drive_letter`
Directs Setup to place temporary files on the specified partition and to install Windows 2000 on that partition.

`/unattend`
Upgrades your previous version of Windows 2000 in unattended Setup mode. All user settings are taken from the previous installation, so no user intervention is required during Setup.

Using the /unattend switch to automate Setup affirms that you have read and accepted the End User License Agreement (EULA) for Windows 2000. Before using this switch to install Windows 2000 on behalf of an organization other than your own, you must confirm that the end user (whether an individual, or a single entity) has received, read, and accepted the terms of the Windows 2000 EULA.

OEMs may not specify this key on machines being sold to end users.

`/unattend[num]:[answer_file]`

Performs a fresh installation in unattended Setup mode. The answer file provides Setup with your custom specifications.

Num is the number of seconds between the time that Setup finishes copying the files and when it restarts your computer. You can use *num* on any computer running Windows NT or Windows 2000.

Answer_file is the name of the answer file.

`/copydir:folder_name`

Creates an additional folder within the folder in which the Windows 2000 files are installed. For example, if the source folder contains a folder called Private_drivers that has modifications just for your site, you can type `/copydir:Private_drivers` to have Setup copy that folder to your installed Windows 2000 folder. So then the new folder location would be C:\Winnt\Private_drivers. You can use `/copydir` to create as many additional folders as you want.

`/copysource:folder_name`

Creates a temporary additional folder within the folder in which the Windows 2000 files are installed. For example, if the source folder contains a folder called Private_drivers that has modifications just for your site, you can type `/copysource:Private_drivers` to have Setup copy that folder to your installed Windows 2000 folder and use its files during Setup. So the temporary folder location would be C:\Winnt\Private_drivers. Unlike the folders `/copydir` creates, `/copysource` folders are deleted after Setup completes.

`/cmd:command_line`

Instructs Setup to carry out a specific command before the final phase of Setup. This would occur after your computer has restarted twice and after Setup has collected the necessary configuration information, but before Setup is complete.

`/debug[level]:[filename]`

Creates a debug log at the level specified, for example, `/debug4:C:\Win2000.log`. The default log file is C:\%Windir%\Winnt32.log, with the debug level set to 2. The log levels are as follows: 0-severe errors, 1-errors, 2-warnings, 3-information, and 4-detailed information for debugging. Each level includes the levels below it.

`/udf:id[,UDB_file]`

Indicates an identifier (*id*) that Setup uses to specify how a Uniqueness Database (UDB) file modifies an answer file (see the `/unattend` entry). The UDB overrides values in the answer file, and the identifier determines which values in the UDB file are used. For example, `/udf:RAS_user,Our_company.udb` overrides settings specified for the identifier RAS_user in the Our_company.udb file. If no UDB_file is specified, Setup prompts the user to insert a disk that contains the $Unique$.udb file.

`/syspart:drive_letter`

Specifies that you can copy Setup startup files to a hard disk, mark the disk as active, and then install the disk into another computer. When you start that computer, it automatically starts with the next phase of the Setup. You must always use the `/tempdrive` parameter with the `/syspart` parameter.

The `/syspart` switch for Winnt32.exe runs only from a computer that already has Windows NT 3.51, Windows NT 4, or Windows 2000 installed on it. It cannot be run from Windows 9x.

`/checkupgradeonly`

Checks your computer for upgrade compatibility with Windows 2000. For Windows 95 or Windows 98 upgrades, Setup creates a report named Upgrade.txt in the Windows installation folder. For Windows NT 3.51 or 4 upgrades, it saves the report to the Winnt32.log in the installation folder.

`/cmdcons`

Adds a Recovery Console option to the operating system selection screen for repairing a failed installation. It is only used post-Setup.

`/m:folder_name`

Specifies that Setup copies replacement files from an alternate location. Instructs Setup to look in the alternate location first and if files are present, use them instead of the files from the default location.

`/makelocalsource`

Instructs Setup to copy all installation source files to your local hard disk. Use `/makelocalsource` when installing from a CD to provide installation files when the CD is not available later in the installation.

`/noreboot`

Instructs Setup to not restart the computer after the file copy phase of winnt32 is completed so that you can execute another command.

Installing on a Fresh Disk (Wipe-and-Load)

Wipe-and-load, a smarmy term for getting a fresh start, is the process of formatting the disk and installing a new copy of Windows 2000 Professional. To do that, you need a way to start the computer so that you have access to Windows 2000 Professional's Setup program, as well as the source files. Two methods come to mind:

- **Bootable MS-DOS disk**   Create a bootable MS-DOS disk that gives you access to the CD-ROM or, if you're installing from a network share, it gives you access to the network.

- **Setup startup disks**   A set of four Setup startup disks come with Windows 2000 Professional. You can make more if you dumped them in the trash.

The entire process goes something like this:

1. Optionally, partition and format the disk, as you learned in "Repartition the Disk." You can partition and format the disk during the setup process, but in order to start the Setup program from the MS-DOS command prompt, you must provide a disk on which the program can put its swap file.

2. Do one of the following:

   - Start the computer using the Setup startup disks, which came with your Windows 2000 Professional CD-ROM. If you don't have all four of these disks, create them as you learn in "Setup Startup Disks." Choose this option if the computer has no formatted hard disks on which the Setup program can put its swap file, or if you don't have a bootable MS-DOS disk that provides access to the Windows 2000 Professional source files.

   - Start the computer by using a bootable MS-DOS disk that provides access to the Windows 2000 Professional CD-ROM or a network share that contains the Windows 2000 Professional source files. You learn how to make such a disk in "Bootable MS-DOS Disk." Choose this option if you do have a hard disk on which the Setup program can store its swap file because it starts the setup process much more quickly than the Setup startup disks. Start the setup program by typing **winnt** at the MS-DOS command prompt. "Winnt.exe," later in this chapter, describes a variety of command-line options that control how the Setup program works.

   - Start the computer by using the CD-ROM. If your computer has a bootable CD-ROM drive, insert the Windows 2000 Professional CD-ROM in the drive and restart the computer. Configure CMOS so that the computer will boot from the CD-ROM, which usually requires that you change the boot order from something like "A,C" to "CD-ROM,A,C".

3. Follow the instructions you see onscreen to install Windows 2000 Professional.

Setup Startup Disks

The package in which you received Windows 2000 Professional had in it four 3.5-inch disks called the Setup startup disks. The first is labeled "Windows 2000 Setup Boot Disk," the second is "Windows 2000 Setup Disk #2," and so on. In most cases, these disks will start the computer, provide access to the CD-ROM drive, and start the Setup program. It's a

slow, painful process, however, which you should use only if you can't create
a bootable MS-DOS disk that will provide access to the Windows 2000
Professional source files, or if you don't want to partition and format a disk
on which the Setup program can stash its swap file.

If you don't have the Setup startup disks—maybe you trashed them—you
can easily create them from the CD-ROM:

1. Grab four formatted 1.44 MB 3.5-inch floppy disks.

2. In the Bootdisk directory on the Windows 2000 Professional CD-ROM,
   Makeboot.bat.

3. Follow the instructions you see onscreen.

Bootable MS-DOS Disk

The key requirements for a bootable MS-DOS disk that you can use to start
the Setup program are these:

- Provides access to the Windows 2000 Professional source files, whether on
  CD-ROM or on the network.

- Runs Microsoft SMARTDrive Disk Cache (Smartdrv.exe) in order to
  quicken the process.

Listings 1.2 and 1.3 show the Config.sys and Autoexec.bat files that I use
in most cases. In fact, with a generic CD-ROM driver, I'm able to boot just
about any computer containing an IDE CD-ROM drive and then use it to
install Windows 2000 Professional. The Config.sys file loads the CD-ROM
device driver; substitute your own device driver in place of *DRIVER.SYS*.
A driver disk comes with most CD-ROM drives, and you can download
device drivers from most vendors' Web sites. The Autoexec.bat file binds
the device driver to the file system driver.

The Autoexec.bat file also loads SMARTDrive, a disk cache that significantly quickens the setup process. Without the disk cache, the process can
take several hours. With the disk cache, the process can take 30 to 60 minutes, depending on factors such as the amount of memory, speed of the
CD-ROM drive, and so on. As of this writing, SMARTDrive isn't available
on the Windows 2000 Professional CD-ROM (it was in a previous beta),
but you can get it from any computer that is running MS-DOS, Windows
95, or Windows 98. Be aware of one "gotcha." If you partition the disk, boot
the computer at Fdisk's request (reloading SMARTDrive in the process), and
then format the disk, SMARTDrive isn't caching the newly formatted disk.

inscrivez vos nom et adresse dans la section prévue à cette fin et conservez une photocopie du recto du billet. Les lots de 300 $ et moins peuvent aussi être réclamés auprès d'un détaillant muni d'un terminal agréé. Les lots jusqu'à concurrence de 990 $ peuvent aussi être réclamés à un casino ou une salle de machines à sous dans un hippodrome de la SLJO, et les lots jusqu'à 250 000 $ inclusivement peuvent être réclamés à un casino ou une salle de machines à sous dans un hippodrome de la SLJO sélectionnés. Les lots de 50 000 $ et moins peuvent aussi être réclamés par la poste, en envoyant le billet à C. P. 877, Sault Ste. Marie (Ontario) P6A 5N5. Tous les lots peuvent (et les lots de 50 000 $ ou plus doivent) être réclamés en personne au Bureau des prix de la SLJO, au 33, rue Bloor E., à Toronto. On peut vous demander de présenter une pièce d'identité au moment de la réclamation du lot.

Tous les lots doivent être réclamés par le porteur légitime du billet dans les douze mois suivant la date du tirage.

Questions ou commentaires? Téléphonez à la SLJO au 1-800-387-0098

Name_____
Nom

Address_____
Adresse

City/Prov._____
Ville/Prov.

Postal Code _____ Tel._____
Code Postal Tél.

KNOW YOUR LIMIT, PLAY WITHIN IT !
THE ONTARIO PROBLEM GAMBLING HELPLINE 1-888-230-3505

DÉPASSER SES LIMITES, CE N'EST PLUS DU JEU !
LA LIGNE ONTARIENNE D'AIDE SUR LE JEU PROBLÉMATIQUE 1-888-230-3505

1620 LT 030105

ONTARIO LOTTERY AND GAMING CORPORATION (OLGC)
www.OLGC.ca

CHECK YOUR SELECTIONS FOR ACCURACY
Rules, odds and other information which regulate all aspects of this lottery game, including limitations of liability and requirements for prize entitlement, are available upon request. The information recorded in the on-line system takes precedence over information recorded on the ticket, validation slip or selection slip. In communicating information regarding any lottery game to a player, a retailer is deemed to be acting on behalf of the player.

No one under 18 is eligible to participate in this lottery game.

TO CLAIM YOUR PRIZE
Complete name/address section and keep photocopy of front of ticket. Prizes of $300 and under may be claimed from an authorised on-line retailer. Prizes up to $990 may also be claimed at any OLGC Casino or Slots at Racetrack facility, and prizes up to and including $250,000 may be claimed at selected OLGC Casino or Slots at Racetrack facilities. Prizes under $50,000 may also be claimed by sending ticket to: P.O. Box 877, Sault Ste. Marie, ON P6A 5N5. All prizes may (and prizes of $50,000 and over must) be claimed in person at OLGC Prize Office, 33 Bloor Street E., Toronto. Identification may be required for all prize claims.

Prizes must be claimed by the lawful bearer within twelve months following the draw date.
Questions or comments? Call OLGC 1-800-387-0098

SOCIÉTÉ DES LOTERIES ET DES JEUX DE L'ONTARIO (SLJO)
www.OLGC.ca

VÉRIFIEZ L'EXACTITUDE DE VOS SÉLECTIONS
On peut se faire communiquer sur demande les règlements, chances de gagner et autres renseignements régissant tous les aspects de ce jeu de loterie, y compris les limitations de responsabilité et les conditions d'obtention des lots. Les renseignements enregistrés dans le système à accès direct l'emportent sur les renseignement portés sur le billet, le coupon de validation ou la fiche de sélection. Pour toutes les communications avec les joueurs au sujet des jeux de loteries, les détaillants sont considérés comme des agents des joueurs.

Aucune personne âgée de moins de 18 ans ne peut participer au jeu de loterie.

POUR RÉCLAMER VOTRE LOT
Inscrivez vos nom et adresse dans la section prévue à cette fin et conservez une photocopie du recto du billet. Les lots de 300 $ et moins peuvent aussi être réclamés auprès d'un détaillant muni d'un terminal agréé. Les lots jusqu'à concurrence de 990 $ peuvent aussi être réclamés à un casino ou une salle de machines à sous dans un hippodrome de la SLJO, et les lots jusqu'à 250 000 $ inclusivement peuvent être réclamés à un casino ou une salle de machines à sous dans un hippodrome de la SLJO sélectionnés. Les lots de 50 000 $ et moins peuvent aussi être réclamés par la poste, en envoyant le billet à C. P. 877, Sault Ste. Marie (Ontario) P6A 5N5. Tous les lots peuvent (et les lots de 50 000 $ ou plus doivent) être réclamés en personne au Bureau des prix de la SLJO, au 33, rue Bloor E., à Toronto. On peut vous demander de présenter une pièce d'identité au moment de la réclamation du lot.

Tous les lots doivent être réclamés par le porteur légitime du billet dans les douze mois suivant la date du tirage.

01-SEP-2004

$2.00

QUICK PICK/MISE-ÉCLAIR

06 17 37 40 42 49

NOT ENTERED/
NON-INSCRIT

203913

9423-0741-7634-0650
002488   039752

LOTTO 6/49 - NOW YOU CAN
WIN $5 BY MATCHING 2/6
PLUS THE BONUS NUMBER
LOTTO 6/49 - GAGNEZ 5 $
EN FAISANT CORRESPONDRE
2/6 ET LE NO COMPL.

That's because it didn't detect a valid disk when you last started the computer. You must give the computer one extra boot in order to get SMARTDrive to cache the disk or type **smartdrv C+** at the command prompt.

Listing 1.2: Sample Config.sys

```
FILES=20
DEVICE=HIMEM.SYS
DEVICE=EMM386.EXE NOEMS
DEVICEHIGH=DRIVER.SYS /D:MSCD001
DOS=HIGH,UMB
```

Listing 1.3: Sample Autoexec.bat

```
MSCDEX /D:MSCD001
LOADHIGH SMARTDRV.EXE
```

Useful Files for Bootable MS-DOS Disks

I've found that these files are quite useful to have available on a bootable MS-DOS disk, particularly when installing an operating system such as Windows 2000 Professional repeatedly (they are all available in MS-DOS, Windows 95, or Windows 98):

Attrib.exe   Useful for showing hidden, read-only, and system files such as Boot.ini.

Chkdsk.exe   Good for scanning the disk for errors prior to starting the setup program.

Edit.com and Edit.hlp   MS-DOS-based text editor that you can use to edit files such as Autoexec.bat, Config.sys, and Boot.ini.

Emm386.exe and Himem.sys   Memory managers that help make sure enough memory is available to run the setup program error-free.

Extract.exe   Utility that extracts compressed files from cabinet files.

Fdisk.exe   Primary way for you to partition a hard disk, preparing it to take a format.

Format.com   Utility for formatting a disk.

Mem.exe   A good way to check the amount of memory available after booting the computer.

More.com   Utility that displays the output of an MS-DOS-based program screens, one at a time.

Mscdex.exe   File system driver that enables MS-DOS to read CD-ROMs.

Ntldr   Blank text file that fools Windows 98 into installing on a computer without asking for a CD key or upgrade credentials.

Smartdrv.exe   Disk cache that makes the setup process go much faster.

Xcopy.exe   Utility that quickly copies an entire directory and its subdirectories to another location.

Winnt.exe

The Setup program, Winnt.exe, is in i386 on the Windows 2000 Professional CD-ROM. This program works only to upgrade 16-bit operating systems to Windows 2000 Professional. Change directories to i386 and then, at the MS-DOS command prompt, type **winnt**, followed by any of the following command-line options, as reported by typing **winnt /?** at the MS-DOS command prompt:

```
WINNT        [/s[:sourcepath]]
             [/t[:tempdrive]]
             [/u[:answer file]]
             [/udf:id[,UDF_file]]
             [/r:folder] [/r[x]:folder]
             [/e:command] [/a]
```

`/s[:sourcepath]`
Specifies the source location of the Windows 2000 files. The location must be a full path of the form x:[*path*] or *servershare*[*path*].

`/t[:tempdrive]`
Directs Setup to place temporary files on the specified drive and to install Windows 2000 on that drive. If you do not specify a location, Setup attempts to locate a drive for you.

`/u[:answer file]`
Performs an unattended Setup using an answer file (requires /s). The answer file provides answers to some or all of the prompts that the end user normally responds to during Setup.

`/udf:id[,UDF_file]`
Indicates an identifier (*id*) that Setup uses to specify how a Uniqueness Database File (UDF) modifies an answer file (see /u). The /udf parameter overrides values in the answer file, and the identifier determines which values in the UDF file are used. If no *UDF_file* is specified, Setup prompts you to insert a disk that contains the $Unique$.udb file.

`/r[:folder]`
Specifies an optional folder to be installed. The folder remains after Setup finishes.

`/rx[:folder]`
Specifies an optional folder to be copied. The folder is deleted after Setup finishes.

`/e`
Specifies a command to be executed at the end of GUI-mode Setup.

`/a`
Enables accessibility options.

Dual-booting Windows 2000 Professional

If you're not quite sure whether you want to give up your current configuration, don't. Users who aren't sure whether their programs will work in Windows 2000 Professional can install the operating system in a dual-boot combination with their current configurations so that they can use both the old and the new.

Windows 2000 Professional supports dual-boot configurations with the following operating systems:

- Windows NT Workstation 3.51
- Windows NT Workstation 4
- Windows 95
- Windows 98
- Windows 3.1
- Windows for Workgroups 3.1
- MS-DOS
- OS/2

Anytime you install Windows 2000 Professional on a computer that is already running a different operating system and you put it in a different folder than the current operating system, you're creating a dual-boot configuration. There's not much to it, really. When Windows 2000 Professional starts, you can choose to continue starting it or to start the previous operating system.

Dual-boot Caveats

Dual-booting isn't without problems, and you should be aware of the long list of restrictions placed on your dual-boot configuration:

- To avoid the possibility that Windows 2000 Professional's Setup program will clobber the original operating system's files, you should install Windows 2000 Professional on a different partition from the original operating system.
- If you're installing Windows 2000 Professional in a dual-boot configuration with Windows NT Workstation 4, each operating system must have a unique computer account on the domain.
- You can install Windows 98 and Windows 2000 Professional in any order, but you must format the boot partition as FAT16 or FAT32.

- You must install MS-DOS first and then install Windows 2000 Professional. Otherwise, the Setup program for MS-DOS destroys the boot sector required to start Windows 2000 Professional.

- You must install Windows 95 first and then install Windows 2000 Professional. Otherwise, Windows 95's Setup program overwrites the boot sector that starts Windows 2000 Professional.

- If you install Windows 2000 Professional on a computer that already has a dual-boot configuration between MS-DOS and OS/2, the Setup program configures the computer in a dual-boot configuration between Windows 2000 Professional and the operating system from which you started the setup program.

- Windows 98 and Windows 2000 Professional are both Plug and Play operating systems and will both try to reconfigure devices as you switch back and forth. This can potentially create hardware conflicts in both operating systems.

- Even though you had already installed your software in the original operating system, you must reinstall any software that you want to use in Windows 2000 Professional.

- Windows NT Workstation 4 Chkdsk and Defrag utilities won't work on NTFS 5 volumes after installing Windows 2000 Professional.

- Files that you create or save in Windows 2000 Professional won't always be available in Windows NT Workstation 4, particularly if you use NTFS 5 features that aren't available in Windows NT Workstation 4.

- Windows 2000 Professional automatically converts removable disks formatted with NTFS 4 to NTFS 5 the first time you mount them. Windows NT Workstation 4 must have Service Pack 4 in order to read these disks.

- You can configure Windows 2000 Professional and Windows NT Workstation 4 in a dual-boot configuration on the same system partition. Make sure that you install each operating system on its own partition.

- You can't reinstall Windows NT Workstation 4 on a partition after installing Windows 2000 Professional on the same partition.

Configuring Dual-boot

To configure Windows 2000 Professional in a dual-boot configuration with the current operating system, click Install a New Copy of Windows 2000 (Clean Install) when the Setup program asks whether you want to upgrade or install a new copy of the operating system. Then, on the Select Special Options dialog box, do the following:

1. Click Advanced Options.

2. On the Advanced Options dialog box, type the directory in which you want to install Windows 2000 Professional. For an error-free configuration, choose a directory on a partition that doesn't contain an operating system.

3. If you want to partition and format another disk during the setup process, select I want to choose the installation partition during Setup.

Automating Installation

Use unattended installation to completely or partially automate the setup process on an individual computer. The script that you use to automate the process is an *answer file*. As the name implies, answer files answer the setup program's prompts on behalf of users. You can use answer files two different ways. First, answer files can provide answers without allowing user intervention. Second, answer files can provide default answers, but allow users to change them. The nice thing about answer files, as opposed to other methods such as disk image replication, is that they work on different computer configurations because the result is little different from running the Setup program on each individual computer.

Listing 1.4 is an example answer file that I use to provide the Setup with program default responses, making short work of the installation process. You can use a similar answer file to install Windows 2000 Professional on your computer. Note the place-holders in Listing 1.4, which you must substitute with your own values:

- *Path*   The path in which you want to install Windows 2000 Professional
- *LocalPassword*   The password you want to assign to the local Administrator account
- *Your Name*   Your name
- *Company Name*   Your organization's name
- *ComputerName*   The name of the computer; on a domain, this is the name of the computer account
- *AreaCode*   Your local area code
- *DOMAIN*   The name of the domain to which you want to join Windows 2000 Professional

- *Administrator*   The name of a user who has enough rights to join the computer to the domain
- *Password*   The password of the *Administrator*

To start the setup program with an answer file, type **winnt /s:***path* **/ u:***answer*. *Path* is the directory that contains Windows 2000 Professional's source files, and *answer* is the path and name of the answer file.

Listing 1.4: Sample Answer File

```
[Data]
    MsDosInitiated="0"
    UnattendedInstall="Yes"
[Unattended]
    UnattendMode=FullUnattended
    OemSkipEula=Yes
    OemPreinstall=No
    TargetPath=path
[GuiUnattended]
    AdminPassword=LocalPassword
    OEMSkipRegional=1
    TimeZone=20
    OemSkipWelcome=1
[UserData]
    FullName="Your Name"
    OrgName="Company Name"
    ComputerName=ComputerName
[Display]
    BitsPerPel=32
    Xresolution=1280
    YResolution=1024
    Vrefresh=72
[TapiLocation]
    CountryCode=1
    Dialing=Tone
    AreaCode=AreaCode
[RegionalSettings]
    LanguageGroup=1
[Branding]
    BrandIEUsingUnattended=No
[URL]
    AutoConfig=0
[Proxy]
    Use_Same_Proxy=0
[GuiRunOnce]
```

```
[Identification]
    JoinDomain=DOMAIN
    DomainAdmin=Administrator
    DomainAdminPassword=Password
[Networking]
    InstallDefaultComponents=Yes
```

Setup Manager

You can create answer files by hand, which you learn about later in this chapter, or you can use Microsoft Setup Manager, which is part of *Windows 2000 Resource Kit* (Microsoft Press). After answering each of Setup Manager's questions, you're left with a text file called Unattend.txt, the answer file, and a batch file called Unattend.bat that starts the setup program with the answer file. The following section describes the format of this file, and "Answer File Parameters" gives you more details about the parameters available in them.

Unattend.bat includes a command that looks like winnt[32] /unattend:*answerfile* /s:*source*. This is the same command that you'd use to run the Setup program with an answer file. The option /unattend indicates the path and file name of the answer file. The option /s indicates the path of Windows 2000 Professional's source files, and the /syspart option specifies where to copy the boot and temporary files, and marks that drive as active.

Answer files look like Setup Information (INF) or Configuration Settings (INI) files. Each contains multiple sections and within each section are numerous items. Each item is a parameter that describes how you want to install Windows 2000 Professional. Listing 1.4 showed an example of a typical answer file. This answer file provides enough information that the Setup program can install the operating system with no intervention. The first section, [Unattended], specifies to install with no user intervention and sets the installation folder to Windows on the system partition. The remaining sections provide answers to questions that the Setup program normally asks, such as an administrator password, time zone, product ID, and computer name. "Answer File Parameters," later in this chapter, describes the purpose of all the parameters you see in this answer file.

Disk Image Replication

As the term implies, *disk image replication* allows you to clone a configuration on multiple computers. This process is the most powerful way to propagate Windows 2000 Professional and is the method that OEMs use to install the operating system on their computers. You install Windows 2000 Professional on a *reference computer* and then use System Preparation Utility (*Sysprep*) to prepare an image of the computer's disk for duplication. *Sysprep* comes with *Windows 2000 Resource Kit* (MSPress, 2000). The method you use to clone the configuration to other computers depends on the tools available to you:

- Duplicate the disk to another disk.
- Distribute the disk image on a network share.
- Distribute the disk image on a bootable CD-ROM.
- Distribute the disk image on a tape.

The only problem with disk image replication is that it works only with computers that have almost identical configurations. Of course, OEMs that are installing Windows 2000 Professional on a line of computers meet this requirement. If you want to replicate the operating system from one computer to another computer that has a different system board, you're out of luck; consider using an answer file to automate the setup process.

The reference computer is the computer containing the configuration that you want to replicate. To prepare the reference computer, install Windows 2000 Professional on it. Then, customize the computer to your requirements, install any applications that you also want to replicate, and configure the operating system to run any post-setup scripts or programs that you want to run the first time users log on to the computer. After you configure the reference computer, use *Sysprep* to prepare the disk image for distribution. The following list describes *Sysprep*:

Syntax: **Sysprep.exe [/quiet] [/nosidgen] [/pnp] [/reboot]**

Options:

`/quiet`	Runs *Sysprep* without displaying any messages and no intervention.
`/nosidgen`	Runs *Sysprep* without generating a new SID. This option is useful only if you're not cloning the computer but are preparing it for end users.
`/pnp`	Causes Windows 2000 Professional to redetect devices on reboot.
`/reboot`	Reboots the computer when finished.

Here's how to distribute the disk image you created using *Sysprep*:

- Put the disk image on a bootable CD-ROM. Users start the computer using the CD-ROM.
- Create a network share and copy the disk image to it. Users access the network share using a network boot disk.
- Replicate the disk using a disk duplication utility. The installation process begins when users start the computer.

When users start a computer that contains a disk created using *Sysprep*, or when they install a disk image from the network or a bootable CD-ROM, the first thing they see is a mini-setup program that configures the computer. The mini-setup program prompts users for and changes settings that are unique from computer to computer. For example, it prompts users for their name, administrator password, and network configuration. It creates a unique security identifier (SID) for the computer and adds an account for the computer to the domain. Just as with unattended installation, you can create an answer file to script answers to the mini-setup program's prompts. From beginning to end, users are ready to log on to the computer within a few minutes.

2

Troubleshooting Setup

THIS IS ONLY THE SECOND CHAPTER in *Inside Windows 2000 Professional*, and you're already reading about troubleshooting. I've got a good reason for putting this chapter here. Although many people have no problem installing Microsoft Windows 2000 Professional, many do have trouble. Often, the kinds of problems that users have are simply a matter of education. For example, you must log on to the computer as a member of the Administrators group in order to change many per-computer settings. Other times, real problems occur and solutions are available. Few users will avoid all of these problems; thus, the reason for a troubleshooting chapter so early in this book.

This chapter does not describe any sort of methodology. It presents problems I've observed, and offers solutions or, at the very least, answers. These are problems that you're likely to encounter during the setup process and immediately after it. Thus, the point of this chapter is to get you up-and-running as quickly as possible. Other chapters in this book offer more specific troubleshooting help for specific parts of Windows 2000 Professional, by the way. For example, Chapter 3, "Configuring Hardware," describes in more detail how to troubleshoot devices, and Chapter 5, "Installing Applications," shows how to troubleshoot applications. These are the two biggest areas where users tend to have trouble.

I've organized this chapter in the order in which you're likely to see problems occur. The setup process is first, followed by starting Windows

2000 Professional, logging on to the operating system, and configuring it. This chapter closes with information about additional sources of troubleshooting help, such as the operating system's extensive troubleshooting wizards and System Information. If you're using an earlier version of Windows and you don't find answers to questions here, take a look at the quick start appendixes: Appendix B, "Quick Start for Windows 98 Users," and Appendix C, "Quick Start for Windows NT 4.0 Users." These quick start appendixes show users how to use features that are new to them.

Windows Installation

For most users, the Setup program doesn't fail. When it does fail, troubleshooting the problem is so frustrating that you might feel like giving up. Don't—because Windows 2000 Professional is worthy of a good effort.

When installing Windows 2000 Professional on ACPI-based computers, BIOS problems are the most common reasons that the setup process fails. More specifically, some ACPI (Advanced Configuration and Power Interface) BIOSes are incompatible with the operating system. These problems usually cause the text-mode phase of the setup process to fail, never allowing the process to move on into the graphical, Windows 2000 Professional phase. The setup program uses a list of good BIOSes to determine whether the operating system should use ACPI, but some BIOSes slip through the cracks and the setup program enables ACPI, even if it won't work properly on that computer.

Steps for resolving this problem on ACPI-based computers include the following:

1. Check for an updated ACPI BIOS from your computer's manufacturer. Often, an updated BIOS will alleviate many installation problems. In some rare cases, you might have to exchange your system board for a more recent version that does work properly with Windows 2000 Professional.

2. Double-check to see that your computer is in Microsoft's Hardware Compatibility List (HCL) in the ACPI section. The hardware compatibility list is on the CD-ROM in Support\Hcl.txt. Also, find a more up-to-date version at http://www.microsoft.com/hcl. If your computer isn't on the list, prevent the Setup program from enabling ACPI.

Some ACPI-based computers just aren't compatible with Windows 2000 Professional. Short of upgrading the computer's BIOS, you can get instant relief by disabling ACPI. The best way to disable ACPI is to do so using the BIOS. This ensures that devices don't wrongly assume that the operating system is using ACPI. Most ACPI BIOSes have an option that allows you to disable ACPI. I've successfully installed Windows 2000 Professional on a few incompatible computers after disabling ACPI in the BIOS. On the computers that don't have such an option, prevent the Setup program from using the ACPI HAL (Hardware Abstraction Layer) when you run the Setup program. During the text-mode phase of the setup process, press F5 at the Setup is inspecting your computer's hardware configuration screen. You have a small window of opportunity to press F5, so react quickly.

If you miss your chance, abort and restart the Setup program. Choose the HAL that's most appropriate for your computer, other than any of the ACPI HALs. For what it's worth, beta testers frequently refer to this process as *F5'ing* the setup process. Alternatively, change Txtsetup.sif, which is in i386 on the CD-ROM, to prevent the Setup program from enabling ACPI. To do so, you must either burn a new CD-ROM or create an installation folder on the network or somewhere in the computer's file system. Search for and change ACPIEnable to 0.

Ensure that no ISA device is using IRQ 9. ACPI uses this IRQ for PCI IRQ steering, and allowing an ISA device to use it creates an IRQ conflict. Either reconfigure the device so it uses a different IRQ or try reserving IRQ 9 for ISA devices using the BIOS.

Other problems that prevent you from installing Windows 2000 Professional aren't caused by ACPI incompatibilities; they are caused by good old-fashioned resource conflicts. In fact, mixing PCI and ISA devices is the second biggest cause for the setup process failing, after incompatible ACPI BIOSes. The operating system doesn't have a reliable mechanism for learning ISA devices' resource settings, causing resource conflicts when it tries to configure PCI devices. The easiest solution, assuming that you know what resources each ISA device uses, is to reserve those resources in the BIOS, preventing the operating system from allocating those resources to PCI devices. The next solution is to remove all ISA devices from the computer until after you install Windows 2000 Professional.

After installing the operating system, use Device Manager to determine what resources are available, and reconfigure your ISA devices to use those resources. If you lost a device's manual and don't know how to reconfigure it, check the independent hardware vendor's (IHV's) Web site or find help using DejaNews, http://www.deja.com.

The third most common reason that the setup program fails is that it might be using incorrect mass-storage device drivers, or your computer's mass-storage devices might be configured incorrectly. The first is common for system boards that are new relative to the release of Windows 2000

Professional that you're using. Most system boards come with disks that contain mass-storage device drivers, though, and you install those drivers early in the setup process. During the text-mode phase of the setup process, press F6 at the Setup is inspecting your computer's hardware configuration screen. Choose a mass-storage device driver from the list or use the device driver that came with your system board. You can also download a mass-storage device driver from the system board's manufacturer and create a disk containing them. The second case is when SCSI devices are configured incorrectly. Check to make sure you don't have any other SCSI devices, such as scanners and removable drives, attached to them and that you've properly terminated the SCSI bus.

Setup Files Are Missing

I had an annoying problem that I reported to Microsoft on a few occasions, and the company's testers insisted they couldn't produce it. After the first boot, the Setup program reported it was missing the installation files.

After digging around, I found that the Setup program created an erroneous Boot.ini file, which is in the root directory of the system partition and contains settings that the boot loader uses to find operating systems. The Setup program misidentified my disks as SCSI disks and wrote `scsi(0)` to this file instead of `multi(0)`. The solution was to start the computer using an MS-DOS disk and then edit Boot.ini to change `scsi(0)` to `multi(0)`. In order to edit this file, you must remove the system and hidden attributes from it and use a text-mode text editor such as the one that comes with MS-DOS. Thus, when you create your bootable MS-DOS diskette, put a copy of Attrib.exe and Edit.exe on it.

See also

- Chapter 3, "Configuring Hardware," for more information about ACPI BIOSes and how the Setup program determines whether a BIOS is compatible with Windows 2000 Professional.

Using the SafeMode Option

The Setup program might stop responding when upgrading from Microsoft Windows 98 to Windows 2000 Professional. This typically occurs during the first part of the setup process, when the Setup program examines the computer's configuration. Using the SafeMode option, the Setup program logs its progress so the next time you run the program, it skips the process that caused the failure. The whole process requires that you run the Setup program three times (you might have to run the Setup program more than three times if more than one process causes the program to fail):

1. Run the Setup program and it fails.

2. Run the Setup program with the SafeMode option, and it fails, creating Setupact.log in *SystemRoot*.

3. Run the Setup program with the SafeMode option, and it uses Setupact.log to avoid the failure.

To use the SafeMode option, start the Setup program using the following command: **winnt32.exe /#u:SafeMode**.

Debugging the Setup Process

During the setup process, failures can occur that don't have easy explanations. If you have access to Microsoft Developers Network (MSDN), you can use checked versions of Migisol.exe to create debug logs that might be useful for locating the problem:

1. Copy the checked version of Migisol.exe to the i386 folder on the installation folder, which must be on a network share or stored locally.

2. Copy the checked version of W95upg.dll to i386\win9Xupg on the installation folder.

3. Create an answer file (call it **Debug.inf**) that contains the lines in Listing AD.1.

4. Run the Setup program using the following command: **winnt32.exe /#u:dolog**.

The Setup program creates two log files, both in the root directory of the system partition. Debug9x.log contains information about the Windows98 phase of the setup process, and Debugnt.log contains information about the Windows 2000 Professional phase of the process. In these files, you find information about hardware detection and compatibility, results of any upgrade packs, and other information relating to the upgrade process. These log files very well might indicate the reason that the Setup program failed.

Listing 2.1 **Debug.inf**

```
[debug]
Debug=0
KeepTempFiles=1
GuiModePause=0
Default Override=POPUP
```

Uninstalling Windows 2000

After the Setup program starts the Windows 2000 Professional phase of the setup process, all bets are off. You can no longer abort the installation, and you can't uninstall Windows 2000 Professional to restore the operating system that you're upgrading.

When upgrading to Windows 2000 Professional, the Setup program wipes out the previous operating system. During the first phase of the setup process, the Setup program migrates settings and files from the existing operating system. During the second phase of the setup process, the Setup program migrates those settings and files back into Windows 2000 Professional. Thus, it leaves few of the previous operating system's artifacts laying around, and there is certainly not enough left to restore it.

If you think for a moment that you might want to remove Windows 2000 Professional, back up the computer before starting the Setup program. The easiest way to back up the computer is to back it up to tape or some other mass storage device, such as a ZIP disk. Alternatively, if you want to try this new operating system without risking your current configuration, install it in a dual-boot configuration with your previous operating system.

See also
- Chapter 1, "Installing Windows," to learn more about installing Windows 2000 Professional in a dual-boot configuration.

Dual-Boot Configuration

Here's a checklist for troubleshooting dual-boot configurations between Windows 2000 Professional and earlier versions of Windows:

- **Earlier versions of Windows won't start** The system partition must use FAT, not NTFS. This is the only file system in common between Windows 2000 Professional and versions of Windows other than Microsoft Windows NT Workstation.

- **All operating systems in a dual-boot configuration are unstable** You must install each operating system on its own partition. Don't try installing Windows 98 and Windows 2000 Professional on the same volume, for example, because this can cause the operating systems to share incompatible files.

- **Windows NT Workstation 4.0 can't read NTFS volumes after installing Windows 2000 Professional** NTFS 5 introduces many new features, and Windows 2000 Professional upgrades all NTFS volumes it finds to NTFS 5 after you install it. Unfortunately, NTFS 5 is not completely compatible with NTFS 4. Thus, you must install Service Pack 4 or greater in Windows NT Workstation 4.0 *prior* to installing Windows 2000 Professional in a dual-boot configuration.

- **You can no longer start Windows 2000 Professional after installing MS-DOS or Microsoft Windows 95** Neither operating system is aware of dual-boot configurations, so you must install both *before* installing Windows 2000 Professional. If you already installed MS-DOS or Windows 95 after installing Windows 2000 Professional, use the repair process, which you learn about later in this chapter, to restore it.

- **Devices no longer work in Windows 2000 Professional after starting Windows 98**   Windows 95 and Windows 98 might reconfigure devices when you run them, and Windows 2000 Professional won't be aware of these changes. This can cause Windows 2000 Professional to assume that the device's configuration has not changed, even though it has. Try using Device Manager to rescan the computer's configuration, which you learn about in Chapter 3, "Configuring Hardware."

- **Applications aren't available in all operating systems**   You must install any applications you want to use in all operating systems under which you want to use them. Each operating system is a separate entity, requiring you to repeat the installation in each operating system.

See also

- Chapter 3, "Configuring Hardware," to learn how to force Windows 2000 Professional to rescan the computer for configuration changes.
- Chapter 1, "Installing Windows," to learn how to install Windows 2000 Professional in a dual-boot configuration with earlier versions o f Windows.

Starting Windows

When Windows 2000 Professional refuses to start, troubleshooting becomes a nefarious process. Because the operating system can't start, you don't have access to many of the troubleshooting tools that it provides. Still, a number of options are available that can help get your computer running in these cases. Mind you, if you've installed a new copy of the operating system, try reinstalling the operating system before sitting down for a painful debugging session; you don't have much to lose. If you upgraded from an earlier version of Windows and Windows 2000 Professional won't start, you probably care a great deal about the files you might lose, so use the tools that you learn about in this section to get things up-and-running again.

If you previously started Windows 2000 Professional and now it won't start due to a change you made during your last session, restoring the Last Known Good Configuration might be just the ticket. For example, if you installed a new device driver and now the operating system won't start, you can restore the Last Known Good Configuration, which restores the operating system's configuration the way it was before you installed the device driver. Did you accidentally disable a service that the operating system requires to start? Restore the Last Known Good Configuration. This nifty capability doesn't restore per-user settings, software settings, or any settings that aren't part of a control set—a portion of the registry that contains hardware and operating settings. Look in the registry at HKLM\System. The Select subkey contains values that define the current control set, the default control set, the control set that last failed, and the last known good control set. Here's how to restore the Last Known Good Configuration:

1. Start the computer.

2. When you see Starting Windows at the bottom of the screen, press F8 to display the Windows 2000 Advanced Options menu.

3. On the Windows 2000 Advanced Options menu, choose Last Known Good Configuration.

4. On the Hardware Profile/Configuration Recovery menu, choose the configuration you want to use.

   If you're using a desktop computer, you're likely to see a single item called Profile 1. If you're using a mobile computer, however, you might see two different items: docked and undocked. Choose whichever option is appropriate.

Windows 2000 Professional has new features that help you troubleshoot problems that keep the operating system from starting properly: Safe Mode and Recovery Console. Windows 2000 Professional uses an Emergency Repair Process that's similar to earlier versions of Windows NT Workstation, but its usefulness is limited if you can't start the operating system after installing it, because you must be able to start the operating system in order to create an Emergency Repair Disk (ERD). To create an ERD, use Microsoft Windows Backup, which you will learn about in Chapter 7, "Managing Disks and Files."

Safe Mode

Safe Mode in Windows 2000 Professional is similar to the same feature in Windows 98. It starts the computer with a minimum of device drivers and services. With Safe Mode, you can start the operating system when a device driver prevents it from starting normally. Keep in mind that most devices (other than the keyboard, mouse, and display adapter) won't work properly while running the operating system in Safe Mode. To start in Safe Mode, restart the computer and, when you see Starting Windows, press F8; then choose one of the following options from the Windows 2000 Advanced Options menu:

- **Safe Mode**   Starts Windows 2000 Professional with a minimum set of drivers and services, and doesn't provide support for network connections.

- **Safe Mode with Networking**   Similar to Safe Mode, but also includes support for network connections.

- **Safe Mode with Command Prompt**   Starts Windows 2000 Professional, but displays the command prompt instead of the desktop and taskbar.

- **Enable Boot Logging**   Logs the drivers and services that Windows 2000 Professional loads or can't load as it boots. It stores the log in a file called Ntbtlog.txt in *SystemRoot*.

- **Enable VGA Mode**   Starts Windows 2000 Professional with the basic VGA driver, which is useful if your faulty display driver is preventing the operating system from starting properly.

- **Last Known Good Configuration**   Restores portions of the registry that the operating system saved the last time Windows 2000 Professional shut down, which is useful if a new device driver prevents the operating system from starting normally.

- **Directory Service Restore Mode**   Restores the SYSVOL directory and the directory service on a Domain Controller (Windows 2000 Server Domain Controllers only).

- **Debugging Mode**   Starts Windows 2000 Professional, but sends debugging information through a serial cable to another computer.

Note

Safe Mode is not useful if one of the devices in the minimum configuration fails. Failing keyboard device drivers will prevent Windows 2000 Professional from starting in Safe Mode. If you're not able to start the operating system in Safe Mode, use Recovery Console, which you will learn about in the next section, to attempt repairing the operating system.

Recovery Console

One of Windows NT Workstation's age-old problems has been that once you change the boot partition's file system to NTFS, you cannot access it from MS-DOS. Thus, creating a bootable MS-DOS disk with which you can examine the file system and repair the operating system was not an option. You couldn't even boot the computer to MS-DOS in order to recover files off the dead volume. Winternals Software, http://www.winternals.com, publishes a utility that allows you to get files off a dead NTFS volume.

Windows 2000 Professional partly goes further with Recovery Console, however. You can start the computer using Recovery Console, which provides commands that you can use to disable services, repair a damaged system volume, or even replace missing system files. It provides limited access to the computer, however, preventing you from copying files to removable drives and restricting you to files in *SystemRoot*. Even though you can't use Repair Console to recover files, you can use it to copy files from a removable disk to any location in *SystemRoot*.

Without planning ahead, the only way to start Recovery Console is via the Setup program. Start the Setup program from boot disks or the Windows 2000 Professional CD-ROM. When the program asks if you want to install Windows 2000 Professional or repair an installation, press **R** to repair an installation, and choose to start Recovery Console. You must log on to Recovery Console using the local Administrator account and password (the Setup program prompted you for the password of the local Administrator account when you installed the operating systems).

Recovery Console supports a limited number of commands. Type **help** at Recovery Console's command prompt to learn more about them, most of which work similarly to the same commands in MS-DOS:

- **Attrib** Changes a file or directory's attributes.
- **Batch** Executes a batch file.
- **Cd** (**Chdir**) Changes directories or displays the name of the current directory.
- **Chkdsk** Scans the disk for errors and optionally repairs errors on the disk.
- **Cls** Clears the screen.
- **Copy** Copies a single file to another directory.
- **Del** (**Delete**) Deletes one or more files.
- **Dir** Displays the contents of a directory.
- **Disable** Disables a service or device driver.
- **Diskpart** Manages partitions on the disk.
- **Enable** Starts a service or device driver.
- **Exit** Exits Recovery Command Console and restarts the computer.
- **Expand** Extracts a file from a compressed file.
- **Fixboot** Writes a new partition boot sector on the system partition.
- **Fixmbr** Repairs the master boot record on the partition boot sector.
- **Format** Formats a disk.

- **Help**   Displays a list of commands that Recovery Command Console supports.
- **Listsvc**   Lists the services available on the computer.
- **Logon**   Logs on to Windows 2000.
- **Map**   Displays drive letter mappings.
- **Md (Mkdir)**   Creates a directory.
- **More**   Displays a text file one page at a time.
- **Ren (Rename)**   Renames a single.
- **Rd (Rmdir)**   Removes a directory.
- **Set**   Displays a list of environment variables or sets an environment variable.
- **Systemroot**   Changes to the root of the Windows 2000 installation to which you're logged on.
- **Type**   Displays a text file.

If you want to make Recovery Console more accessible, install it as a choice in the list of available operating systems. This is like installing Recovery Console and Windows 2000 Professional in a dual-boot configuration, except that you install both on the same partition. This makes Recovery Console available as an operating system each time you start the computer. To install Recovery Console, use the following command to run the Setup program: **winnt32.exe /cmdcons**.

Options in Boot.ini

Boot.ini is a file in the root directory of the system partition that describes the operating systems you can choose and any options that apply to them. The lists of operating systems that you see when you start computers in dual-boot configurations result from this file. Listing 2.2 shows a typical Boot.ini file.

Listing 2.2: **Boot.ini**

```
[boot loader]
timeout=30
default=multi(0)disk(0)rdisk(0)partition(1)\WINDOWS
[operating systems]
multi(0)disk(0)rdisk(0)partition(1)\WINDOWS="Microsoft Windows 2000 Professional"
/fastdetect /SOS
C:\CMDCONS\BOOTSECT.DAT="Microsoft Windows 2000 Recovery Console" /cmdcons
```

Boot.ini supports options that might help you figure out why Windows 2000 Professional won't start. If the system partition uses the FAT file system, edit Boot.ini by using a text-based editor after starting the computer with MS-DOS. Also, if the system partition uses the NTFS file system, you must start another copy of Windows 2000 Professional or Windows NT Workstation 4.0 with Service Pack 3 in order to edit Boot.ini. In either case, you must reset the file's system and hidden attributes in order to edit it. In Listing 2.2, the first item under [operating systems] indicates the location o f Windows 2000 Professional. It includes two options: /fastdetect and /sos. You learn about these two options and a few others that are useful for troubleshooting why the operating system doesn't start in the following list:

/BASEVIDEO	Starts Windows 2000 Professional using the standard VGA display driver. This option is useful if, after installing a new video device driver, the operating system doesn't start properly.
/MAXMEM:*N*	Sets the maximum amount of memory that Windows 2000 Professional will use. This option is useful if you suspect a memory chip is damaged.
/NUMPROC=*N*	Sets the maximum number of processors that Windows 2000 Professional will use on a multiprocessor computer.
/FASTDETECT=COM*x*	Prevents Windows 2000 Professional from searching the serial ports for a mouse. Use this option if you have no mouse connected to a serial port. Using /FASTDETECT alone prevents the operating system from looking for a mouse on any serial port.
/SOS	Displays the names of device drivers that Windows 2000 Professional loads as it loads them. This option is useful for figuring out which device driver is failing.

Using Windows 2000 Professional

Configuring Hardware

3

MICROSOFT WINDOWS 98 GIVES USERS AMPLE CHOICES of hardware. Two reasons are the market's expectations and its size. The market, of course, contains consumers who use computers not for business, but at home. They play games, they use the Internet, and they entertain their children. They expect the operating system to support a plethora of devices, and Microsoft delivers. Because the market is so large, independent hardware vendors tend to focus first on Windows 98 device drivers and frequently neglect other business-oriented operating systems. And Microsoft made device drivers easy to develop for Windows 98 versus its other operating systems, providing further impetus for independent hardware vendors (IHVs) to focus their efforts on Windows 98.

Contrast that with Microsoft Windows NT Workstation 4.0, which is undeniably better suited to business than home entertainment. Businesses have simpler requirements: network-connected computers that support the devices users require for doing their jobs: displays, keyboards, pointing devices, and so on. Seldom does that mean they need the latest 3D gaming card. And recent demand isn't for hand-numbing joysticks, it's for devices that have practical business uses and more instrumentation built into already existing devices. Add on top of low demand for oddball devices the fact that device drivers are harder to build for Windows NT Workstation 4.0. The operating system's best features, stability and security, prevent IHVs from realistically developing device drivers for some classes, particularly when they'd be servicing a market so small as to make the venture unprofitable.

Microsoft Windows 2000 Professional straddles the line somewhere between Windows 98 and Windows NT Workstation 4.0. In fact, this is one of the media's favorite targets when criticizing Microsoft; they say that in trying to be all things to all people, Microsoft has made a product that's not fit for home *or* business. Regardless, Windows 2000 Professional supports many more device classes and many more devices than Windows NT workstation 4.0 does. In rough terms, the operating system supports more than 6,500 devices, including 65 percent more legacy devices such as printers, scanners, and digital cameras. Broad support like this is due mostly to architectural changes to the operating system. A new driver model, Win32 driver model, makes it possible for IHVs that once limited themselves to Windows 98 to develop device drivers that work in Windows 98 *and* Windows 2000 Professional. And servicing both markets with one bang means that users are likely to see more device drivers for Windows 2000 Professional. Plug and Play, appearing for the first time in an operating system based on NT technology, allows users to install devices easily. Windows 2000 Professional is still a business-oriented operating system, but now it supports the hardware that home users want to use.

This chapter describes Windows 2000 Professional's new hardware features. It covers obvious topics such as how to install new devices and how to configure them, yes. Most of this chapter covers less-obvious topics, however, such as troubleshooting and how to pick a computer that works well with Microsoft's latest desktop operating system. As with many topics, exceptions are more frustrating than the rules, so this chapter focuses on exceptions. For example, one of the most troubling issues for new users installing Windows 2000 Professional for the first time is BIOS compatibility. This chapter addresses this issue in great detail.

Maintenance

In an ideal world, you'd use nothing but Plug and Play devices that are on the hardware compatibility list and would therefore have little maintenance. Windows 2000 Professional automatically recognizes and configures Plug and Play devices. How you install a Plug and Play device depends on its type, though. Internal devices, such as video adapters, require that you shut down the computer before you install them. Install the device and then restart the computer. To install external devices, such as those you connect to USB ports or those that you insert in PC Card slots, plug in the device. An exception is SCSI devices, which usually require you to turn off the computer so you can set the device's SCSI ID, attach the device to the bus, and properly terminate the bus before restarting the computer. In all cases, when you restart the computer, the operating system recognizes new devices, starts the Found New Hardware wizard, configures the devices, and prompts you for device drivers only if it doesn't find them on the computer.

The goal is a computer that's maintenance-free. You don't want to juggle resources between devices or troubleshoot hardware that doesn't work. To that end, the best advice I can give you is not to mix Plug and Play and legacy ISA devices. Doing so minimizes the operating system's capability to configure the computer's hardware correctly. The reason is that legacy devices, which you must manually configure using jumpers and switches, don't report to the operating system the resources they're using. The operating system often allocates those same resources to Plug and Play devices, causing resource conflicts that are time-consuming and frustrating to repair. For example, if you use a legacy network adapter and set its jumpers so it uses IRQ 7, the operating system is likely to cause a conflict by assigning IRQ 7 to a Plug and Play device because it doesn't know that the IRQ is allocated. The symptom is usually that your network connection doesn't work, but these problems can cause the operating system to fail. At home and in some shops, people are still stuck with legacy devices, though. If you must use legacy devices, here's the best way to install them:

1. Remove all legacy (ISA) devices from the computer.

2. Install and configure Windows 2000 Professional, making sure that all devices work properly and the operating system allocated resources to them.

3. Determine what resources are available, and then make a note of the resources you want to allocate to each legacy device. Do one of the following:

   - In Device Manager, on the View menu, click Resources by type and then note resources that are available under each type. Figure 3.1 is an example, showing which devices are using which resources. To open Device Manager, in Control Panel, double-click the Administrative Tools icon, double-click the Computer Management icon, and then click Device Manager.

   - In Computer Management, in the tree pane, double-click System Tools, double-click the System Information, and then click Hardware Resources. Examine each node to see what resources are available.

4. Reconfigure each legacy device using the resource you allocated to it in the previous step, and then install the device in your computer.

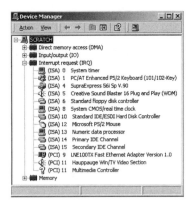

Figure 3.1   There are some resources that you should never allocate.
Those include IRQ 2 and IRQ 9 on ACPI-based computers.

You might require some legacy ISA devices in order to install Windows
2000 Professional. If you're installing the operating system from a network,
for example, and you use a legacy network adapter, you must install the
adapter before running the setup program. In those cases, note the resources
that you've configured those devices to use and then use the computer's
BIOS setup utility to reserve them for legacy ISA devices. To reserve
resources on computers containing an Award BIOS, choose PNP/PCI
CONFIGURATION from the BIOS setup utility's main menu, change
Resources Controlled By to Manual, and then indicate each resource that
you want to reserve by changing it to Legacy ISA. Reserving resources
using other BIOSes is a similar process. The operating system won't allocate
those resources to Plug and Play devices because the BIOS reserves them
for legacy devices. Even after all this, the operating system probably won't
recognize the device, so you'll have to install it manually, which you will
learn how to do in the next section, "Installing."

Note

Device Manager, by default, does not show non-Plug and Play device drivers. To view them, on the View menu,
click Show Hidden Devices and then double-click Non-Plug and Play Drivers. Not only do you see non-Plug and
Play device drivers, but you see legacy software drivers, too. Device Manager allows you to start and stop each
device driver and change its startup type: automatic, boot, demand, system, and disabled.

Installation Security

In early beta versions of Windows 2000 Professional, Plug and Play ran in the user context, requiring users to log on to the computer as an administrator in order to install devices on their computers. Microsoft received floods of complaints, particularly from mobile users because it created a lot of extra work each time they changed their computers' configurations, which they do often. It also caused a bit of a hole in the operating system's security by making logging on as an administrator for normal daily use of users computers more likely (just the thing Microsoft wants to prevent).

In the final release of the operating system, Plug and Play runs in the system context, if possible. This means that users can install new hardware without requiring users to log on to their computers as an administrator. A few rules govern this capability, though. First, the device driver's installation must present no user interface. All the files that the operating system requires to install the device driver must already be present on the computer. The device driver must have a digital signature, and it must return no errors during installation. If any of those conditions fail, the operating system restarts Plug and Play in the user context, requiring them to be an administrator in order to continue installing the device.

These changes have other positive implications. If a driver for a device is already present on the computer, which is the case for any device for which Microsoft put a driver on the Windows 2000 Professional CD-ROM, the operating system doesn't present a user interface when it detects the device; it just installs the device and carries on with business. And now the operating system can automatically install device drivers before users log on to their computers because Plug and Play runs in the system context initially and doesn't require a user context present. The operating system does a better job of detecting devices such as keyboards *before* users have to log on to the computer.

Administrators can disable automatic installation, if necessary. Although there isn't a setting they can use to accomplish this, they can force installation out of the system context and into the user context by causing one of the conditions described earlier to fail. The easiest way is to remove Driver.cab from *SystemRoot*\Driver Cache\i386. This forces users to log on to the computer as an administrator in order to install hardware. This also means that users will have to keep Windows 2000 Professional's CD-ROM handy.

Installing

Just because a device isn't working, don't automatically assume that the operating system didn't recognize the device and then set off installing it manually. If the operating system finds a Plug and Play device but can't find a device driver for it, the operating system still recognizes it but can't enable the device. The easiest way to get this device working is by using Device Manager to install its device driver, which presumably came on a disk with the device (or you must get it from the device's manufacturer). In Device Manager, double-click the device and then click Update Driver on the

Driver tab. You can also use the Add/Remove Hardware Wizard to troubleshoot the device: In Control Panel, double-click the Add/Remove Hardware icon, click <u>N</u>ext, click <u>A</u>dd/Troubleshoot a device, and then follow the instructions you see on the screen. This gives you the opportunity to enable the device by starting the Updated Device Driver wizard.

If Windows 2000 Professional does not automatically detect and configure a device, and the device isn't already listed in Device Manager, it's probably a legacy ISA device. You must manually install these devices using the Add/Remove Hardware Wizard. In Control Panel, double-click the Add/Remove Hardware icon and follow the instructions you see onscreen. The wizard displays a list of devices that are installed. But because a legacy ISA device isn't likely to be in this list, you want to add a new device and select the device from a list or provide third-party device drivers that you have on a disk. The operating system does provide drivers for many legacy devices and just might be your only source for them because some IHVs aren't updating older device drivers for Microsoft's latest and greatest operating system.

Tip
You can force Device Manager to rescan the computer for hardware changes. On the <u>A</u>ction menu, click Rescan for hardware changes.

Device Manager and the Add/Remove Hardware Wizard are the two primary user interfaces you use to configure and troubleshoot hardware. Both require that you log on to the computer as an administrator, but you can use Device Manager to *view* your computer's configuration otherwise. Use Device Manager to manually set devices' resources and do some unguided troubleshooting. This is the tool for power users because they tend to know more about hardware and how Plug and Play allocates resources to devices. Use the Add/Remove Hardware Wizard to do the same, but with more guidance from the operating system and also to install new hardware that the operating system didn't detect automatically. Both are equally useful for removing hardware, which you learn about in the next section, but Device Manager is the quickest route.

Removing

The fact that I've included a section about removing hardware must indicate that there's more to it than you might imagine. Yes and no. Although in almost all cases, you simply unplug the device, you should realize that Windows 2000 Professional does not uninstall the device driver or any services associated with it. Device drivers remain fully installed, but the operating system doesn't start them if the device is missing from the computer. Services still start, however, and they tend to display errors and log errors in the event log if their corresponding device drivers aren't running. Thus, the only way to permanently remove a device is by using Device Manager or the Add/Remove Hardware Wizard.

To remove a device, do one of the following:

- In Device Manager, double-click the device you want to remove; and on the Driver tab, click Uninstall. Follow the instructions.

- In Control Panel, double-click the Add/Remove Hardware icon, click Next, click Uninstall/Unplug a device, click Next, and click Uninstall a device. Follow the instructions.

The order in which you remove a device and remove its device drivers is important. Windows 2000 Professional doesn't load a device driver if the device is missing from the computer's current configuration. That also means that the device driver doesn't show up in Device Manager and isn't available for removal. Thus, remove the device driver *before* removing the device from the computer. Also, make sure that you remove the device from the computer before restarting the computer again, so you can prevent the operating system from detecting the device again and reinstalling its device driver.

Caution

You can remove most hot-pluggable devices while the computer is running. Keep in mind that some devices require you to use the Add/Remove Hardware Wizard before removing them, however, because the operating system needs a chance to flush any cached data and close any connections to the device. If in doubt, check the device's documentation to see if removing a hot-pluggable device without using the Add/Remove Hardware Wizard might cause data loss. Never remove any hot-pluggable storage device without using the Add/Remove Hardware Wizard, however, because doing so will almost certainly lead to damage.

Unplugging

Unplugging devices is different from removing them. Windows 2000 Professional doesn't uninstall their device drivers, ensuring that they're ready to go the next time you plug them in to the computer. For most devices, you simply eject or unplug the device, and the operating system automatically detects that you've unplugged the device and reconfigures the computer accordingly. Some devices, however, particularly storage devices, require a user interface to unplug or eject them, making it safe to remove the device without losing data by flushing cached data and closing connections to it. The user interface merely shuts down the device nicely.

To unplug a device, do one of the following:

- In Control Panel, double-click the Add/Remove Hardware icon, click Next, click Uninstall/Unplug a device, click Next, and click Unplug/Eject a device. Follow the instructions.

- In the taskbar, double-click the Unplug/Eject icon. Windows 2000 Professional automatically adds this icon when your computer has PC Card slots or if you select the Show Unplug/Eject icon on the taskbar icon in the Add/New Hardware Wizard.

Ejecting or unplugging portable computers from docking stations is a bit different. On the Start menu, click Eject PC and then wait until you see a message that says undocking your computer is safe. Of course, you won't see this command on the Start menu if you're not actually using a docking station, and Windows 2000 Professional seems a little picky about the portable computers for which it displays it. Rumor has it that you can force the operating system to display this command by removing the portable computer from Device Manager, however.

DirectX 7 (Gaming Comes to Windows 2000 Professional)

DirectX is a set of Application Programming Interfaces (APIs) that programmers use to develop games and multimedia applications for the Windows family of operating systems. It has two layers. The DirectX Foundation layer provides access to high-performance hardware features such as 3D acceleration chips and sound cards. By abstracting the hardware, DirectX allows developers to write generic code that works with almost any hardware the operating system supports. The second layer, the DirectX Media layer, supports animation, streaming video, and multimedia coordination on a much higher level. Together, both layers enable developers to create great games—the aspect for which most people know DirectX.

Windows NT Workstation is limited to DirectX 3, which requires Service Pack 4. Most games sold today require newer versions of DirectX and won't run on this operating system.

DirectX 7 makes its long awaited debut in Windows 2000 Professional. You just might be able to play your favorite games in Windows 2000 Professional, but not all games that use DirectX will work properly in Windows 2000 Professional. In particular, poorly behaved games won't work, but many of the most popular and best-designed games do work well. Don't expect that you can take home from the computer store just any game and it's going to work, however. Microsoft did not develop Windows 2000 Professional as a gaming platform, and other operating system limitations will prevent some games from working at all. If in doubt, make sure the game you want to play has the Windows logo before purchasing it, and double-check other users' experiences with the game by searching DejaNews, http://www.deja.com. You can also check compatibility on Microsoft's Web site, http://www.microsoft.com/windows2000/upgrade/compat/search/default.asp.

For DirectX 7 to work properly, you must have DirectX device drivers for your video adapter and sound card. If you don't have these, you can usually get them from the manufacturers. You can test your drivers, as well as DirectX in general, using DirectX Diagnostic Tool. At the command prompt, type **dxdiag.exe**. Each tab tests different portions of DirectX and allows you to tune DirectX settings such as hardware acceleration. DirectX Diagnostic Tool also reports DirectX features such as acceleration that aren't available. Often, DirectX will emulate a feature even if that feature isn't available in your hardware, however.

BIOS Compatibility

Windows 2000 Professional supports both ACPI and APM BIOSes, although its support for ACPI is more complete and more robust than its support for APM. Some BIOSes, ACPI and APM, are not compatible with the operating system, however. The most notable problems are with ACPI BIOSes because the technology is new relative to APM, and many IHVs failed to design their computers to be 100 percent compatible with the ACPI specifications.

Problems run the gamut between not being able to install Windows 2000 Professional at all to blue screens of death (BSOD) popping up from time to time. The former is more menacing than the latter, no matter how frustrated you get while trying to install the operating system. Worse is that some ACPI-based systemboards have such huge problems that you must actually return them to the manufacturer so they can *rework them* in order to work properly with the operating system's ACPI hardware abstraction layer (HAL). For example, in order to use certain versions of ASUS dual-processor systemboards with the ACPI HAL, you must return them to the distributor so that ASUS can rework them. This actually involves moving a resistor from one location on the systemboard to another (are you handy with a soldering iron?). Fortunately, most users get off with nothing more than BIOS upgrades. And, in most cases, even if the computer doesn't work with the ACPI HAL, you can install Windows 2000 Professional with the APM HAL, and everything works handily.

Which leads me to the fact that Windows 2000 Professional maintains a list of compatible BIOSes. When the setup program detects that you're installing the operating system on a computer with a good ACPI BIOS, it installs the ACPI HAL. When it doesn't find the BIOS in the *good BIOS list*, it installs the APM HAL. The good BIOS list, which you learn more about in the following section, does a good job of catching most problems In my tests, however, it didn't identify the ASUS dual-processor systemboard as having an incompatible ACPI BIOS. This prevented the operating system from installing properly and required me to manually install the APM HAL during installation.

Checking the Lists

Figure 3.2 shows how the Setup program checks to see whether an ACPI BIOS is compatible with Windows 2000 Professional. The good and bad BIOS lists that you read about in these steps is in Txtsetup.inf, which is located in the i386 from which you installed the operating system:

1. The Setup program checks the bad BIOS list. If the version number of the current BIOS is newer than the version number in the list, the Setup program installs the ACPI HAL; otherwise, it installs the legacy APM HAL. The bad BIOS list is the section [NWACL], which contains an item for

each BIOS that indicates another section containing more specific information about the BIOS. Examine this table if you're unclear about why the Setup program is not installing the ACPI HAL.

2. The Setup program examines the date of the BIOS. If it's a recent BIOS (newer than 1/1/99), the Setup program assumes that it's a good BIOS list (it's already checked the bad BIOS list), and installs the ACPI HAL.

3. The Setup program did not find the BIOS on the bad BIOS list and it's an older BIOS, so the Setup program examines the good BIOS list to determine whether this older BIOS passed Microsoft's testing. The good BIOS list is in the section [GoodACPIBios] and each item indicates another section that has more specific information about the BIOS other than just its name. You can examine this list to determine whether the Setup program will install the ACPI HAL prior to actually running it.

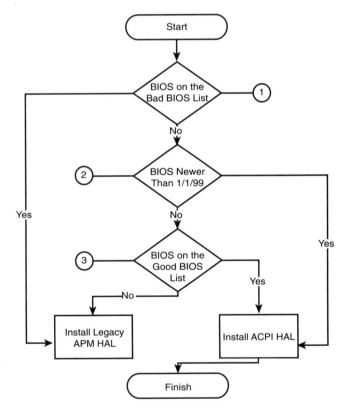

Figure 3.2 Microsoft assumes that any recent BIOS is compatible, even though that is not always true and causes problems.

BIOSes end up in the bad BIOS list when Microsoft finds that the BIOS doesn't work with Windows 2000 Professional or an IHV reports that its BIOS is not compatible with the operating system. The problems vary, but symptoms include hardware that doesn't work properly, an instable system that hangs frequently, or BSODs that cause data loss. Even though I show you how to override the bad BIOS list, doing this is not a good idea unless you're very sure that using the ACPI HAL with your BIOS is safe and won't cause you to lose any data. Microsoft provides no support in these cases, and you have to assume that the BIOS ended up on the list for a reason. Still, to force the setup program to accept your BIOS as a good BIOS and install the ACPI HAL, change ACPIEnable=2 to ACPIEnable=1. You must make this change at the installation point prior to installing the operating system, which implies that you are installing from a network share, a local folder, or a customized Windows 2000 Professional CD-ROM. As a result, the section [ACPIOptions] will look like this:

Listing 3.1 **[ACPIOptions]**

```
; [ACPIOptions]
; This section lists options that affect the installation of ACPI on x86
;
; ACPIEnable
;     0 - ACPI will be disabled at install time regardless of the BIOS
;     1 - ACPI will be enabled at install time if an ACPI BIOS is present
;     2 - ACPI will be enabled based on the GoodACPIBios list, the NWACL
;         and ACPIBiosDate
;
; ACPIBiosDate = mm,dd,yyyy
;     Supplies the date that a BIOS must have to be considered good if it is
;     not in the GoodACPIBios list. If a BIOS has a date greater than this and
;     is not in the NWACL list, then it will be used unless ACPIEnable = 0
;
[ACPIOptions]
ACPIEnable = 1
ACPIBiosDate = 01,01,1999
```

Upgrading BIOSes

If you're ACPI BIOS is in the bad BIOS list or if it's older than 1/1/99 and not in the good BIOS list, you might gain ACPI functionality by upgrading your BIOS. The process is similar for any BIOS:

1. Download the BIOS update from the systemboard's manufacturer, not from the BIOS's manufacturer.

2. Unzip the disk to a bootable 3.5-inch disk.

3. Restart the computer and follow the instructions you see on the screen. *Do not restart the computer while the flash software is updating the BIOS!*

Caution

A few cautions are in order because human error while upgrading your BIOS can render your computer dead, requiring you to return it to the manufacturer for repair. First, if you're updating a portable computer's BIOS, make sure that you plug the computer into a power outlet. If the BIOS decides that the computer has been idle long enough and shuts down the computer before the upgrade process finishes, you might not be able to start the computer again. You might also make sure that you have configured the BIOS using the BIOS setup utility to shut down an idle computer, even if it's connected to a power source. If in doubt, tap one of the Shift keys every once in awhile to keep the computer awake. Second, and for the same reason, if you have a UPS available, attach it to your computer whether it's a portable or desktop computer, protecting the computer from power outages that could also render the computer useless. Finally, don't shut down the computer until the upgrade process is complete.

Most BIOS manufacturers don't offer upgrades anymore because systemboard vendors usually customize their BIOSes. Thus, you must go to the systemboard's manufacturer for an update. If you know the manufacturer's Web site, you can usually find BIOS updates quickly. If you don't know the systemboard's manufacturer, restart the computer and pay attention to the screen as it first starts. This screen will usually indicate the name of the manufacturer or, at the very least, the systemboard's version number, which can easily lead to a manufacturer. With a version in hand, I can usually track down the manufacturer by searching the Web using the version as the keyword.

To make upgrading your BIOS easier, Microsoft, Compaq, and Dell co-sponsor a Web site that makes it easier to locate BIOS upgrades: http://www.Hardware-Update.com. You must know your computer's manufacturer, make, and model in order to use this site. After providing this vital information to the site, it displays information about the update; the setup for updating your BIOS, tips and tricks; and (the most important thing of all) a link to the BIOS update itself. As of this writing, the following manufacturers offer updates via this Web site (the Web site is open to all manufacturers, so you can expect more to participate by the time you read this book):

Compaq	IBM
Dell	Micron
Fujitsu	NEC
Gateway	Toshiba
HP	Others

Driver Compatibility

The single biggest barrier to getting all of your hardware working properly is device driver compatibility. Windows 2000 Professional ships with thousands of drivers that do work well with the operating system, but so many devices don't yet have device drivers and don't work well with it. For example, at this writing, no device drivers are available for ATI TV cards, frustrating many users. To be fair, ATI does promise that it will make drivers available by the time the operating system ships, but those drivers aren't going to be available on the Windows 2000 Professional CD-ROM.

Compatibility is an issue for many reasons. Windows 2000 Professional introduces a new driver model, for example. The format of Setup Information (INF) files is different, forcing IHVs to update their products' INF files. New features such as Windows File Protection prevent some device drivers from installing properly because they can't overwrite protected system files. Still others refuse to install in Windows 2000 Professional because they don't like the operating system's version number. The way to get most devices working, particularly when you see that big yellow question mark and exclamation point in Device Driver, is to get updated device drivers. The best source is the device's manufacturer. Visit the Web site, and you can usually download device drivers.

Note

Microsoft online hardware compatibility list, http://www.microsoft.com/hcl, is the best way to verify whether a particular device works well with Windows 2000 Professional. It's worth much more than that, however. It's also the best source for finding updated device drivers. Look up a device and click it. You'll see a list of certification levels for each operating system that Microsoft sells and notes about using the device. Best of all, for each operating system, you'll find links to updated device drivers if they're available. Other Web sites are notorious for making beta device drivers available, and the two that I use most are Frank Condron's World O'Windows (http://www.worldowindows.com) and BetaOS.com (http://www.betaos.com). Both are good sources for device drivers that haven't yet made it on to Microsoft's online hardware compatibility list.

See also

- Chapter 5, "Installing and Using Applications," to learn more about Windows File Protection.

Troubleshooting

If your difficulty is with the setup process, take a look at Chapter 2, "Troubleshooting Setup." The help you find in this chapter is specifically for troubleshooting hardware *after* you have successfully installed Windows 2000 Professional. Chapter 2 includes information about installing the APM HAL, for example.

Most problems reflect themselves in Device Manager. If devices aren't working properly, you see exclamation points next to them. Double-click the device and you'll see an error message and code in the Device Status area. Knowing what those codes really mean and what steps you should take in fixing them is key to fixing those problems. The following list shows the codes and their descriptions:

1   Windows 2000 Professional did not find a suitable driver for the device. Make sure that Driver.cab is in *SystemRoot*\Driver Cache\i386. If Driver.cab is present, the operating system doesn't provide a device driver and you must get one from the device's manufacturer. If updating the device driver doesn't remove this error, assume that the registry is corrupt and restore it.

3   Either the device driver is corrupt or does not have enough memory to work properly. Update the driver. If that doesn't help, verify that the computer has enough memory.

10   This is one of the most common errors; it indicates that the driver is incompatible with Windows 2000 Professional. Get an updated device driver from the manufacturer. A less common cause is a device that's actually damaged.

12   Windows 2000 Professional cannot allocate to the device the resources that it needs. The most common reason is that there simply aren't enough resources available, such as when you've used all the available IRQs. Often, shuffling resources around can fix this problem because some devices work only with specific ranges of resources, and changing another devices' resources might free the resources that the offending device wants.

14   You see this error when you haven't yet restarted the computer after installing a device that requires you to do so. Restarting the computer usually removes this error.

16   Windows 2000 Professional isn't communicating well with the device driver, and this is due to an incompatible device driver or failed hardware. Update the device driver and, if that doesn't resolve the error, replace the device. Even if the error message says that you should manually allocate resources to the device, don't do it. This action will limit the usefulness of Plug and Play.

17   This error code usually displays because of a bad device driver. Update the device driver.

18   If you upgraded to Windows 2000 Professional from an earlier versions of Windows, you might see this error if the Setup program couldn't replace the device driver with one that works in the new operating system. You might also see this message if you install a

device, but can't install the device driver because you must log on to the computer as an administrator. In either case, do as the message suggests: Install a driver for the device.

19   This is a serious error, indicating that your registry might be corrupt. Removing and reinstalling the device might repair the problem. Otherwise, resource the Last Known Good Configuration, as described in Chapter 2, "Troubleshooting Setup."

21   Device Manager displays this error when you try to open a device that it's removing. Restarting the computer usually fixes it.

22   You manually disabled the device in the current hardware profile. Enable the device.

24   You usually see this error when using a bad device driver. Update the device driver.

28   Like many other errors, this one usually results from an incompatible device driver. Update the device driver.

29   This error message is a bit misleading. It usually means that you disabled the device in the BIOS, but the BIOS still reports the device to Windows 2000 Professional. To fix this problem, update the computer's BIOS.

31   A faulty device driver is the usual culprit. Contact the device's manufacturer to obtain a device driver that actually works.

32   A misleading error message that says a device driver is not required; this really indicates that the device driver depends on a service that is disabled. Enable the service. You can usually locate the service by checking the event log or by looking for services that seem to be related to the device.

33   This error code usually displays because of bad device driver. Update the device driver.

34   You see this error code as a result of using legacy ISA devices that don't report their settings to the operating system. Verify the devices settings and make sure that the settings on the Resources tab match them.

35   Your computer's BIOS requires an update. If an update isn't available, you won't be able to use this device. If the BIOS allows you to switch between MPS 1.1 and MPS 1.4, switch to MPS 1.4. (MPS is Microsoft Platforms Support.)

36   You reserved a resource for a legacy ISA device, but a PCI device is using it. Use the BIOS's setup utility to reconfigure the BIOS. If you find no fault with these settings, update the computer's BIOS.

4

Personalizing Windows

I LAY NO CLAIM TO BEING A USER-INTERFACE expert—I couldn't build an easy-to-use toothpick if I tried. I do know a lot about user interfaces, however, because I use them. So, too, do you. I know that we never read manuals and infrequently use online help. I know that if a feature isn't so obvious that it whacks us upside the head, it must be discoverable or we'll never use it. I know that more powerful computers mean more complexity, and that most companies don't realize the cost savings that are possible due to various innovations.

Discovery must therefore be an important part of user interfaces. Microsoft spends a lot of research dollars on discovery and puts a lot of energy into making Microsoft Windows 2000 Professional's features easy to use. A good thing because operating systems are the one type of software that all users must use, and thus has a more direct impact on usability and total cost of ownership. Some features do miss the discoverability boat, however, but this chapter will help you get on board.

In Windows 2000 Professional, there are many bold changes to Microsoft's already innovative user interface. The majority help make finding files and folders easier by anticipating your needs and adapting to how you use the computer. A new menu for opening files in different programs, integrated searching, and a more useful My Network Places folder are examples. Other features are more subtle adjustments to existing features, such as better Help and smarter error messages. Many of these Windows

2000 Professional features were inherited from innovations made by
Microsoft Internet Explorer 4. Other new features are requests made by users
or are based on feedback given during the beta process. This chapter
describes the new features you find in the operating system's user interface.

Windows Explorer

Few people find the fact that Microsoft buried Microsoft Windows Explorer
deeper in the Start menu more annoying than me. In earlier versions of
Microsoft Windows, this ubiquitous file manager had a prominent position in
the Programs menu. In Windows 2000 Professional, you must click the Start
button, point to Programs, point to Accessories, and then click Windows
Explorer. I'm so peevish about its new location (because I rely on Windows
Explorer for just about every task) that the first thing I do after installing the
operating system is drag the shortcut to the top of the Start menu. I also drag
a copy of the shortcut to the Quick Launch toolbar. On the other hand, a
couple of other ways you can open Windows Explorer might satisfy you
(Microsoft is good about providing different ways to access a feature, each of
which is appropriate for different levels of users):

- Using a Windows keyboard, press Windows+E (Windows is the Windows
  key, between the Ctrl and Alt keys).
- Click Explore on any folder's shortcut menu, including the My Computer
  and My Network Places icons.
- Put a shortcut to Explorer.exe on the desktop or a QuickLaunch toolbar.
  SystemRoot\explorer.exe is the path. Then, double-click the shortcut or
  click the button on the toolbar.
- In the Run dialog box or at an MS-DOS command prompt, type
  explorer and press Enter.

Regardless of the lower esteem in which Microsoft seems to hold Windows
Explorer, it has a wealth of new features and an overhaul of existing fea-
tures that'll make the last of the holdouts stop dreaming about Microsoft
File Manager. My favorite is the reorganized namespace, which is the
outline you see in the left pane. Upon mentioning my discovery to a
Microsoft developer, he said, "Who cares? The change is minimal." I was
crushed. My Computer now contains only drives and Control Panel.
Printers, Scheduled Tasks, and similar folders are under Control Panel. Also,
My Documents is now at the top of the hierarchy, rather than stuck smack
dab in the middle of it, making users more likely to actually use the folder.

This is certainly a minimal change, but it leads me to believe that someone at Microsoft was thinking about us.

Microsoft borrowed many of Windows Explorer's renovations from Internet Explorer 4 and carried forward with version 5. Explorer bars, folders that look like Web pages, and the nifty single-click interface are examples. Figure 4.1 shows an Explorer bar in Windows Explorer. Close it altogether, leaving a simple view of the folder that has more space for displaying its contents, or replace it with a different Explorer bar. In the <u>V</u>iew menu, click the name of the Explorer bar you want to open: <u>S</u>earch, <u>F</u>avorites, <u>H</u>istory, or F<u>o</u>lders. Alternatively, click the Search, Folders, or History button in the toolbar. All but the Search bar have been around long enough and are simple enough that I won't discuss them in this chapter. Searching using the Search bar, also known as Search Assistant, is new and not always intuitive; you learn about it in "Integrated Searching" later in this chapter.

One of Windows Explorer's best features is also one of its worst, an irony repeated throughout Windows 2000 Professional. On the left side of the current folder, Windows Explorer displays useful information about the item you selected. In most cases, the information reflects what you see in the Name Properties dialog box. In other cases, it might include a pie chart, describing how much space is available on a disk, or links to other folders and programs that are related. Great, but here's the rub: although the information is certainly useful, it gobbles up too much real estate and leaves little room to display a folder's contents. I'd say that Microsoft missed this one in its usability labs,

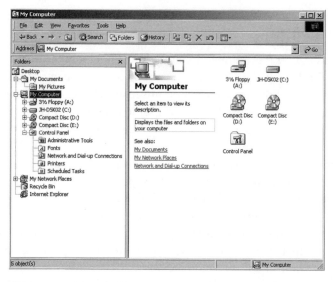

Figure 4.1   The capability to open and close Explorer bars makes viewing the contents of a folder without scrolling easier.

except that Windows Explorer *is* smart enough to realize when this added information makes viewing the folder impossible and removes it so that you can see more of the folder's content in the window. You can also quickly toggle the Folders bar on and off by clicking the Folders button in the toolbar, freeing up additional space for the folder's contents.

Weird Science

A key part of making Windows 2000 Professional easy to use is discoverability. *Discoverability* is a measure of how obvious a feature is to users at the right time. In other words, when users need a particular feature, will they find it on their own without any additional help? Does the feature meet users' expectations? If so, the feature is discoverable. The My Documents folder is a discoverable feature, for example, because it's obvious and appears when users need it.

Microsoft doesn't just come up with this stuff out of thin air. The company tests new features to make sure they're easy to use and highly discoverable. On the Redmond campus, the company has more than 25 usability labs that are staffed with more than 100 usability engineers. Each lab has two sections, separated by a soundproof barrier: a section for observers and one for the participant. Observers watch the participant through a one-way mirror. They communicate via an intercom. Each month, more than 750 participants complete a series of tasks, thinking out loud and discussing their experiences with the engineers. The result is that the engineer better understands participants' expectations and thought processes. For all their trouble, they get to visit Microsoft's campus and receive a free gift, usually a Microsoft product.

The backgrounds of Microsoft's usability engineers are telling. They include engineers with degrees in human factors psychology, social psychology, industrial engineering, technical communications, developmental psychology, information science, and computer science. These are people whose careers are making computers and software easier to use.

Files and Folders

Windows 2000 Professional has numerous improvements that make accessing files and folders easier. You'll say it's about time for many of them, and some are innovative. Some enhancements are massively sweeping, touching all tasks, whereas others dribble into the tiniest nooks and crannies of the operating system and are delightful surprises when you find them (but aren't worth discussing here).

Windows 2000 Professional makes substantial changes to the way it stores class information in the registry, all to support the various enhancements that make accessing files and folders easier. The biggest difference is that the registry now contains two different groups of class information—per-user and per-computer—allowing you to customize file associations without affecting other users who share the computer. The operating system merges into HKCR the contents of the per-computer class information, HKLM\SOFTWARE\Classes, and per-user class information, HKCU\Software\Classes. Per-user class information has a higher priority than per-computer class information.

A higher priority is `FileExts\.ext`, a subkey underneath
`HKCU\Software\Microsoft\Windows\CurrentVersion\Explorer`. When you use the
File Types tab of Windows Explorer's Folder Options dialog box to change
the program that opens a file, the operating system stores that choice in
`FileExts\.ext` as a `REG_SZ` value called `Application`, not in the per-user class
information. Thus, the operating system looks in `FileExts\.ext` before looking in `HKCR` to determine with which program to open a file. When you click
Restore to restore the file type, the operating system merely removes
`Application` from `FileExts\.ext`. What you can gather from all this is shown
in Figure 4.2. This diagram shows the order in which Windows 2000
Professional uses different subkeys to determine the program with which it
will open a file, based on the file's extension. The operating system first looks
in `FileExts` to see whether you changed the program with which you open
files having that extension. It then looks in `HKCR`, which is a combination of
`Software\Classes` in `HKCR` and `HKLM`. Clicking any program on the Open With
menu skips `HKCR`.

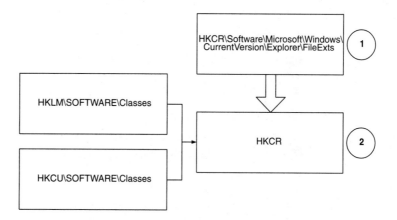

Figure 4.2   File associations are far more complex than they were in
earlier versions of Windows, even Microsoft Windows 98.

In Windows 2000 Professional, many tasks don't change much from earlier
versions of Windows. Moving, copying, renaming, and deleting files are no
different. With a few exceptions, the shortcut menus are roughly the same.
The operating system's drag-and-drop feature is identical to the same feature
in earlier versions of Windows. All told, your learning curve will be short;
however, the following sections describe any significant changes that you
should be aware of.

Common Dialog Boxes

The common dialog boxes, Open and Save As, have a new look. The changes
are more than just skin deep, however, as shown in Figure 4.3. The buttons
you see on the left side make jumping to certain folders quicker. Each represents a folder in which you're likely to store documents, so they're a good
way to locate important files or to make sure you save them in the right
place.

I have a hunch that Microsoft added these buttons to the common dialog
boxes to cover up a small flaw that frustrates many users. You can go to any
folder by clicking its name in the Look in or Save in lists, but Windows
2000 Professional can take several seconds to open it. It must enumerate
each disk and network drive to which you've connected and usually waits a
few seconds for the CD-ROM to spin up. Clicking the shortcuts is much
less frustrating and definitely much quicker. Thus, a potential cover-up turns
out to be a great feature.

Figure 4.3   The new buttons in the Open (shown in the figure)
and Save As dialog boxes make jumping from folder to folder easier.

History Lists

Most recently used (MRU) lists are another name for history lists. Windows
2000 Professional uses them more pervasively than do earlier versions of
Windows; they're everywhere. Anywhere that the operating system prompts
for a filename keeps a history. The Run, Open, and Save As dialog boxes are
but a few examples. The operating system constrains the list to the type of
file that you're opening or saving. For example, if you're opening a file with
the .txt extension, you see a history of files with that extension.

Windows 2000 Professional keeps histories in the registry. They're scattered
helter-skelter, but all have the same general form. A subkey contains numerous

values, each of which represents a single item in the history. The value's name is irrelevant, and its data contain the filename, path, or other history data. Usually, each subkey has an extra value, called something like `MRUlist`, which describes the order of the history data. In all cases, history lists are per-user data, meaning that your history is separate from other users'. See the subkey `HKCU\Software\Microsoft\Windows\CurrentVersion\Explorer\RecentDocs` for an example of a history list.

Are you paranoid that other users will snoop around and see what you're doing? Because Windows 2000 Professional keeps a separate history list for each user and users can access only their own profiles, this isn't a problem. Of course, if everyone knows your password or if you walk away from the computer without locking it, they can take a peek. If you're still worried or you want to clear the history lists just to keep things tidy, Tweak UI has several settings that give granular control over which lists the operating system clears and when it clears them.

Tip

The Favorites folder isn't just for Internet shortcuts. It's useful for files and folders that you open frequently. In Windows Explorer, select the file or folder you want to add to the Favorites folder, and then click Add to Favorites on the Favorites menu. This beats history lists as a way to open your most-often-used files and folders.

AutoComplete

Windows 2000 Professional automatically completes filenames as you type them. This feature, *AutoComplete*, is available anywhere that the operating system prompts for a filename. Here's how it works: begin typing a file or folder name and the operating system opens a list of files in the current folder that match it. It doesn't replace what you typed; you click one of the files in the list or continue typing. In the Open and Save As dialog boxes, this feature's usefulness is questionable because clicking the file's name is easier than typing its name. This feature proves most useful in dialog boxes that don't display a list of files. Figure 4.4 shows an example with several files in the list. Drag the handle to change the size of the list.

A similar feature is available at the MS-DOS command prompt. Begin typing a file or folder name, press the key assigned as the completion character (typically Tab), and the command-line editor replaces what you typed with the first match it finds. Each time you press the key, the editor replaces what you typed with the next match. Windows 2000 enables this feature by default but, if for some odd reason it isn't enabled, use Tweak UI, a must-have utility. You can also enable it by adding to the subkey `HKCU\Software\Microsoft\`

Command Processor a REG_DWORD value called CompletionChar. Change this value to the ASCII code representing the key you want to use to complete a file or folder's name. For example, to use the Tab key to complete a name, use 0x09.

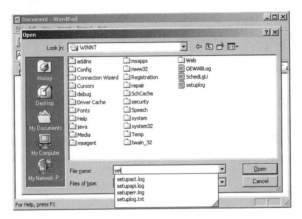

Figure 4.4   Navigate quickly to any file or folder by starting with a backslash (\) and choosing each folder in the path.

Open With Menu

Earlier in this chapter, you learned a bit about the Open With menu, but you haven't yet learned why this menu is so innovative or about the problems it solves. The registry associates each file extension with a single file type, which describes how to open the file with a particular program. Many programs can open the same type of file, however. Text files are an example. You can open them in Microsoft Notepad, Microsoft Word, or any other text editor. Windows 2000 Professional associates text files only with Notepad, however, which limits your choices.

In earlier versions of Windows, the solution to this problem was to add a new command to the file type, a task for which you use Registry Editor or Windows Explorer's Folder Options dialog box. Neither is satisfactory because they're slow and cumbersome to use. Both solutions also clutter shortcut menus with commands you might use only on occasion. Another solution was to create a shortcut to the program in the Send To folder so that you can *send* a file to the program by pointing to Send To on the file's shortcut menu and clicking the program's shortcut. The problem here is that the shortcuts in the Send To folder apply to all files, regardless of their extensions.

Along comes the Open With menu. You don't have to customize file associations using Registry Editor or the File Types tab of Windows Explorer's Folder Options dialog box. You don't have to create shortcuts in the Send To folder, either. In fact, all you have to do is choose a program with which you want to open the file, and Windows 2000 Professional remembers your choice. For files that don't yet have an Open With menu, click Open With on its shortcut menu and then choose the program with which you want to open the file. Otherwise, point to Open With and then do one of the following:

- Click the name of the program with which you want to open the file.
- Click Choose Program to choose a different program with which to open the file.

The Open With menu changes class information in the registry and also uses `FileExts\.ext`, a subkey of `HKCU\Software\Microsoft\Windows\CurrentVersion\Explorer`. First, `HKCR\Applications` contains the list of programs you see in the Open With dialog box. When you use this dialog box to open a file in a program of your choosing, the operating system stores the program's filename in `FileExts\.ext`, where *ext* is the extension of the file you opened. Also, when you click Open With on a file's shortcut menu, the operating system looks up the file's extension in `FileExts` and adds each program it finds in `FileExts\.ext` to the menu. When the user clicks one of the programs, the operating system looks up that program in `HKCR\Applications` to find the command that opens it.

Special Folders

Until recently, users put documents anywhere they liked. Most of the time, they kept documents in the same folder as the program they used to create them. They also kept documents in the system folder or in a variety of other places that would make an administrator cringe when it was time to back them up. Calls to the help desk saying that they couldn't find an important document were common because users didn't have or didn't use a central place for it. Microsoft Windows 3.1 and Microsoft Windows 95 didn't do anything to help. Windows 98 introduced My Documents, however, and for the first time users had an operating system-sanctioned central place to put all their stuff.

Windows 2000 Professional extends the idea. Not only do you have a place to put your documents, but the folder is also part of your user profile folder. Every user has their own My Documents folder, and they can't view any other user's My Documents folder. Your stuff is safe from prying eyes.

Using roaming profiles, your stuff follows you from computer to computer, as long as you connect to the network. Your user profile contains other special folders, too, which make organizing and finding information easier. More about all of these is in the following sections.

My Documents

Windows 2000 Professional provides My Documents as a central place to store your documents. Programs that use the common Open and Save As dialog boxes automatically use this folder. Note that Windows 2000 Professional does not automatically direct older programs that do not use the command dialog boxes.

You see My Documents at the top of Windows Explorer's hierarchy and on the desktop. This is a shortcut, more or less, to the folder. The physical folder is in your user profile, *UserProfile*\My Documents. You're free to use a different folder for your documents unless Group Policy prevents you from doing so (see your administrator, if that's the case):

1. On My Document's shortcut menu, click Properties.

2. On the Target tab, shown in Figure 4.5, click Move and select the folder in which you want to store your documents.

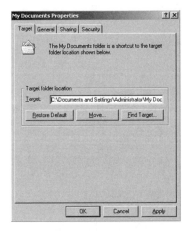

Figure 4.5   Administrators can redirect My Documents to a different folder using Group Policy.

My Pictures

My Pictures does for images what My Documents does for documents. It provides a central place to store your pictures, and it has some exciting features that make it more interesting to use than My Documents. First of all, it allows you to see images without having to open them with any other program. You can zoom, pan, print, and do other things with images, all from the comfort of Windows Explorer. Figure 4.6 shows an example. Notice that instead of using the image file's icon, Windows Explorer displays a thumbnail of the image. To use thumbnails that allow you to see numerous images at one time, click Thumbnails on the View menu. Work with thumbnails as you would any file's icon.

Point to any image file in the folder; the left side of the folder shows a preview of it. The top part provides information that's similar to the image's Name Properties dialog box. Particularly useful are the image's dimensions. The bottom part shows a preview of the image. Click Zoom In, Zoom Out, Actual Size, or Best Fit Size to change the size of the image. Click Full Screen Preview to open the image in a new full-screen window. Last, click Print to print the image on the default printer.

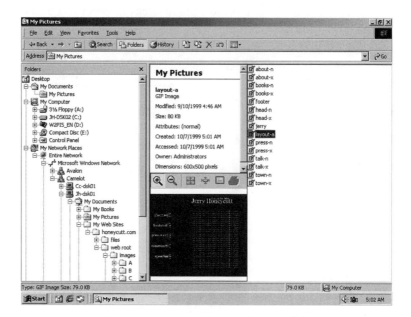

Figure 4.6 You can customize other folders
so that they work just like My Pictures.

> **Note**
>
> My Pictures supports any type of image that Internet Explorer 5 can display. That includes GIF, JPG, BMP, and others. There are many types of images that it doesn't support, including PCX files, as well as most proprietary and vector graphics formats.

My Network Places

My Network Places replaces Network Neighborhood from earlier versions of Windows. The name is consistent with the names of other folders such as My Computer and My Documents. It also represents a bit of an overhaul, making it easier to manage your network connections.

As shown in Figure 4.7, the organization of My Network Places is a bit different from Network Neighborhood. At the top, you see Entire Network. Below that, you see a folder for each network client, along with a folder that contains each directory. Below each client is a folder for each domain with which the computer has a trust relationship or, if the computer isn't on a business network, the name of the workgroup in which it participates. Below that are the names of individual computers, followed by each computer's shares. This organization is more of a strict hierarchy than was Network Neighborhood's, but it requires too many clicks in order to get things done.

Figure 4.7 Although this organization is more structured, it's clumsy.

That's where links help. When Windows 2000 Professional notices that you use a particular resource repeatedly, it adds a link to it in My Network Places. The operating system doesn't even ask; it just does it.

For example, open \\avalon\public enough times and the operating system creates a link to it in My Network Places, so you don't have to slog through four different folders to get the information you want. You can also create your own links in My Network Places. The traditional methods don't work, however. You can't drag a shortcut to My Network Places; clicking Create Shortcut on a resource's shortcut menu puts the shortcut on the desktop and not in My Network Places. In My Network Places, double-click the Add Network Places icon instead. Note that links to network places work differently from shortcuts. Opening a shortcut opens the file or folder to which the shortcut refers. A link is an actual folder in which Windows Explorer displays the target. The operating system stores your links in *UserProfile*\NetHood.

Mapping network drives is as common as it is useful, but Windows 2000 Professional still does not provide the same level of support as Novell NetWare.

You can map only the root of each share, not a folder. *Map Root* is a common name for this feature, and administrators have begged for it since Microsoft first introduced Microsoft Windows NT some years ago. The importance of it becomes clear when you try to create home directories using a single share rather than creating potentially thousands of shares, one for each user. Windows 2000 Server eases this burden very little. Mapping a network drive is similar to doing so in earlier versions of Windows: On the share's shortcut menu, click Map Network Drive, and then choose a drive letter for it. If you want a permanent connection, select the Reconnect at logon checkbox. Windows Explorer displays the drive with all the others, sorted by letter.

You can rename links and you can rename resources to which you make permanent connections. Renaming either is just like renaming any other file or folder.

Administering Computers

Administrators see extra shares that normal users don't. Look again at Figure 4.7, and you'll see a share under JH-DSK01 called Schedule Tasks. This allows administrators to schedule tasks on the remote computer.

Other shares don't show up at all, but they are available if you know their names. C$ is the root of drive C on the remote computer. ADMIN$ is *SystemRoot* on the remote computer. The reason you don't see either in My Network Places is because they end with a dollar sign ($). To use either share, the account you're using must have administrator rights on the remote computer. If not, Windows 2000 Professional asks for a set of credentials that does have those rights.

Because you don't see C$ or ADMIN$ in My Network Places, you must open it Page: 1 using the Address bar, Run dialog box, or even the MS-DOS command prompt. Type the full path, including the computer's name. \\JH-DSK01\C$ opens the root of drive C on a remote computer called JH-DSK01, for example. Note that you can also map a drive to a hidden share using any of the methods you learn about in this book.

Integrated Searching

One of Windows 2000 Professional's most notable changes to the user interface is Search Assistant. I must admit that I was a bit resistant to accepting this new feature. I liked the Find dialog box. It was separate from Windows Explorer, had a nice tabbed user interface, and was easy to use. By comparison, the Search bar (Search Assistant's user interface) is a little clumsy to use and doesn't feel quite as crisp. After I stopped stomping my feet, I quickly realized the merit of this new approach, however. Rather than searching by using a separate user interface, you can flip back and forth between viewing the computer's contents and viewing the results of your search. In other words, searching is fully integrated into Windows Explorer and doesn't require you to go elsewhere.

To display the Search bar, click the Search button in the toolbar. Figure 4.8 shows an example. Provide as much information about the item for which you're searching and then click Search Now. Each type of search prompts for different types of information. Chapter 7, "Managing Disks and Files," shows you how to search faster by enabling Indexing Service, which catalogs the contents of your computer. Windows Explorer displays the results in the right pane. If you replace the Search bar with the Folders bar, you'll see a new folder at the top of the hierarchy, immediately beneath Desktop, which contains the most recent results. As long as you don't close Windows Explorer, you can always return to the search results by clicking this folder. After closing Windows Explorer, this folder goes away until you search again.

You find thorough descriptions of the different search types in other chapters:

- For more information about searching for files and folders, see Chapter 7, "Managing Disks and Files."
- For more information about searching for computers on the network, see Chapter 9, "Networking Your Computer."
- For more information about searching for printers on the network, see Chapter 6, "Printing Documents and Images."
- For more information about searching for people, see Chapter 12, "Connecting to the Internet."
- For more information about searching the Internet, see Chapter 12, "Connecting to the Internet."

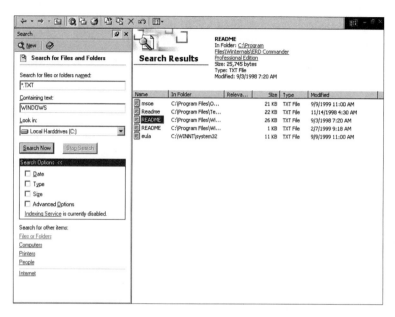

Figure 4.8   Search Assistant gives a fuller view of each
search's results than did the old Find dialog box.

But Wait! There's More

Windows 2000 Professional contains hundreds of tiny enhancements that are by themselves too small to notice. Maybe, but someone somewhere is going to look at one of them and think they're the cat's meow. For example, the attrib command now works on folders. Most people say, "Who cares?" I set the read-only attribute on all files and folders in network installation points and couldn't use the attrib command to do it. This one was a big enhancement for me.

Notepad is another example. Open the Find dialog box by pressing Ctrl+F instead of dancing through menus. Repeat the search by pressing F3. Not a huge change, but enough to stop me from reassociating text and log files with Wordpad. The same goes for Registry Editor. You can now save subkeys in the Favorites menu and then go to any of your most-often-used subkeys by clicking the name rather than wading through the registry.

Guidance for Users

Microsoft gets a lot of criticism for "dumbing down" Windows 2000 Professional. According to many analysts, in trying to make the operating system easy for everyone to use, they've made it difficult for proficient users.

I couldn't disagree more.

Most of the aid that Windows 2000 Professional provides isn't through features that are crippled with too much hand-holding. I've found few features designed to the lowest common denominator. If anything, some of the operating system's new features are so complex as to make them difficult for advanced administrators to figure out. Instead, I've found more extensive guidance for users who need it—guidance that stays well out of the way of users who don't need it.

Help

Windows 2000 Professional's help is more extensive and more complete than any earlier version of Windows. According to Microsoft, they designed it with the following goals in mind:

- Provide balloon help that appears when users point at objects on the screen.
- Use more consistent style, organization, and terminology throughout to avoid confusion.
- Streamline the Contents tab and provide fewer levels so users can find help faster.
- Provide a more thorough index.
- Include better troubleshooters that are well-integrated into the operating system.
- Provide more emphasis on common tasks and more shortcuts in those tasks that start programs.
- Include more cross-referencing in the form of related-topic links to make navigation easier.
- Build a more extensive index, making sure that users can find help using varieties of common words.

Figure 4.9 shows the new Help window. The Contents, Index, and Search tabs are the usual suspects. You can use Boolean keywords in the Search tab, which helps narrow down your searches even more. Keywords include *and*, *or*, *not*, and *near*. The Favorites tab is new and allows you to save shortcuts to topics so that you can quickly return to them later. To save the current topic, click Add on the Favorites tab. In Topics, double-click a topic to which you want to return.

Note

Windows 2000 Professional's Help makes most books about the operating system useless. A majority of them regurgitate information that's already available in Help. This book tries to avoid this by not overly duplicating information that's already available. My goal is to provide additional insight that's not already at your fingertips.

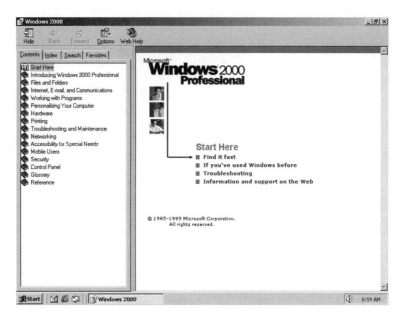

Figure 4.9   Help relies on Internet Explorer 5.

Error Messages

No version of Windows is known for its terrific error messages. They're usually cryptic, sometimes misleading, and almost always useless. The fault isn't Microsoft's alone. Trapping errors, diagnosing their causes, and recovering from them are more difficult than they seem. Imagine heading out to work in the morning, only to discover that you have a flat tire that was the result of a slow leak. By the time the tire is flat, you have no idea what caused the leak, much less at what intersection or even in what part of town you got it. The same goes for some errors. By the time the symptoms appear, figuring out who, what, why, when, and where is difficult.

Let's give Microsoft a break on this one.

Especially because they put a lot of effort into making the error messages in Windows 2000 Professional much more friendly. They give more specific instructions and make better distinctions between errors that affect stability and messages that are just informational. Messages that are informational dismiss themselves automatically after a time, requiring you to take no action at all. More serious errors provide instructions for recovering from the error and preventing it in the future. They also contain links to related tools and Help topics.

5

Installing and Using Applications

MAKING NO BONES ABOUT IT, USERS EXPECT their applications to work. It's their biggest concern, other than whether their hardware will work properly. Expectations are high. Like magic, "poof." Also, administrators won't deploy Microsoft Windows 2000 Professional, if doing so means that they're going to have to visit individual desktops in order to repair broken applications. Thus, Microsoft invested a lot of energy toward making sure they do work. The issue has two sides. First, what happens to applications when users upgrade from an earlier version of Microsoft Windows? Will they migrate properly? Second, will applications work when users install them in a new copy of Windows 2000 Professional?

Oddly enough, the biggest problem is the latter. Microsoft notes that while testing applications, the most pervasive problems were applications that refused to install in Windows 2000 Professional because the Setup program didn't like the operating system's version number. These applications work flawlessly when users install them in Windows 98 first and then upgrade to Windows 2000 Professional. They failed to install in a new copy of Windows 2000 Professional, however. This is just a sample of the stupid problems that you might encounter using your favorite application in Windows 2000 Professional; this chapter starts off describing more.

After you learn about the most typical reasons why applications fail and how you can circumvent some of those problems, this chapter describes some of Windows 2000 Professional's stability improvements and then goes on to show you how to perform various tasks. It wraps up by showing how to troubleshoot application failures, how applications store their preferences in the registry, and how to track down the changes that applications make to your configuration. You also learn about some of the new application-oriented technologies that Windows 2000 Professional introduces, such as Windows Installer.

Typical Failures

Most well-behaved applications work gloriously in Windows 2000 Professional. Not all applications are well-behaved, however, not even all of Microsoft's applications. So it is ironic that Microsoft coined the term *well-behaved*.

Why then do these applications work properly in other operating systems such as Microsoft Windows 98, but fail in Windows 2000 Professional? The problem has many faces. First, Windows 98 was more tolerant of behavior problems. Any user could install an application without regard for rights or permissions, for example. Windows 98 had holes in its memory manager that allowed applications to tread where they shouldn't, and the operating system wouldn't complain a lick. Second, very subtle changes in Windows 2000 Professional, which shouldn't affect any application, break a surprising number of misbehaved ones. An example is a change to the heap manager that causes applications that make fundamental memory-management mistakes to start failing in Windows 2000 Professional—the problem was always present but doesn't show up until now. Third, Microsoft made changes that they knew would break some applications, but they did so to improve the operating system's reliability, which is a higher priority for Microsoft than application compatibility. Last, some applications rely on Windows 98-specific features. When running applications that are bound to Windows 98, users might see error messages about missing entry points, which indicate that a particular API is unavailable.

To ferret out these types of problems, Microsoft dedicated numerous resources to test varieties of applications. I include the results of those tests in this section. Keep in mind that not all applications are afflicted with these problems. They're pretty much limited to poorly designed or misbehaved applications, which do include Microsoft offerings in some cases. Out of the 100 or so applications that I tested, only a handful failed to run in Windows 2000 Professional. If you do encounter any of the following problems, contact the independent software vendor (ISV):

- **Checking versions**   Although it's understandable that certain types of programs are bound to a particular version of Windows (disk utilities are an example), some applications refuse to run in Windows 2000 Professional because it reports its major version number as 5 and they've erroneously bound themselves to version 4. This is the most common reason that applications fail to install.

- **Replacing system files**   Applications that rely on replacing system files, files in *SystemRoot*, are in for an unpleasant surprise. Windows File Protection, which you learn about later in this chapter, restores protected files as soon as an application replaces them. Some applications won't work properly unless they can replace system files, and so they fail. This is such a big change that you learn more about it later.

- **Assuming too much about components**   Applications that assume certain components will or will not exist because, well, that's the way it's always been, are going to fail. Assumptions like that are unsafe in Windows 2000 Professional because the operating system has dropped some components and added others. For example, by default, the operating system now includes DirectX but doesn't include MAPI (Mail Application Programming Interface). Some applications refuse to install in Windows 2000 Professional because they assume it doesn't include DirectX. Other applications fail after they don't find MAPI on the computer.

- **Hard coding folder locations**   Even Microsoft's own applications are guilty of making assumptions about the location of shell folders. Have you ever wondered why the My Documents folder keeps popping up in the root folder of Drive C, even though it's in a user profile folder? That's because some misbehaved applications hardcode the locations of shell folders such as My Documents. This behavior is not safe in Windows 2000 Professional, though, because most of them have new locations under Documents and Settings. Some applications might fail and others are likely to confuse users.

- **Failing to handle long filenames**   Too many applications fail to handle long filenames properly. Earlier versions of Windows stored profiles in *SystemRoot*\Profiles. Not a huge problem, but Windows 2000 Professional stores profiles in Documents and Settings, and some applications don't like that because paths are more likely to have spaces in them. Another symptom is that misbehaved applications don't provide a big enough buffer for filenames and fail because paths are now longer due to the new location of user profiles. Other problems result from misbehaved applications not supporting long filenames properly; these were just samples.

- **Requiring Administrator credentials**   Some applications require users to log on as Administrator, which is wholly unacceptable. Companies want to reserve the Administrator account for administrators while still allowing users to install applications. The problem is two-fold. First, some setup programs require users to log on as Administrator, a lazy way of avoiding the permissions problem, whereas some applications use portions of the registry that are accessible only by Administrator. Either way, the application fails for most users.

- **Overwriting memory by accident**   This is the scariest application failure because it doesn't end with application errors; it ends with corrupt data. Microsoft has changed how it puts memory back into the pool when an application releases it. Earlier versions of Windows put it at the bottom of the list and Windows 2000 Professional puts it back on top. Some applications erroneously continue to use memory even after they free it. Because Windows 2000 Professional relocates that memory to the application more quickly now, those applications are more likely to write over its own data than it was in earlier versions of Windows. This is another case of changes in the operating system showing up application errors that already existed. Other failures are likely to result.

- **Limiting stack space available**   To date, many programmers used the smallest stack possible in order to improve their application's performance. They tuned the stack size so that just enough was available to squeak by. Windows 2000 Professional uses worldwide binaries now, and as a result uses more Unicode strings (see Chapter 16, "Using Multiple Languages"). The effect is that the operating system requires more stack space, and those applications that don't provide enough space fail.

- **Using undocumented capabilities**   Applications that use undocumented APIs are sometimes getting caught short. Microsoft has changed some of these APIs, and applications that use those are failing in Windows 2000 Professional. An interesting twist to this problem is applications that rely on events occurring in a specific order, even though Microsoft never guaranteed any sort of order to them. For example, a few applications rely on a specific sequence of messages from the operating system before they close their own processes. These applications no longer close themselves properly, even if they close their windows. Users can't restart those applications until they identify and kill the hung processes.

A plethora of other problems lurk in some applications, particularly those married to Windows 98. Few problems are full-blown failures, but they are more like annoyances. For example, some applications won't install their fonts properly, requiring users to restart the computer. Other applications aren't able to display their own help files or don't register their uninstallers properly.

More significant annoyances occur when applications rely on registry settings that are unique to Windows 98. One example is an application that doesn't find a default printer because of differences between Windows 98 and Windows 2000 Professional's registries. None of these problems makes the application unusable.

Although not really a failure, it is troubling to me that many applications based on earlier versions of Windows give bad advice in their dialog boxes and help. It's not the applications' fault. In Windows 2000 Professional, many features have new homes, particularly administrative tools. An application that tells users how to configure a device will probably give users incorrect information. Those that instruct users how to create dial-up connections will also give bad advice. The bottom line is that because the instructions for using so many features are different in this version of Windows, don't rely on the advice that applications might give in their dialog boxes or in help. Always consult Windows 2000 Help instead.

Note

Windows 2000 introduces new application programming interfaces (APIs) that help counter many of the problems you just read about. For example, the operating system includes `VerifyVersionInfo`, a new API for checking the operating system's version. It includes new APIs for working with Windows File Protection—such as `SfcIsFileProtected` and `SfcGetNextProtectedFile`, which help applications identify protected system files. The problem with these new APIs, of course, is that they're available only in Windows 2000, so applications must make sure that they're available before using them.

See also

- Chapter 3, "Troubleshooting," to learn how to repair failures that prevent the computer from starting properly.

Upgrade Reports

One way you can take advantage of Microsoft's testing efforts is to create a compatibility report *before* you upgrade to Windows 2000 Professional. You can, of course, determine whether applications are compatible by checking Microsoft's directory of Windows 2000 applications, but doing so case-by-case is too much work. An upgrade report checks each application installed on your computer, tells you whether you can expect problems, and tells you how to fix any problems that it finds. It certainly won't catch every problem, but it will leverage Microsoft's test results to help you find incompatible applications. Do check the directory of Windows 2000 applications before purchasing new software, in order to prevent disappointment.

Tip

Potentially, the best sources of information about whether an application works well in Windows 2000 Professional are other users' experiences. UseNet users are usually vocal about their experiences and also offer a lot of assistance. Try searching UseNet by using a service such as DejaNews, whose address is http://www.deja.com. For keywords, use a combination of *Windows 2000* and the name of the application about which you're inquiring.

As you learned in Chapter 1, "Installing Windows," you don't have to actually upgrade in order to create an upgrade report. To generate an upgrade report, which Microsoft sometimes calls a *compatibility report*, run Winnt32.exe with the /checkupgradeonly command-line option. The upgrade report, which is limited to the applications that the Setup program can identify, lists those application that won't work as well in Windows 2000 Professional as they did in the version of Windows from which you're upgrading. It also makes suggestions for fixing those problems, solutions that might include upgrade packs, reinstalling applications, or getting upgrades from the ISV.

To check numerous network-connected clients for compatibility problems, use the answer file in Listing 5.1 to run Winnt32.exe in unattended mode. Put the command in users' logon scripts. Don't forget to replace *path* with the network location you want to write the upgrade report: *server\share*. Because the Setup program uses the same filename for each upgrade report, set AppendComputerNameToPaths to Yes, causing the Setup program to create a unique folder for each computer. After executing the script on each computer, you'll have a collection of upgrade reports that help you determine which applications you must upgrade and which machines contain those applications.

Listing 5.1 Answer File to Create Upgrade Reports

```
[unattended]
win9xupgrade=yes
[win9xupg]
ReportOnly=yes
SaveReportTo=Path
AppendComputerNameToPaths=yes
```

See also

- Chapter 1, "Installing Windows," for more information about upgrade reports and upgrading to Windows 2000 Professional from earlier versions of Windows, including Windows 98.
- Chapter 13, "Deploying to Many Users," to learn how to upgrade to Windows 2000 Professional by pushing answer files in users' logon scripts.

Upgrade Packs

The Setup program is likely to recommend *upgrade packs*. Upgrade packs migrate applications from earlier versions of Windows to Windows 2000 Professional. Upgrade packs might be necessary in two instances: applications that are and applications that are not compatible with Windows 2000 Professional. In the first case, those applications can't handle changes in the operating system, even though they work properly in both operating systems. By updating their files and adjusting their settings so they work in the new operating system, upgrade packs prevent you from having to reinstall applications. In the second case, upgrade packs replace Windows 98-specific files to make those applications work properly in Windows 2000 Professional. In either case, the result is that your applications continue to work after upgrading the operating system to Windows 2000 Professional.

One way that ISVs figure out what their upgrade packs must do is to install their products on both operating systems and then compare the differences between them. They use snapshot utilities such as *Sysdiff* to compare the file systems and registries on both installations, using the results to implement their upgrade packs. Do the setup programs install different binaries for each operating system? Do the setup programs create different subkeys and values in each operating system's registry? Do the applications require services in Windows 2000 Professional that they didn't require in Windows 98? These are just some of the issues that ISVs discover by comparing their applications in both operating systems.

In their simplest form, upgrade packs are nothing more than migration DLLs (dynamic link libraries). In fact, their filenames are all the same: Migrate.dll. ISVs create migration DLLs to very strict specifications that determine how they exchange information with the Setup program, the order in which they complete tasks, and the APIs that they expose to the setup program. Their sizes vary from 100 kilobytes to several megabytes, and depend on the complexity of the application and the amount of work that they must perform. Even if they can preset users' interfaces, most don't do so because they don't usually require them. Migration DLLs themselves are actually pretty dull—in most cases, they do nothing more than change files and registry settings. Figure 5.1 illustrates the migration process.

The following provides an overview of the migration process:

1. Acquire upgrade packs for applications that require them in order to migrate successfully from Windows 98 to Windows 2000 Professional.

2. During the Windows 98 phase of the setup process, you provide the path to a directory that contains your upgrade packs to the setup program. The setup program runs each upgrade pack and passes it to a file called

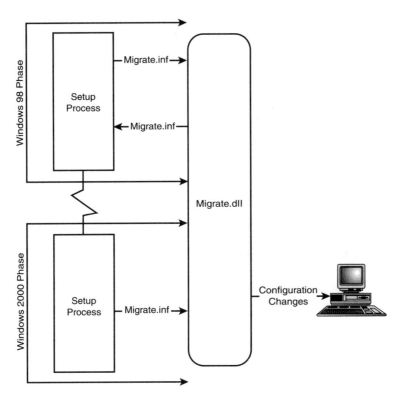

Figure 5.1   Upgrade packs do most of their work during the Windows 2000
Professional phase of the setup process.

Migrate.inf. Each upgrade pack writes to Migrate.inf information about
the work it must do in order to migrate the application from Windows 98
to Windows 2000 Professional. It doesn't do any work yet, though. The
setup program displays any messages that it finds in the Migrate.dll files in
the upgrade report.

3. During the Windows 2000 phase of the setup process, the setup program calls each migration DLL again, passing it the Migrate.dll file that
   it created during the first phase of the setup process. The migration
   DLL uses the information in Migrate.inf to migrate the application.

As indicated, Migration DLLs communicate with the setup program via
Migrate.inf, a setup information (INF) file that looks similar to other INF files
in Windows 2000 Professional. During the first part of the setup process, the
Windows 98 phase, the migration DLL adds a list of files, directories, and

registry settings that it will move or change to Migrate.inf. This file also contains messages that the migration DLL wants the setup program to add to upgrade reports. For example, it might include a message that informs you that you must reinstall the application in order for it to work properly. Just as likely is a message that tells you about the changes the migration DLL is going to make to your configuration. Migrate.inf also indicates the migration DLL's space requirements so that the Setup program can add that amount of disk space to the Setup program's overall requirements.

Microsoft naively anticipates that most ISVs will distribute upgrade packs, free of charge, via their Web sites. Technically speaking, upgrade packs are a terrific idea. They help ensure that users' applications work as well after upgrading to Windows 2000 Professional as they did in Windows 98. I'm not so confident about their usefulness, however. Many ISVs choose to ignore the capability to help their customers upgrade to Windows 2000 Professional, putting their efforts into new versions of their products rather than existing versions. Also, Microsoft doesn't support the Migration DLL AppWizard, a Microsoft tool that developers use to create migration DLLs—which doesn't seem like a good way to encourage companies to create and distribute upgrade packs to their customers. After searching the Web for upgrade packs, I found none, and Microsoft has no plans to post upgrade packs on their Web sites. In fact, the only upgrade packs that I found were the handful on the Windows 2000 Professional CD-ROM in i386\Win9xmig. The outlook is bleak. Also keep in mind that you must collect all of the upgrade packs you require in advance of upgrading Windows 98 to Windows 2000 Professional because you can apply them only during the setup process—an obvious weakness of the approach.

If you forget to use an upgrade pack for an application when you upgrade to Windows 2000 Professional, reinstalling the application usually fixes most problems.

See also

- Chapter 1, "Installing Windows," to learn how to use upgrade packs during the setup process.
- Chapter 13, "Deploying to Many Users," for more information about deploying upgrade packs to many users along with Windows 2000 Professional.

Logo Compliance

A simple logo, the now infamous Windows logo, is the single best thing Microsoft ever did for users. ISVs display the logo on certified applications' packaging. Microsoft also keeps a directory of certified products, and users can search the directory to determine whether Microsoft has certified a particular product. The logo indicates that applications bearing this badge of honor have passed the rigors of the *Application Specification for Windows 2000.* The implications are important.

By giving ISVs requirements to meet, the specification helps ISVs develop those applications without shooting in the dark. It ensures that those applications work and play well with Windows 2000 Professional, not to mention other applications that run on the operating system. It means that those applications are more stable, better able to repair themselves, cause fewer DLL conflicts, provide a better experience for roaming and mobile users, and are much easier to manage on a network. It also means that those applications migrate smoothly from earlier versions of Windows. What a deal.

The *Application Specification for Windows 2000* is a result of a collaboration between Microsoft and numerous ISVs, implying that these aren't just Microsoft edicts but a set of standards owned by varieties of companies. Table 5.1, which I quote from the specification, is an overview of its contents. You can read the specification for yourself; it's at `http://msdn.microsoft.com/winlogo`. Microsoft maintains two versions of it: a core specification for desktop applications and a more comprehensive specification for distributed applications. You're concerned primarily with the first specification because you're reading about Windows 2000 Professional.

Things can get a bit confusing when you see Microsoft's description of the three different application levels: certified, ready, and planned. *Certified* applications meet or exceed the requirements of the *Application Specification for Windows 2000,* and a third-party testing company, VeriTest, Inc., verifies them. This is the only level in which ISVs can license the logo from Microsoft, and they pay good money for that license. Microsoft will certify applications for any combination of Windows 2000 Professional, Windows NT Workstation 4.0, Windows 95, and Windows 98—as long as the application at least works in Windows 2000 Professional. The logos that Microsoft licenses to ISVs show the versions of Windows on which they certified the products. *Ready* applications are those that ISVs tested on their own and plan to support on Windows 2000 Professional but have not yet received certification from Microsoft. *Planned* applications are those that ISVs plan to deliver for Windows 2000 Professional in the future, but those versions are not yet available. Check an application's level at `http://www. microsoft.com/windows2000/upgrade/compat/search/default.asp`.

Table 5.1 **Application Specifications for Windows 2000**

95	98	NT 4	2000	Requirement
				Windows Fundamentals
X	X	X	X	Perform primary functionality and maintain stability
X	X	X	X	Provide 32-bit components
X	X	X	X	Support long filenames and UNC paths
X	X	X	X	Support printers with long names and UNC paths
	X		X	Do not read from or write to Win.ini, System.ini, Autoexec.bat, or Config.sys on any Windows operating system based on NT technology
X	X	X	X	Ensure that non-hidden files have associated file types; and all file types have associated icons, descriptions, and actions
X	X	X	X	Perform Windows version-checking correctly
X	X	X	X	Support AutoPlay of compact disks
			X	Kernel mode drivers must pass verification testing on Windows 20000
	X	X	X	Hardware drivers must pass WHQL testing
				Install/Uninstall
X	X	X	X	Install using a Windows Installer–based package that passes validation testing
X	X	X	X	Observe rules in componentization
X	X	X	X	Identify shared components
X	X	X	X	Install to Program Files by default
X	X	X	X	Support Add/Remove Programs properly
X	X	X	X	Ensure that your application supports advertising
X	X	X	X	Ensure correct uninstall support
				Component Sharing
			X	Do not attempt to replace files that are protected by System File Protection
	X		X	Component producers: build side-by-side components
	X		X	Application developers: Consume and install side-by-side components

continues

Table 5.1   **Continued**

95	98	NT 4	2000	Requirement
X	X	X	X	Install any non side-by-side shared files to the correct locations
				Data and Settings Management
X	X	X	X	Default to My Documents for storage of user-created data
X	X	X	X	Classify and store application data correctly
		X	X	Degrade gracefully on access denied
		X	X	Run in a secure Windows environment
			X	Adhere to system-level Group Policy settings
			X	Applications that create ADM files must properly store their ADM file settings in the registry
				User Interface Fundamentals
X	X	X	X	Support standard system size, color, font, and input settings
X	X	X	X	Ensure compatibility with the High Contrast option
X	X	X	X	Provide documented keyboard access to all features
X	X	X	X	Expose the location of the keyboard focus
X	X	X	X	Do not rely exclusively on sound
X	X	X	X	Do not place shortcuts to documents, help, or uninstall in the Start Menu
	X		X	Support multiple monitors
				OnNow/ACPI Support
	X		X	Indicate busy application status properly
	X		X	Respond to sleep requests from the operating system properly
	X		X	Handle sleep notifications properly
	X		X	Handle wake from normal sleep without losing data
	X		X	Handle wake from critical sleep properly
				Application Migration
X	X	X		Application must continue to function after upgrade to Windows 2000 Professional without reinstall

Get Great Applications Online

Even though I recommend that you stick with applications that sport the Windows logo, I must point out an exception. Few shareware and freeware vendors, who often produce best-of-breed applications and utilities, can have the resources required to get the logo, even if their applications come close or already meet the logo's requirements. They don't sell their software in boxes anywhere, so where do you expect them to display the logo? When searching out quality shareware and freeware products, the Web site I use most is ZDNet Downloads at `http://www.zdnet.com/swlib`.

If you're more in the market for commercial applications that you can buy and download now, try one of the many software e-commerce sites. Beyond.com is one the most famous example, which is at `http://www.beyond.com`. Purchase software by using a credit card and then install it immediately. Beyond.com has been on a buying spree recently, so you won't find as many strong competitors as in the past. Amazon.com does sell software, but its selection isn't nearly as strong as Beyond.com's selection.

A feature that many users liked in Microsoft Windows 98, one that's missing from Windows 2000 Professional, is Quick View. This handy utility allows you to view a document without actually owning the application. Add Quick View back to Windows 2000 Professional by purchasing Quick View Plus from Inso Corporation, `http://www.inso.com`.

Stability Improvements

Windows 2000 Professional includes varieties of enhancements that make it more stable. Stability is, after all, one of Microsoft's prime selling points for its new operating system. The improvements that make applications more stable usually involve DLLs or system files:

- **Application Isolation**   The capability to isolate the files of applications that don't implement side-by-side DLLs, so they don't harm other applications that rely on different versions.

- **Side-by-side DLLs**   The capability for setup programs to install a private copy of a DLL that it doesn't share with other applications, which prevents version conflicts that affect stability.

- **Windows File Protection**   A feature of Windows 2000 Professional that prevents applications from replacing system files, therefore improving the overall stability of the operating system.

You learn about these improvements in the following sections: "Application Isolation," "Side-by-Side DLLs," and "Windows File Protection." Windows 2000 Professional has many other improvements that make it a more stable platform. Driver-signing makes device drivers more stable. Enhancements to NTFS make the file system more stable. Substantial enhancements to the operating system's networking features make it more stable. New management features not only make it more stable, but also make it a substantially more manageable platform.

Application Isolation

Most users and all administrators have been in "DLL hell:" a term coined by someone at Microsoft to describe the terrible havoc that version conflicts wreak on users' configurations. DLL hell starts when users install two different applications, each of which requires a unique version of the same common DLL. Usually what happens is that one setup program overwrites a DLL that another setup program installed with a newer version. If the first application requires a different version of the DLL, it's going to fail. A version conflict is born and vanquishes the user to DLL hell. This problem doesn't occur with private DLLs—those that applications install for their own use in their own program directories.

In the old days, users had to choose one or the other program. In Windows 2000 Professional, Microsoft enhanced the `LoadLibrary` API to support DLL redirection, however. Administrators can now redirect an application's request to load DLLs from one location to a different one. For example, an administrator can force an application to load DLLs from its own program directory instead of from *SystemRoot*\System32, where many common DLLs reside. The result is DLLs isolated to the application, requiring them and preventing version conflicts with other versions of the same DLLs. After identifying applications that don't work well together in the same configuration, here's how you isolate an application's DLLs:

1. Identify the DLLs that are causing problems.

   This task isn't as daunting as it seems. You'll usually see an error message that indicates an offending DLL. The error message might be an application error or it might be a dialog box that says an entry point is missing from a DLL. If the application caused an application error, look at Dr. Watson's log files to determine the DLLs.

2. Extract from the CD-ROM the version of the DLLs that the application requires to work properly.

3. Put the DLLs in the application's directory.

4. In the application's program directory, create a file named *Filename*.exe.local, where *Filename* is the name of the application's .exe file.

   If you don't know the name of the application's .exe file, look at the shortcut you use to run the application. If you don't find a shortcut for the application, look in its program directory.

The result of creating *Filename*.exe.local in the application's program directory is that LoadLibrary looks for DLLs there first, regardless of the path that the application gave to LoadLibrary. If the API doesn't find the DLL in the application's program directory, it then looks in the path that the application gave it as well as other common locations of DLLs such as System32.

Side-by-Side DLLs

Side-by-side DLLs is a developer solution to DLL hell. This is in fact the solution that Microsoft recommends and requires for certification. It's the solution that the company is adopting for its own applications, too.

Side-by-side DLLs allow multiple versions of a DLL to run at the same time. The concept is simple and goes back to the ways of Microsoft MS-DOS, when setup programs wrote all of an application's files to its program directory. We've come full circle, it seems. From your perspective, it means that applications use the DLLs with which ISVs tested their products and not DLLs that some other setup program installs on the computer. Applications are no longer at the mercy of other setup programs, which puts control over an application's stability back into the hands of the application's developer.

Of course, many applications don't yet implement side-by-side DLLs. If these applications send you into the abyss of DLL hell, you can still use application isolation to prevent version conflicts, a process you learned about in the previous section.

Note

Speaking of changes in the way Microsoft develops its products, it has hinted at changes other than side-by-side DLLs that eliminate *feature creep*. The company hints that it will no longer bury new features in service packs, for example, which is always a mischievous problem for administrators. In the future, the company intends to limit service packs to fixes, but will release a new version of the operating system in order to distribute new features. The company also hints that it will restrict the products through which it will distribute different components. This means you might not find Microsoft FrontPage Server Extensions on quite as many CD-ROMs as before. The goal of all these changes is to minimize *installation hell*—expanding on the term DLL hell—in which the installation order of different service packs and components significantly impacts the operating system's stability. This is a bit more like the distribution model that Microsoft uses for its consumer operating systems. Better days are coming!

Windows File Protection

DLL hell affects more than applications; it also treads on the operating system's stability. Applications usually replace system files—files in *SystemRoot* that are vital parts of the operating system—because they require newer versions of those files than the operating system uses. The result is that the operating system becomes fragile, left to the whim of a programmer who takes little or no responsibility for the operating system his code affects. Wanting to control Windows 2000 Professional's stability, Microsoft introduced Windows File Protection (System File Protection). It restores system files when it detects that something has changed them.

Windows File Protection has two facets. First is the service that runs quietly in the background, monitoring system files for changes. To recognize changes, Windows File Protection compares each system file's signature to the signature it expects. If the two are different, it replaces the file from the DLL cache. The DLL cache is in *SystemRoot*\System32\dllcache and also includes Security Catalog (CAT) files that contain the expected signatures. If Windows File Protection doesn't find the system file it needs in the DLL cache, it looks for it on the network or on the Windows 2000 Professional CD-ROM, prompting you to insert the CD-ROM if it's not already in the drive. If you don't have access to either, download system files from Microsoft's new DLL Help Web site, which you can access via http://support.microsoft.com. Windows File Protection will use files that you download from this Web site as long as their signatures match the signatures in the DLL cache's CAT files.

Other than official mechanisms for updating system files, Windows File Protection allows no exceptions. None. It protects more than 2,700 files having the .sys, .dll, .exe, and .ocx extensions, as well as a few font files. Mechanisms that Windows File Protection supports for updating system files include service packs, hot fixes, operating system upgrades, and Windows Update. ISVs that must replace system files aren't out of luck, however. They can still use versions of DLLs other than those that Windows 2000 Professional uses; the trick is for them to implement side-by-side DLLs or for you to use application isolation, which you learned about earlier.

The second facet is System File Checker (Sfc.exe). It's a utility that scans protected system files for errors and also populates the DLL cache with proper copies of system files. This is also the tool you use to change the size of the DLL cache and set other options. The following describes System File Checker's command-line options:

Syntax: sfc [/scannow] [/scanonce] [/scanboot] [/cancel]
                    [/quiet] [/enable] [/purgecache] [/cachesize=*N*]

Options:

/scannow	Scans protected files now
/scanonce	Scans protected files one time at the next boot
/scanboot	Scans protected files each time the operating system starts

/cancel	Cancels all pending scans
/quiet	Replaces incorrect protected files without prompting first
/enable	Enables the default operation of Windows File Protection, which is to prompt users before replacing protected files
/purgecache	Purges and repopulates the DLL cache with proper system files
/cachesize=N	Sets the maximum size of the DLL cache in megabytes (requires you to restart the computer in order to take effect)

You must log on as Administrator or be a member of the Administrators group to use System File Checker.

The default size of the DLL cache is 50 megabytes. Change its size by using the /cachesize option or by storing it in SFCQuota, a REG_DWORD registry setting that you find in HKLM\SOFTWARE\Microsoft\Windows\CurrentVersion\Winlogon. Setting it to 0xFFFFFFFF causes Windows File Protection to cache all protected system files, just over 2,700 of them. With the default size, it caches about 1,400. Table 5.2 describes other registry settings that you can use to further configure Windows File Protection, including one that allows you to disable the feature the next time you start the operating system. All of these values are in Winlogon, along with SFCQuota.

Table 5.2 **Windows File Protection Settings**

Value	**Type**	**Settings**	
SFCDisable	**REG_DWORD**	0	enable
		1	disable but prompt to enable at the next boot
		2	disable at the next boot only and enable without prompting first
		4	enable without prompts
SFCScan	**REG_DWORD**	0	don't scan at boot
		1	scan at every boot
		2	scan files once
SFCQuota	**REG_DWORD**	size of cache in megabytes	

continues

Table 5.2 **Continued**

Value	Type	Settings
SFCDllCacheDir	**REG_EXPAND_SZ**	path of the folder that contains the dllcache
SFCShowProgress	**REG_DWORD**	0 don't display progress meter while scanning
		1 displays progress meter while scanning

Note

Uncontroversial? Windows File Protection is not. Although it certainly improves Windows 2000 Professional's stability, it can break many applications that *must* replace system files in order to work properly. Those applications fail in Windows 2000 Professional because the operating system immediately restores the original version of the file. Also, for certification, Microsoft requires developers to add code that detects whether the operating system is protecting a particular file to their applications and, if the application must use a different version, they must implement it as a side-by-side DLL. This is a lot of work that ISVs hadn't originally counted on doing. Still, by stomping its feet and forcing ISVs' hands, Microsoft is preventing one of the biggest threats to the operating system's stability.

See also

- Chapter 7, "Managing Disks and Files," for more information about features that enhance Windows 2000 Professional's stability even more.
- Chapter 14, "Managing Individual Computers," to learn more about service packs and hot fixes, and how to slip stream both types of updates.

Installing Applications

Installing applications on a standalone computer running Windows 2000 Professional is no different from installing them in any recent version of Windows. The Add/Remove Programs dialog box does look a wee bit different, but the general process is the same. Thus, after a quick list of methods for installing applications, the rest of this section deals with the hellish issues that power users might encounter when installing applications. To install an application, do one of the following:

- Insert the application's CD-ROM in the drive and follow the directions you see on the screen.
- In Control Panel, double-click the Add/Remove Programs icon, click Add New Programs, and follow the directions you see onscreen.

- In Windows Explorer, double-click the Setup program's icon, and then follow the directions you see on the screen.

- On the Start menu, click Run, and then type the path and filename of the setup program. Follow the directions you see on the screen.

The Add/Remove Programs dialog box has a new look. Click Change or Remove Programs to display the applications you installed. Sort this list by clicking a sort order in the Sort by list. If you sort by size (useful for finding monster applications that you can remove to free disk space), the dialog box displays each application's size. Sort by frequency of use (useful for removing applications that you no longer use), and the dialog box displays how often you use the application: rarely, occasionally, or frequently. Sort by date last used, and it displays the date you last used the application. In the Currently installed programs list, click applications to highlight them. The Add/Remove Programs dialog box displays selected applications' size, frequency of use, and the date you last used them. Click Change/Remove to reconfigure the application or remove it altogether. Be wary, though, because some applications' setup programs automatically remove the application when you click Change/Remove without first confirming the action.

No matter how you install the application, you can still remove it by using the Add/Remove Programs dialog box. All certified and most non-certified applications register their uninstall programs in the registry; thus, the method that you use to run the setup program has no bearing on whether you can remove it or not. Using Control Panel is usually the easiest way to remove an application, but you can also start its uninstall program manually. It most cases, you find it in Program Files in the application's program folder. To see the uninstall programs registered on your computer, look at the subkey HKLM\SOFTWARE\Microsoft\Windows\CurrentVersion\Uninstall.

Using Windows 2000 Professional on a managed, Windows 2000-based network makes installing applications more convenient, assuming that the network's administrators take advantage of Group Policy. Using Group Policy, they can assign or publish applications to users within any site, domain, or organizational unit; and they can assign applications to computers. When administrators assign applications, you see shortcuts for those applications in the Start menu, even if the application isn't yet installed on your computer. The first time you click the shortcut or the first time you try opening a document that the application associates with itself, Windows 2000 Professional installs the application from the network. The technology partly responsible for this capability is the Windows Installer service, which you will learn about later in this chapter. Applications that administrators publish are in the Add/Remove Programs dialog box. These are applications that they make available to users on the network, but installing them is optional. Figure 5.2 shows the Add/Remove Programs dialog box. In the Add programs from your network list, you see three applications that are available on the network. This list is always empty unless your computer is connected to a managed network; on a peer-to-peer network, you can't assign or publish applications.

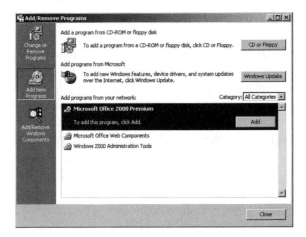

Figure 5.2   Using this dialog box, you can install applications locally or publish applications from the network.

Note

ISVs build too much *bloatware*—software products that contain too many useless features and waste entirely too much space on users' disks. Microsoft is the biggest culprit (consider Microsoft Office 2000). The solution is to make sure you don't accept the default options that these applications' setup programs present, even though they recommend you install all of them. Limit the number of components that you install and you'll find that you have more space available and the software is actually easier to use.

See also

- Chapter 15, "Managing Networked Computers," for more information about managing Windows 2000 Professional on a network.

Best Install Locations

Some applications don't install in their proper places by default. The current version of America Online installs in the root directory, for example. This is undesirable if you want a well-organized disk that's easy to manage. Aside from the root directory's appearance in Microsoft Windows Explorer, installing applications in the root directory dodges Windows 2000 Professional's security. Windows 2000 Professional gives full control of the root directory to everyone while it limits access to Program Files. Administrators have full control, of course, whereas power users can modify Program Files and users can only read files in Program Files. Even though some setup programs install their applications in the root directory, you can almost always redirect the setup program to install the application in Program Files.

Some users install applications on a volume other than the one that contains Windows 2000 Professional. They create a smallish volume for Windows 2000 Professional (one that's just big enough for the operating system to work properly), another volume for their applications, and sometimes yet another volume for their documents. The result is that the operating system is more stable because applications and documents are on separate volumes. Note that this configuration goes against Microsoft's policy of installing applications in *SystemDrive*\Program Files and documents in *UserProfile*\My Documents.

View Program Files in Windows Explorer, and you see the nag shown in Figure 5.3. The purpose of this nag isn't to frustrate power users; it's to prevent novices from making changes that break their applications. Microsoft doesn't call it a nag, of course; they have two different names for it: *soft barrier* and *barricade*. Windows 2000 Professional redirects users to Control Panel to manage their programs, and allows them to view Program Files by clicking Show Files. As a power user, you can disable the soft barrier so that the operating system immediately displays the contents of Program Files when you click it in Windows Explorer's Folders bar. Edit Folder.htt, replacing `!gFolder.HaveToShowWebViewBarricade` with **true**. Folder.htt is in Program Files, but you'll have to display hidden and super-hidden files in order to open it. The quickest way to edit this file is using Microsoft Notepad, which you can associate with .htt files by clicking Open With on the file's shortcut menu. The following listing shows what the excerpt of this file looks like after changing it:

```
// INITIALIZATION

function Initialize(introText) {
    gIntroText = introText;
    gFolder = FileList.Folder;
    gShowFiles = true;
    gFolderPath = Info.innerHTML;
    Thumbnail.style.display = "none";
    Info.innerHTML = NoneSelected();
```

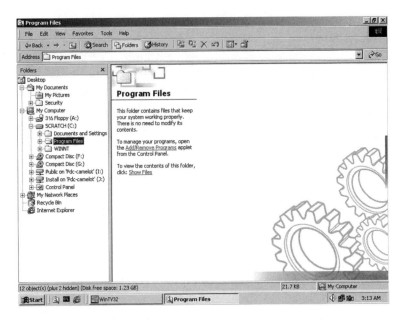

Figure 5.3   Microsoft designed this *soft barrier* to prevent novice users from accidentally harming their configurations.

See also

- Chapter 7, "Managing Disks and Files," to learn more about how Windows 2000 Professional organizes its files and how to display super-hidden files.

Dual-Boot Configurations

Dual-boot configurations present special problems all their own. When installing earlier versions of Windows in dual-boot configurations, the convention was to reinstall the application in the same location for both operating systems. That way, you stored only one copy of the application's program files, even though the application stored settings in both operating system's registries.

This approach doesn't work when using Windows 2000 Professional in dual-boot configurations with earlier versions of Windows such as Windows 98. Chances are good that the application won't install the same binary files in both operating systems, having different requirements for Windows 2000 Professional. Great confusion and many problems are possible; thus, to ensure a reliable dual-boot configuration, you must install applications twice (once for each operating system) and in different locations for each operating system.

For example, if you install Windows 98 and Windows 2000 Professional in a dual-boot configuration, you installed Windows 98 on the first partition and Windows 2000 Professional on the second, out of necessity. The first partition is most likely FAT32 and the second is NTFS. To install Office 2000, you'd install it twice. Install it in Windows 98—to Windows 98's Program Files directory. Install it in Windows 2000 Professional to that operating system's Program Files directory. The result is that you have two different copies of the application, but fewer problems down the road.

See also

- Chapter 1, "Installing Windows," for more information about dual-boot configurations.

Rights and Permissions

Any discussion of the rights and permissions that users require in order to install applications must start with a refresher course on the basic types of groups: Users, Power Users, and Administrators. Users' accounts are members of one or more of these groups. The groups to which an account belongs determine what a user who logs on to the computer using that account can do. Although this isn't new information for Windows NT Workstation 4.0 users, it's certainly new for Windows 98 users. Accounts in the following groups have different capabilities that affect their ability to install applications:

- **Users** Members of this group can do very little in Windows 2000 Professional. They have permission to read most files and registry settings, but no other permissions, such as write, delete, etc.
- **Power Users** Members of this group can change most files and registry settings, but Windows 2000 Professional still limits them in annoying ways.
- **Administrators** Members of this group have full control over the computer, including almost all of the computer's files and registry settings.

Ordinary users don't expect much. They know that they can't install applications. Administrators don't have a care in the world. Windows 2000 Professional tests Power Users' patience, however. Although they can install most applications without a hitch, the operating system doesn't give them sufficient permissions to all portions of the file system and registry in order for them to install many applications. Power Users can't install Microsoft Money 2000, for example. They can't install applications that install from Setup Information (INF) files, either. Until the very last release candidate of Windows 2000 Professional, only administrators could install Office 2000 because Power Users didn't have permission to modify Win.ini. If you're using the account that Windows 2000 Professional's Setup program prompted you to create, your account is a member of this group.

This problem is chock-full of paradoxes. First, Microsoft wants to prevent users from using accounts that are members of the Administrators group on a routine basis. The company wants them to log on as a member of the Power Users group for routine tasks and log on as Administrator when they must perform a task that requires elevated permissions. The idea is that this approach avoids human errors and viruses that must have elevated permissions to do their harm. The second paradox is that when users log on to the computer as Administrator, they're using that accounts user profile, not their normal ones. Thus, any per-user changes that they make do not affect the user profiles that they use on a daily basis. This means that when users log on to the computer as Administrator to install a per-user application, the application won't be available when they log on to the computer using their regular accounts. Microsoft is still forcing users to add themselves to the Administrators group in order to get productive use of their computers, which is precisely the situation that the company hoped to avoid.

Eventually, you're going to become frustrated after continually seeing error messages telling you that you don't have enough permission to install an application. In order of preference, here are a few ways around the problem:

- Temporarily add your account to the Administrators group, install the application, and then remove your account from the Administrators group. Other than extra work, this doesn't have the same limitations as the rest of the options in this list.

- Use Secondary Logon to run the Setup program using an account that has the required permissions. Press Shift and right-click the program's icon; then click Run as. Realize that the Setup program sees the user profile of the account you're using to run the Setup program, not your normal user profile. Thus, if the program only puts shortcuts in the current user's Start menu, you won't see those shortcuts in your Start menu.

- Log on to the computer as Administrator and then run the application's setup program. This has the same limitations as the previous bullet.

- Use Group Policy to install applications using elevated permissions. This applies to applications that administrators assign or publish.

- Permanently add your account to the Administrators group so that you can install any application and change any setting without further complaints from Windows 2000 Professional.

See also

- Chapter 7, "Managing Disks and Files," for more information about file system security, including how to assign permissions to users and groups.
- Chapter 10, "Securing Your Computer," to learn more about security in Windows 2000 Professional. This chapter shows you how to add users to groups.

More Software Rights

File permissions aren't the only thing you must worry about. You must also have a license to install the application at all. I'm referring to software piracy, which, according to Software and Information Industry Association, costs independent software vendors (ISVs) billions every year.

The penalties for pirating software are stiff. It's a felony offense that might include prison terms of five years and fines up to $250,000. Civil penalties can be as large as $100,000 for each infringement, and don't forget to throw in attorney fees. The only exception to the copy law is that you may copy products in order to make backup copies. That's all.

Some forms of piracy are obvious. A fellow at the flea market stamping out copies of a CD-ROM is an example. Other forms are insidious, though. A coworker borrowing your Microsoft Office 2000 CD-ROM is an example of what you might think of as innocuous distribution of software over cubicle walls. This is where ISVs are losing most of their money, though.

As a user, complying is easy: Don't install the application if you don't have a license for it. Companies have a big challenge, however, even if they really want to do the right thing. You can enforce compliance using a few simple steps, though. Document usage policies and distribute those to the company's employees. Set up procedures for getting licenses and documenting them (particularly in licensing programs such as Microsoft's Open License program). Assign responsibility for managing licenses to an employee. Empower them to perform regular audits using one of the audit programs that the Software and Information Industry Association recommends at http://www.siia.com.

6

Using Printers
and Fonts

THE IMPROVEMENTS TO MICROSOFT WINDOWS 2000 Professional's
printing and font features are subtle but nevertheless a boon for you. The
core set of features remains largely unchanged. Yet, finding and installing
printers is easier. Documents print exactly as expected. Colors look the
same on paper as they do onscreen. Innovative features such as OpenType
fonts and Internet Printing make the operating system a document-
producing machine.

Experienced users such as you will be immediately comfortable with
routine tasks such as adding printers, printing documents, and managing
fonts. Therefore, after providing an overview of these routine tasks, this
chapter focuses on nuances that are a bit obscure or are not immediately
obvious. In this chapter, you learn how to search your organization for
printers that suit your needs. You learn how to print documents over
the Internet. Also, you learn how to troubleshoot printer problems that
afflict users in various situations.

Installing Printers

Whether you're connecting to a local or network printer, you must install
the drivers for that printer. Local printers are those that you physically
attach to your computer. Network printers are those attached to a network
server or attached to the network via internal or external network adapters.

Either way, there are three different ways to install printer drivers: allowing Plug and Play to detect the printer, using the Add Printer Wizard, or using Point and Print to install a network printer.

The requirements for installing local printers are similar to installing any other hardware, except for installing network printers:

- In most cases, you don't have to log on to the computer as an Administrator to install a network printer or any printer for which Windows 2000 Professional provides drivers. To install a local printer using drivers that the operating system does not provide, you must log on to the computer as an Administrator, however.

- In order to install a network printer, you must have appropriate permissions. To connect to a network printer requires that the printer's administrator gave you permission to do so, either implicitly through a group that's in the printer's access control list (ACL) or explicitly by adding your account to the printer's ACL.

Note

When two or more users share a computer, each user must individually install printers. If I install a printer, for example, other users won't see that same printer when they log on to the computer and install it themselves. On a nicer note, users will never have to log on as an Administrator in order to install a printer after someone else installs it because the drivers will already be available on the computer.

See also

- Chapter 2, "Configuring Hardware," to learn more about when you must log on to the computer as an Administrator in order to install new hardware.
- Chapter 10, "Securing Your Computer," for more information about access control lists.

Local Printers

Installing local printers isn't any different from installing them in Microsoft Windows NT Workstation 4.0 or Microsoft Windows 98. Windows 2000 Professional automatically detects and configures thousands of Plug and Play printers, so check the Printers folder to make sure the printer isn't already installed. If it's not already installed, use Add Printer Wizard in the Printers folder under Control Panel:

1. In Control Panel, double-click the Printers icon and then double-click the Add Printer icon.

2. In Add Printer Wizard, click Next, click Local printer, and then click Next again.

Add Printer Wizard first searches for any Plug and Play printers. If it doesn't find any, click Next to manually install the printer; pick the printer port, select a printer driver, and choose whether you want to share the printer.

After installing a local printer, you can share it with other users on the network. To share a printer, you must have Manage Printer rights on the computer. Click Sharing on the printer icon's shortcut menu, click Shared as, and then type a name for the printer. Other ways to configure printer sharing include the following:

- If you want to make the printer particularly easy for other users to find, select the List in the Directory check box, which only applies if you connect to a network that uses Active Directory.

- When other users connect to your printer, if they're also using Windows 2000 Professional, they don't have to provide drivers for it because the operating system downloads the drivers from your computer. If you want users of other operating systems to be able to use the printer, however, you can install additional drivers for them; click Additional Drivers to do so.

- If you want to control which users can access the printer, click the Security tab of the printer Properties dialog box, shown in Figure 6.1. Then, do one of following:

  - Click Add to add a user or group, whether local or domain, to the printer's ACL.

  - Click the name of a user or group and then click Remove to remove it from the ACL.

  - Click the name of a user or group and then select the check boxes corresponding the permissions you want to assign to it in the Permissions list. You can explicitly allow or deny Print, Manage Printers, and Manage Documents permissions for each user or group. If you want to have finer control over the printer's ACL, click Advanced.

See also
- Chapter 10, "Securing Your Computer," to learn more about managing access control for printers, files, and folders.

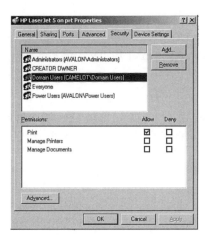

Figure 6.1 You don't usually need to worry much with printers' ACLs unless you want to specifically prevent access to an individual user or a group of users.

Network Printers

You can choose between two different ways to install network printers. The simplest way is to locate the printer in the My Network Places folder and then click Connect on its shortcut menu. The operating system installs the printers' drivers and associates them with the appropriate network share automatically, usually requiring no user interaction at all.

If you prefer, you can use Add Printer Wizard to install a network printer. In Add Printer Wizard, click Type the printer name or click Next to browse for a printer. Then, type the UNC name of a printer on the network (UNC names look like *servername**printername*) or click Next and browse for a printer on the Browse For Printer page. Searching the directory is useful if you're connected to a network that Windows 2000 Server manages and you can't locate the printer you want to use. In that case, if the printer is listed in Active Directory, you can easily search for the printer as follows:

1. In Control Panel, double-click the Printers icon and then double-click the Add Printer icon.

2. In Add Printer Wizard, click Next, click Network printer, and then click Next.

3. On the Locate Your Printer page, click Find a printer in the Directory and then click Next.

4. In Find Printers, provide as much information as you can about the printer for which you're searching on the following tabs and then click

Find Now. If you don't provide any information on any of these tabs, the operating system displays all of the printers listed in Active Directory:

- **Printers** Type the printers' name, location, or model. All this information is optional and usually not necessary if your organization has only a few printers. If it has a lot of printers, be as descriptive as you can so the list will be shorter.

- **Features** Describe the features for which you're looking: double-sided printing, color printing, stapling, paper size, minimum resolution, and minimum speed.

- **Advanced** Search for printers based on any of the fields that describe printers in the Active Directory. Fields for which you can search include Asset Number, Owner Name, Paper Available, and Web Page Address.

5. On the Printers tab shown in Figure 6.2, choose which printer you want to install. Click Connect on its shortcut menu.

Figure 6.2 If you don't provide any search parameters, Add Printer Wizard displays all printers listed in Active Directory.

Note

Using Active Directory, administrators have a fair amount of control over printers. They can automatically install printers for you or they can prevent printers from being listed in the directory. For more information about these capabilities, see *Inside Windows 2000 Server*, published by New Riders.

Internet Printers

Internet printing is a hot new feature that I think has a lot of potential—but not yet. The idea is that it's an alternative to faxing, e-mailing, or sending documents via overnight mail. Imagine being able to make reservations at your favorite hotel by printing them. Imagine printing documents at the office while you're on the road. It's a great idea that's going to take awhile to develop because using a printer over the Internet requires companies to prepare their servers and publish those addresses.

Internet printing is based on a new protocol, *Internet Printing Protocol* (IPP). IPP creates remote procedure call (RPC) connections to printers over the Internet.

Installing or printing to an Internet printer is really no different from any network printer. In Add Printer Wizard, click Network printer, click Next, click Connect to a printer on the Internet or on your intranet, and type the printer's URL in URL. Essentially, you provide a URL instead of a UNC name. After installing an Internet printer using Add Printer Wizard, it downloads the drivers from the Internet, installs the printer, and you're ready to go. After you installed the printer, printing to it is no different from printing to any other printer, which you learn about later in this chapter.

Note

In order for a printer to be accessible via the Internet, it must be attached to a server computer running Windows 2000 Server that's accessible from the Internet. Also, Internet Information Services (IIS) must be running on the server and the administrator must install and share the printer.

You can view information about Internet printers over the Internet. Open the printer's URL to see its status. Open `http:/servername/printers` to see all the printers that are available over the Internet on that server. An easier way to view a printer's status is to double-click its icon in the Printers folder, however. This is the same user interface you're already accustomed to using.

Managing Printers

The following sections discuss printer queues, printer preferences, and printing documents.

Printer Queues

Managing a printer's queue is no different from earlier versions of Windows. In the Printers folder, double-click the printer to open its queue. When you open the printer queue, you see a list of the documents that are printing or are queued to print. Click any document to select it and then do one of the following:

- To pause a document, click Pause on the Document menu.
- To print a paused document, click Resume on the Document menu.
- To restart a document from the beginning, click Restart on the Document menu.
- To cancel a document, click Pause on the Document menu.
- To view a document's properties, click Properties on the Document menu.

   This command allows you to change the document's priority, schedule when the document prints, and view the document's printing preferences.

The remaining commands apply to all of the documents in the queue. These are available only if you have Manage Printers permission for the printer, which you probably have if you installed the printer locally and probably don't have if you're using a network printer. To pause the printer, for example, click Pause Printing on the Printer menu. To cancel all print jobs, click Cancel All Documents on the Document menu.

Printer Preferences

If you're using more than one printer, make sure you select the one that you want to use as the default. To do so, in the Printers folder, click Set as Default Printer on its shortcut menu. That way, output automatically goes to that printer if you don't select a printer.

More preferences are available than just setting the default printer. Click Printing Preferences to configure things such as default paper orientation and quality. The first tab of the printer Printing Preferences dialog box allows you to change the orientation of the paper, whether it prints on both sides of the paper; as well as the page order, front-to-back or back-to-front. On this tab, click Advanced to set printer-specific options. The next tab, Paper/Quality, allows you to choose the paper source or tray. Note that the options that are available on this dialog box are different, depending on the driver you installed. One printer's driver might include just a few basic options, whereas another printer's driver will include several different options.

On a printer's shortcut menu, click Properties to configure the printer. The options here are a bit more administrative than printing preferences, which describe how you want documents to print. For example, you can configure the printer share, determine when the printer is available, set the printer's ACL to control which users or groups can use and manage the printer, and set device settings such as printer memory. However, once you've installed and shared a printer, there aren't that many good reasons to spend much time configuring a printer because the default settings are usually preferable. Note that you must have Manage Printers permission for the printer to change any of these settings.

Printing Documents

To print a document in most applications, click Print on the File menu. The application then displays the Print dialog box. Although some applications do modify the Print dialog box, most don't. Figure 6.3 shows what it looks like. In the Select Printer list, you see the same icons that you see in the Printers folder: one icon for each printer to which you can print and the Add Printer icon. If you forgot to install the printer you want to use, you don't have to go back to the Printers folder—just double-click the Add Printer icon to install it. If you'd rather search the directory for a printer, click Find Printer, which opens the Find Printers window (refer to "Network Printers" earlier in this chapter). All other options on this dialog box are the same as in earlier versions of Windows, including Windows 98.

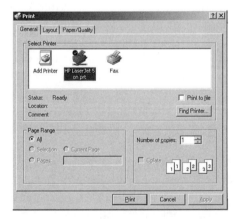

Figure 6.3 The Layout and Paper/Quality tabs allow you to adjust printing preferences for this document only.

Other ways you can print documents include these:

- On a program's File menu, click Print.
- On a document's shortcut menu, click Print.
- Drag a printer icon from the Printers folder to your desktop to create a shortcut for it and then drag a document to the shortcut.
- Drag a printer icon from the Printers folder to your SendTo folder, which is *UserProfile*\SendTo. Click Send To on a document's shortcut menu and click the name of the printer.

Managing Fonts

OpenType fonts are the latest addition to Windows 2000 Professional's collection of fonts. OpenType is a standard that Microsoft developed in conjunction with Adobe, combining technologies such as TrueType and Type 1, which brings the benefits of those fonts to all platforms. New features, including subsetting and font-compression, make OpenType fonts particularly applicable to the Internet, and more specifically the Web, because they're quicker to download and look good in a Web browser. To ensure an OpenType font's integrity, each is digitally signed. (Signatures are available only for OpenType fonts and, in fact, if a font doesn't have a digital signature, it's not an OpenType font.) Getting that digital signature requires that the font pass tests to verify the integrity of its hinting algorithms, suggesting a good-looking font.

In Windows 2000 Professional, managing fonts is not unlike other versions of Windows. You install, remove, and preview fonts the same way. The following sections show you how to perform those tasks and describe any problems you might encounter.

See also

- Chapter 16, "Using Multiple Languages," to learn more about Windows 2000 Professional's single set of world-wide binaries. Each language edition of the operating system comes with at least one font that enables you to write documents using any language supported by the operating system.

Installation

Fonts are in *SystemRoot*\Fonts, but you can also view them in Control Panel. In Control Panel, double-click the Fonts icon. Installing a font is as simple as dragging the font file to this folder. Windows 2000 Professional automatically installs the font and adds the appropriate information to the registry. Other ways that you can install a font include the following:

- At the MS-DOS command prompt, copy the font file to the Fonts folder. If Microsoft Windows Explorer isn't open when you do this, Windows 2000 Professional won't register the font until after you restart the computer.

- With the Fonts folder open, click Install New Font on the File menu. Using this command doesn't make sense because it's more complicated than simply dragging the font file to the Fonts folder.

- Administrators can install additional fonts via answer files, which are scripts that allow you to install Windows 2000 Professional with little or no interaction.

To remove a font, simply delete the file from the Fonts folder. Windows 2000 Professional automatically cleans up the font's settings from the registry.

See also
- Chapter 1, "Installing Windows," to learn more about answer files and how to write them.

Font Previews

Within the Fonts folder, you can view a sample of any font by double-clicking its icon. The window that Windows Explorer displays describes the type of font, whether it's signed, its typeface name, file size, version, and copyright information. It also displays a basic set of characters and the string "The quick brown fox jumps over the lazy dog. 1234567890" at various sizes so you can get an idea of what the font looks like. What it doesn't do, and I wish it did, is display a list of each character in the font. This would be particularly handy if you use any of the symbol fonts, such as WingDings.

7

Managing Disks and Files

O N THE SURFACE, MICROSOFT WINDOWS 2000 Professional doesn't introduce any dramatic new features to disk and file management—nothing as radical as changing from Microsoft File Manager to Microsoft Windows Explorer. You manage disks and files as you did in earlier versions of Microsoft Windows, using Windows Explorer. Shortcut menus and properties dialog boxes are similar, with exceptions you learn about in this chapter. Any user, novice or advanced, will be *quite* comfortable immediately after installing the operating system. For that reason, this chapter doesn't cover obvious features that you already know how to use. For example, it doesn't discuss moving, copying, or renaming files because these are obvious.

Dig a bit lower than the surface and you find a lot of changes that cause one or two headaches but, on the whole, put more power in your hands. This chapter shows you how to get the most out of those changes. Volume management is a bit different because of dynamic volumes. Disk management has new features and a new location—it's a snap-in in the Computer Management console. Microsoft threw the encrypting file system, directory junctions, and other innovations into the mix. The list of other new disk and file-management features is large. On the whole, most users don't use many of these features, though. After installing Windows 2000 Professional, most are happy just to leave the disk alone and do their work or play their games. The most common tasks that users perform are defragmenting their disks, checking disks for errors, compressing files, and cleaning disks to regain lost or wasted space. Thus, these are the tasks that this chapter focuses on most. This chapter also shows you how to schedule these tasks to happen automatically.

Defragmenting Disks

Defragmenting disks greatly improves their performance, particularly defragmenting the disk containing Windows 2000 Professional's boot files and your numerous program files. Microsoft Windows 98 users have long enjoyed the benefits of defragmenting their disks because it included a utility for that purpose. Microsoft Windows NT 4.0 users were out of luck or else they had to purchase a third-party tool for the same purpose, something they seldom did. Windows 2000 Professional brings you into parity with Windows 98 users, though; it includes Disk Defragmenter, which does an admirable job.

First, let me explain the big deal about defragmenting disks. The file system divides disks into clusters. The size of a cluster depends on variables such as the size of the disk and the way you format the disk. Ideally, when the operating system writes a file to the disk, it would write the file to contiguous clusters, one after another. That way, when the operating system reads the file, it doesn't have to look all over the disk for it. In the real world, though, the next available block of clusters isn't always big enough to contain the file it's trying to write. So, the operating system writes as much of the file to that block of clusters as it can and then moves on to the next free block of clusters. The result is a file that's fragmented and takes longer to load. A few fragmented files don't make much of a difference, but several thousand do.

Use Disk Defragmenter to make your computer work faster by reorganizing files so that they use contiguous space, as follows:

1. In Control Panel, double-click the System Tools icon and then click the Computer Management icon.

2. In Computer Management, double-click Storage and then click Disk Defragmenter.

3. Click the disk that you want to defragment and then click Defragment.

Using Disk Defragmenter requires that you log on to the computer as an administrator. Otherwise, it's usually a rosy process. Be aware of the following caveats, though:

- You can use Disk Defragmenter to defragment one disk at a time, not multiple disks, and you can't use the utility on remote computers' disks.

- Don't interrupt Disk Defragmenter while it's working. Doing so might cause it to start an already painful and long process over gain. Things that can interrupt this utility are running other programs and letting the screen saver open, both of which can cause Disk Defragmenter to think that it needs to rescan the disk for changes.

- Disk Defragmenter can't defragment some files, so they'll always appear in the program's report. Those include ShellIconCache, Safeboot.fs, Safeboot.csv, Safeboot.rsv, and Bootsec.doc. Three files are unmovable system files: the NTFS Master File Table (MFT), the NTFS Master File Table Mirror, and the virtual memory paging file.

- You can't schedule Disk Defragmenter to run automatically, not even via a script, which is a significant limitation for those folks who obsessively schedule this program in Windows 98 to keep their computer running well.

Disk Defragmenter fails to live up to expectations in two special situations. First, defragmenting fails if the paging file is very active. Second, it doesn't do a good job with disks that don't have a large amount of free space. The following two situations help you get around these problems.

Paging File

An extremely fragmented paging file can cause Disk Defragmenter to fail. Windows 2000 Professional keeps locks open over active page files, and Disk Defragmenter can't defragment them if they are locked for exclusive use. The way to get around that is to create a new one (which requires that you have more than one volume):

1. In Control Panel, double-click the System icon.

2. On the Advanced tab, click Performance Options.

3. In the Performance Options dialog box, click Change in the Virtual memory area.

4. Change the paging file to another drive by setting the original paging file to 0 megabytes and making a temporary paging file on another drive. Figure 7.1 shows what this looks like. Make very sure that you create a page file on another drive because the operating system will not start properly if it doesn't find a page file.

5. Restart the computer so Windows 2000 Professional uses the new paging file.

6. Use Disk Defragmenter on the original disk to defragment its existing drives and consolidate the free space you created by moving the paging file.

7. Re-create the original paging file on the original drive and remove the temporary paging file by setting its size to 0 megabytes.

8. Restart the computer to use the new paging file.

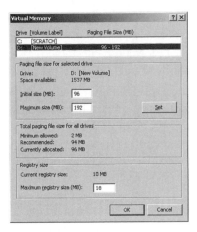

Figure 7.1 To defragment the paging file, move it to a temporary disk and then restore it to the original disk.

Full Disks

Disk Defragmenter doesn't work well on disks that don't have plenty of free space or are extremely fragmented. It requires a good amount of disk space to store parts of files until Disk Defragmenter is ready to recombine them in contiguous clusters. You know that this is a problem when you see a message that suggests defragmenting the disk even after you've already done so, or if you see an error that says you should make more space available. In any case, if Disk Defragmenter doesn't have enough disk space, it defragments only a small portion of the disk.

The easy solution is to remove the megabytes of temporary files that you've certainly collected. "Recovering Wasted Space," later in this chapter, shows you an easy way. In most cases, this frees enough space for it to work well.

Another solution is to temporarily move highly fragmented, large files to another volume, and then move them back to the original volume after defragmenting it. You can identify highly fragmented files by analyzing the disk and viewing the report using Disk Defragmenter. The last solution, which really isn't much of solution, is to repeatedly defragment the disk. You can repeat this process many, many times and never fully defragment the disk, however.

Checking Disks for Errors

Checking a disk for errors is similar in all recent versions of Windows:

1. In My Computer, click Properties on a drive icon's shortcut menu.
2. On the Tools tab, click Check Now.
3. In the Check Disk dialog box, click Start.

The Check Disk dialog box has two options. I don't suggest that you select the Automatically fix file system errors check box because this is a process that you're better off controlling yourself. If you want to scan the disk for physical errors, select the Scan for and attempt recovery of bad sectors check box.

Before checking your disk for errors, make sure that you close all running applications. Most applications lock files open, preventing Check Disk from working properly. If you forget, Check Disk asks you whether you want to schedule it to run the next time you start the computer. If you do, Check Disk runs prior to your logging on to the computer, ensuring that no applications are running. The only caveat is that you can't use the computer at all while Check Disk is working because you can't log on to Windows 2000 Professional. After starting the computer, Check Disk does give you a few seconds to change your mind before it gets to work.

You're not going to have many occasions to use Check Disk with NTFS, except for the random, dramatic power outage. Check Disk comes in handy, however, if you're still using the FAT file system. During the beta, users reported some problems with FAT that were easily remedied. When you do run Check Disk on an NTFS volume, it replaces bad clusters automatically and stores duplicate copies of key information for all files on the drive.

Can't start Windows 2000 Professional? If you suspect the problem is a disk error, you can run Check Disk from Recovery Console. For more about Recovery Console, see Chapter 2, "Troubleshooting Setup." The operating system also supplies a command-line Check Disk, which is often more convenient. Its options look like this:

Syntax: CHKDSK [*drive*[[*path*]*filename*]]] [/f] [/v] [/r] [/x] [/i] [/c] [/l[:*size*]]

Options:

drive	Drive letter (including colon), mount point, or volume name
path	Path of file to check for fragmentation (FAT only)
filename	File to check for fragmentation (FAT only)
/f	Fixes errors on the disk

/v	Displays the full path and name of each file on the disk (FAT only)
/r	Finds bad clusters and attempts to recover information from them (this option requires /f)
/x	Forces Check Disk to dismount the volume before scanning it
/i	Check index entries less vigorously (NTFS only)
/c	Skips checking for cycles in folders (NTFS only)
/l[:*size*]	Changes the size of the log file to *size* bytes (displays size if you don't provide *size*)

Most users simply use the command **chkdsk /f /r**, which automatically scans the disk for errors and repairs any that it finds.

See also

- Chapter 2, "Troubleshooting Setup," for more information about Recovery Console and other Windows 2000 Professional troubleshooting tools.

Compressing Disks and Files

NTFS compression can conserve dramatic amounts of disk space. In a scenario such as mine, in which I have hundreds of megabytes of manuscripts, I reduce the size of documents by about 50 percent. Although pure binary files don't compress quite as much, compression might mean the difference between chocking out a few hundred dollars for a new hard drive and being able to use Disk Defragmenter. Note that because of the large sizes of disks that come with most computers today, disk compression isn't generally required. It's more useful for servers than it is for desktop computers because few people actually find a way to fill 13 gigabytes.

Windows 2000 Professional's compression feature differs from similar features in other software. It doesn't limit you to compressing entire drives. Compress individual directories and files, too. As well as NTFS compression's flexibility, compression is built in to the NTFS file system, which results in a scheme that performs better than others. To compress a drive, directory, or file on an NTFS volume (you can't do this on FAT volumes), do one of the following:

- To compress a drive, click Properties on its shortcut menu, and select the Compress drive to save disk space check box (see Figure 7.2).

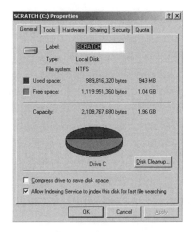

Figure 7.2   Compressing files is much easier and much safer to do in
Windows 2000 Professional than it is in Windows 98.

- To compress a directory, click Properties in its shortcut menu, click
  Advanced, select the Compress contents to save disk space check box, and
  then do one of the following:
  - To compress only the selected folder and its files, select the Apply
    changes to this folder only check box.
  - To compress the selected folder and all its subfolders and files, select the
    Apply changes to this folder, subfolders, and files check box.
- To compress a file, click Properties on its shortcut menu, click Advanced,
  and select the Compress contents to save disk space check box.

Windows 2000 Professional doesn't report the results of compression as a
percentage. Click Properties on a disk, directory, or file's shortcut menu; on
the General tab, note the size and size on disk. With compression, the size is
greater than the size on disk. To get an actual percentage, divide the difference between the size and size on disk by the size: (size—size on disk/size).
For example, the compression percentage of a 49-kilobyte file that the operating system compressed to 28 kilobytes is around 43 percent. Not bad at all.

   Windows NT 4.0 users are familiar with its compression feature, which is
the same in Windows 2000 Professional. If you're upgrading from Windows 98,
however, be aware of the differences in the way both implement this feature:

- Windows 98 supports only compressed drives. It doesn't allow you to
  compress individual files and directories. Windows 2000 Professional
  supports compressing individual files and directories on existing NTFS

volumes, on the other hand, which means that if you have a particularly big file or a directory containing big files, you can compress them individually without compressing the drive.

- In Windows 98, you use DriveSpace or DoubleSpace to create compression volumes on host drives. It then stores the entire compressed drive's contents in that compressed volume, which is a single file. Windows 2000 Professional stores compressed files on the existing NTFS volume without requiring you to create a compressed volume on a host. Windows 2000 Professional does not support DriveSpace or DoubleSpace disk-compression.

- Although Windows 2000 Professional's compression feature uses algorithms similar to Windows 98, it's more efficient. It doesn't significantly degrade the operating system's performance.

Note

Two key Windows 2000 Professional features are mutually exclusive of compression. First, the operating system can't compress encrypted files; you can't have your cake and eat it too! You also can't compress offline files. Even if you compress the offline files cache, the operating system doesn't compress its contents. The reason is that the operating system might hang or not update the cache properly if it allowed you to compress the cache.

Recovering Wasted Space

You have more disk space available than you think. It's just wasted. Unused temporary files tend to gobble up huge amounts of space because too many programs don't clean up their temporary files when they're done with them. Microsoft Word 2000 frequently leaves several megabytes of temporary files lying around in a documents directory. When most programs crash, and it happens often, they don't clean up after themselves. Rampaging through your file system and manually removing temporary files isn't a good idea because you're more likely to make mistakes.

Disk Cleanup is a tool that safely removes temporary and otherwise unnecessary files. Recently, it removed over half a gigabyte of space for me. Here's how to use it:

1. On a drive's shortcut menu, click Properties, and then click Disk Cleanup.

   Expect a long pause while Disk Cleanup scans the disk to see how much space it can free. When it finishes, you see the dialog box shown in Figure 7.3.

Figure 7.3   Disk Cleanup is the fastest way to reclaim disk space.

2. On the Disk Cleanup tab, select the check box next to each type of temporary files you want to remove in the Files to delete area. Choices are the following:

   - Downloaded Program Files

   - Temporary Internet Files

   - Recycle Bin

   - Temporary Files

   - Temporary Offline Files

   - Offline Files

   - Compress Old Files

   - Catalog Files for the Content Indexer

When you select all but the last two items in the Files to delete list, click View Files to see a list of the files that Disk Cleanup proposes to remove. Using Disk Cleanup is usually quiet and safe, but check this list if you have any doubt about what it's going to do.

The last two items, Compress Old Files and Catalog Files for the Content Indexer are special and require a bit more discussion. When you select the Compress Old Files check box, Disk Cleanup compresses a file that you haven't used in 50 days. To change the length of time after which it compresses a file, click Options. Don't do this right after installing Windows 2000 Professional, however, because it will compress a lot of files that you probably don't want to compress. Wait a few months and then use Disk Cleanup to compress old files; you can then be sure that it compresses only infrequently used files. The next option, Catalog Files for the Content Indexer, causes Disk Cleanup to remove files that the Indexing Service created when it indexed the disk's files.

Tip

After using Disk Cleanup, the file system will have many, many holes in it left by the files that the utility removed. It's thus a good idea to consolidate used and free disk space using Disk Defragmenter. You get more space and a faster computer.

Managing Disks and Volumes

Windows 2000 Professional supports two different kinds of disks, both of which you manage using Disk Management:

- **Basic disks** Basic disks are physical disks that contain primary partitions, extended partitions, and logical drives. These are the kinds of disks that you've been using all along and created using Fdisk.exe. In Windows 2000 Professional, FT Disk manages basic disks as it did in Windows NT Workstation 4.0. Windows 2000 Professional can use volume, mirror, and stripe sets (with or without parity) on basic disks, but cannot create them. As well, the operating system can't extend basic disks online; you must restart the computer.

- **Dynamic volumes** In Windows 2000 Professional, Logical Disk Manager (LDM) manages dynamic disks. These are physical disks that contain dynamic volumes instead of partitions and logical drives. You create and manage logical disks using Disk Management. Because Windows 2000 Professional is the only Microsoft operating system that supports dynamic volumes, don't plan on using dynamic volumes in a dual-boot configuration with another operating system. Still, they have some nice features of basic disks. You can extend volumes online without restarting the computer. They support fault tolerance, disk mirroring, and disk striping.

Types of dynamic volumes are simple, spanned, mirrored, striped, and striped with parity (RAID-5). *Simple volumes* aren't fault-tolerant; they can also span multiple disks. When a simple volume spans multiple disks, it's a *spanned volume. Striped volumes* alternate data across two or more physical disks, bettering the computer's performance by dividing the work between two disks. The enhancement to your computer's performance can be significant. *Mirrored volumes* protect your data against disk failure. They duplicate data on multiple disks so that if one disk fails, the computer still operates properly. Windows 2000 Professional doesn't support RAID-5, by the way; this is an honor reserved for Windows 2000 Server.

You manage basic and dynamic disks using Disk Management. To use this tool, you must log on to the computer as an administrator. Figure 7.4 shows it with four drives, a basic fixed disk, a dynamic fixed disk, and two CD-ROM drives. To start Disk Management, double-click the Administrative Tools icon in Control Panel, double-click the Computer Management icon, and click Disk Management. Windows NT Workstation 4.0 users should already be familiar with this tool's capabilities. Just note that you access a disk's shortcut menu by right-clicking the disk and a volume's shortcut menu by right-clicking the volume.

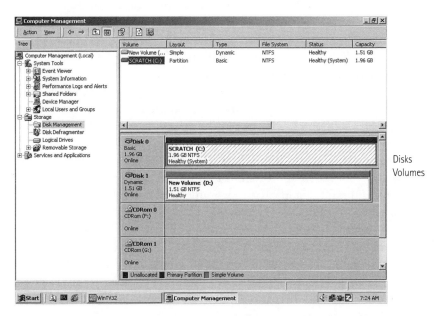

Figure 7.4   Click a disk's shortcut menu to manage the disk. Click a volume's shortcut menu to manage the volume.

File Systems

Windows 2000 Professional supports varieties of file systems on basic and dynamic disks. It introduces a new file system, Universal Disk Format (UDF), and extends NTFS to version 5. And, yes, it still supports all the old file systems such as FAT, FAT32, and CDFS:

- **FAT** Otherwise known as FAT16, FAT has been around since the dawn of Microsoft MS-DOS. In Windows 2000 Professional, the maximum partition size for FAT is 4 gigabytes.

- **FAT32** Microsoft introduced FAT32 with Microsoft Windows 95 OSR2. It uses cluster sizes that are smaller than FAT16, making about 20 percent more disk space available. The maximum partition size is 2 terabytes, but Windows 2000 Professional can create FAT32 partitions only up to 32 gigabytes.

- **CDFS** CD-ROM File System (CDFS) is the file system that the operating system uses to read CD-ROM drives. In Windows 2000 Professional, CDFS meets the Organization for Standardization (ISO) 9660 specification.

UDF, a new file system defined by the Optical Storage Technology Association (OSTA), is compliant with the ISO-13346 specification. It's the successor to CDFS. ISO designed this file system for use by digital videodiscs (DVD) and CD-ROMs, as well as for exchanging data between incompatible operating systems. It supports long Unicode filenames. Windows 2000 Professional supports UDF 1.5, but the operating system can only read UDF at the moment.

Nothing new about NTFS; it's been a part of Windows NT since its first version. Windows 2000 Professional introduces version 5 of NTFS, however, and this is the file system that I recommend you use. It's secure, it has native file compression built into it, files are recoverable when errors occur, and it supports encryption. The list of reasons why you should use NTFS is endless. The only reason that you might not use NTFS is if you created a dual-boot configuration with Windows 2000 Professional and another operating system, such as Windows 98, that can't read NTFS volumes. To learn more about the differences between each of the file systems, see Table 7.1. For each file system, it shows the minimum partition size, maximum partition size, and maximum file system. It also shows the operating systems that support each.

Table BD.1   **File Systems**

	Minimum Partition Size	Maximum Partition Size	Maximum File Size	OS
FAT16	N/A	2 GB	2 GB	Windows 3.1 Windows 95 Windows 98 Windows NT 3.1 Windows NT 3.5 Windows NT 3.51 Windows NT 4.0 Windows 2000
FAT32	512 MB	2 TB	4 GB	Windows 95 OSR2 Windows 98 Windows 2000
NTFS 4	20 MB	15 EB (exabytes)	N/A	Windows NT 3.1 Windows NT 3.5 Windows NT 3.51 Windows NT 4.0 Windows 2000
NTFS 5	20 MB	15 EB	N/A	Windows NT 4.0 Windows 2000

See also

- Chapter 1, "Installing Windows," contains much more information about each file system, which helps you determine which file system to choose as you're installing the operating system.

Mount Points

Mount points are one of the most innovative new features in NTFS 5. They allow you to graft a volume onto any directory, which causes the operating system to resolve that directory to the root of the mounted volume. In other words, rather than assigning a drive letter to a volume, you assign a path to it. This abolishes the limit of 26 drive letters. With mount points, instead of using a drive letter to identify a volume, you use its path.

Microsoft built mount points for administrators to simplify their lives. It allows them to add storage to a computer without overly disturbing a volume's namespace and without that awful restriction on drive letters. They can scale up the storage for user profiles, for example, by mounting additional volumes to an existing volume. Microsoft uses the term *sticky* to refer to mount points, meaning that changes in the device's name, which occur due to configuration changes, don't break it. They're just as useful for power users, though. You can move all your documents to a second volume, for example, and then mount it to *UserProfile*\My Documents\Personal. Another example is mounting a second volume to Program Files so you can better manage your applications.

You must log on to the computer as an Administrator to mount volumes because you do so using Disk Management. The process is somewhat like assigning a drive letter to a volume. On its shortcut menu, click Change Drive Letter and Path, and click Add to add a mount point or click Edit to change the current one. For example, you can leave the volume's existing drive letter assignment alone and add a mount point. You can also replace the current drive letter assignment with a mount point.

Tip

Windows 2000 Professional provides a command-line utility for creating mount points. For more information, type **mountvol /?** at the MS-DOS command prompt.

Backing Up Files

Microsoft Windows Backup is a significant improvement that administrators probably love more than power users. Still, if you have useful backup media and you're good about backing up your computer, you'll appreciate how much easier and more reliable this utility is now. Even if you don't have useful backup media, you can now back up files to another disk or to the network. Aside from shedding the archaic look of its predecessor by using a tabbed user interface that's similar to Windows 98's backup utility, it also includes a handful of wizards that make the backup process painless.

Some of Windows Backup's features are more useful for Microsoft Windows 2000 Server. Active Directory is an example. Remote Storage Service is another that's more useful in a server environment, so I don't discuss it here. The remaining features of Windows Backup are appropriate for Windows 2000 Professional. It can archive files and folders, restoring them when necessary. It can create emergency repair disks that help you start the operating system when something has gone terribly wrong. It can make a copy of the computer's system state, which includes the registry, boot files, and Certificate Services database. You learn about these features in the following sections.

As with most system tools in Windows 2000 Professional, you must have the appropriate rights. You must log on to the computer as a member of the local Administrators or Backup Operators groups to back up or restore any file or folder on the local computer. If you're a member of the domain Administrators or Backup Operators groups, you can back up or restore any file or folder on any computer in the domain, assuming that it has a two-way trust relationship with the domain (member workstations usually do). If you aren't a member of either group, you must have no less than read permission to any file that you want to back up, or you must have the following rights on the domain or locally:

- Back up files and directories
- Restore files and directories

Files and Folders

To start Windows Backup, on the Start menu, point to Programs, followed by Accessories and System Tools, and click Backup. Then, do one of the following:

- To back up your computer, click Backup Wizard and follow the instructions you see onscreen.
- To restore your computer, click Restore Wizard and follow the instructions you see onscreen.

Here are some additional notes:

- As an Administrator or Backup Operator, you can back up and restore all files, even if you don't have read permission for them. When you restore those files, whether to the same or a different computer, the Backup program restores their original permissions and you won't be able to read files that you couldn't already read.
- Windows Backup can back up encrypted files. The program stores them encrypted on the tape or backup media—it doesn't decrypt them first—and also restores them encrypted. If you're looking for a way to recover a file when you've lost the certificate required to decrypt it, see the section "Encrypting Files" later in this chapter.

Windows 2000 Professional doesn't back up all files in every folder; Windows Backup keeps in the registry a list of files and folders that it and other Windows 2000-compatible backup utilities exclude. The two subkeys, FilesNotToBackup and FilesNotToRestore—both subkeys of

HKLM\SYSTEM\CurrentControlSet\Control\BackupRestore—are where Windows Backup stores this information. Each contains REG_MULTISZ values whose contents indicate a file or a folder to exclude from the backup. Note that Windows Backup has similar settings for registry subkeys that it won't restore in KeysNotToRestore.

Caution

Some of the more ill-behaved applications might not work properly after restoring a full system backup. These applications don't use long filenames properly and rely solely on short filenames. Recall that Windows 2000 Professional appends a tilde and a number, name~N, to distinguish between short filenames. It does this if two files' short filenames would be identical even though their long filenames are not: All My Stuff.doc and All My Stuffing.doc. When Windows Backup restores files, it does so in alphabetical order and creates new short filenames for them. Because you didn't necessarily create those files and folders in the same order, these programs might not find the files for which they're looking.

Emergency Repair Disks

Emergency Repair Disks (ERDs) are limited. They can help you start a computer when other methods fail. An ERD has no data, program files, or settings; but it contains enough information to make basic repairs to the system files, partition boot sector, or startup environment. Start the Setup program and then use the ERD to restore these core system files. There is a catch, though. You must create the ERD while the computer is healthy and before something bad happens, requiring you to maintain it on a regular basis. Waiting until your computer fails is not the time to decide you need to update its ERD. Also, all computers must have their own ERDs and you can't use one computer's ERD on another, no matter how desperate you are to fix it and get a raise. Even with all the limitations, the first thing you should do immediately after changing your computer's configuration is to update your ERD.

The program you used in Windows NT Workstation 4.0 to create ERDs, Repair Disk Utility, is not available in Windows 2000 Professional. Microsoft Windows Backup is the program responsible for that capability now. Adding Repair Disk Utility to Windows Backup is sensible because backing up a computer and creating an ERD are similar in nature. To create an ERD using Windows Backup, click E_mergency Repair Disk on the Welcome tab.

Windows Backup does not create a copy of the ERD in *SystemRoot*\ Repair as Repair Disk Utility did, and it does not copy the registry hive files to the ERD at all. Instead, if you choose to do so on the Emergency Repair Diskette dialog box, it backs up the registry hive files to *SystemRoot*\Repair\ Regback—the same location to which it backs them up when you back up System State data. Also, *SystemRoot*\Repair always contains a copy of the original hive files that the Setup program created when you first installed Windows 2000 Professional. You should never change or remove these files because you might need them to troubleshoot the computer in extreme circumstances or if you change the administrator password and forget it. The files on the ERD, which are small in number, include the following:

Autoexec.nt *SystemRoot*\System32\Autoexec.nt, which Windows 2000 Professional uses to initialize MS-DOS environments

Config.nt *SystemRoot*\System32\Config.nt, which Windows 2000 Professional uses to initialize MS-DOS environments

Setup.log Log file indicating the files installed, as well as a cyclic redundancy check (CRC) that helps the emergency repair process determine whether core system files are corrupt

Using an ERD to repair the computer relies on the Setup program, but it is really not difficult. First, start the Setup program—Winnt.exe and not Winnt32.exe—by starting the computer with MS-DOS and running it, by starting the computer with the Setup boot disks, or by booting the computer with the Windows 2000 Professional CD-ROM, if you happen to have a bootable CD-ROM drive. If the Setup program doesn't find any disks with a FAT partition, you must use one of the latter two options because the Setup program complains that it can't find a place for its swap file if you start it from MS-DOS and don't have any FAT partitions. When the Setup program first starts, it asks whether you want to install Windows 2000 or repair an installation. That's where the following instructions begin:

1. Press **R** to start the emergency repair process.

2. Press **R** again to choose the emergency repair process, not the recovery console, and do one of the following:

   - Press **M** to choose whether you want to repair the system files, partition boot sector, or startup environment. I don't recommend this option.

   - Press **F** to automatically repair the system files, partition boot sector, startup environment, and registry, as long as a backup copy of the registry hive files exist in *SystemRoot*\Repair\Regback.

System State

Windows Backup puts the registry and other data together, calling the whole thing *System State data*. System State data include the registry, the COM+ Class Registration database, and boot files. Windows 2000 Professional adds

even more to System State data. Backing up and restoring System State data is an all-or-nothing deal. However, you can restore System State data to alternative locations and then restore portions of it manually. Windows Backup restores only the registry, SYSVOL directory, and boot files to an alternative location—not the remaining parts of System State data.
Here are the different ways to back up System State data:

- To back up System State data as part of a regular backup, select the System State check box on the Backup tab, as shown in Figure 7.5.

- To back up selected files on the computer, including System State data, click Back up selected files, drives, or network data in Backup Wizard and then select the System State check box on the Backup tab.

- To back up all files on the computer, including System State data, click Back up everything on my computer in Backup Wizard.

- To back up only System State data, click Only back up the System State data in Back Wizard.

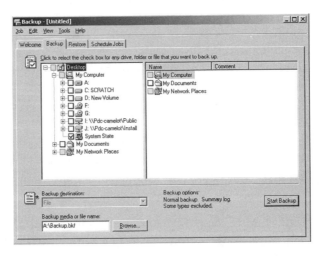

Figure 7.5   Select the System State data check box to back up the Windows 2000 Professional's System State data.

Windows Backup does back up the entire registry, but doesn't necessarily restore it all. It identifies hives using HKLM\system\CurrentControlSet\ Control\hivelist. The backup data therefore includes HKU, the hive that contains per-user settings for each logged-on account. Windows Backup copies hives to static files, and adds the static files to the backup data. Restoration is more complicated. Subkeys of HKLM\SYSTEM that

Windows Backup does not copy from the old registry to the new are in HKLM\SYSTEM\CurrentControlSet\Control\BackupRestore\ KeysNotToRestore. The result is that Windows Backup does not restore any subkey listed in KeysNotToRestore. And Windows Backup doesn't restore any subkey in this list that ends with a backslash (\). If a subkey ends with an asterisk (*), Windows Backup doesn't restore it or any of its subkeys, the whole subtree.

Windows Backup can't back up System State data on remote computers. It backs up files on remote computers via their administrative shares (ADMIN$, C$, D$, and so on), but doesn't have capabilities to access a remote computer's registry via RPCs (remote procedure calls), as does Microsoft Registry Editor. Don't rely on it as a way to protect client computers' System State data unless you actually run Windows Backup on each locally.

Verify, Verify, Verify

Don't lull yourself into a false sense of security just because you back up System State data. Media go bad and errors happen. Make sure you verify backup data to ensure that it matches what's on the disk. By default, Windows Backup doesn't verify backup data. To force it to do so after backing it up, click Options on the Tools menu and then select the Verify data after the backup completes check box on the General tab.

Second, check the log file to make sure the backup data includes everything it should. After Windows Backup finishes a job, click Report on the Backup Progress dialog box. *UserProfile*\Local Settings\Application Data\Microsoft\Windows NT\NTBackup\data is where it stores log files—not the most convenient location in the world. Windows Backup opens the log file in Microsoft Notepad, though. By default, the report contains a few measly statistics about the backup data. If you want more information, such as what files are in the backup data, click Options on the Tools menu and then click Detailed on the Backup Log tab.

Restoring System State data is the same process in reverse. Be careful, however, because System State data get out-of-date rather quickly. Use Restore Wizard and, in the What to restore list, select the System State check box. You can do likewise on the Restore tab. Windows Backup restores System State data, including the registry, COM+ Class Registration database, and boot files. You might still run into problems with programs losing their settings, but this happens only if you installed the application after you made the backup data you're restoring. Most applications can restore their settings in the registry, however.

8

Managing
the Computer

MANAGING COMPUTERS MEANS MANY THINGS TO many people.
Everyone can find some common ground, though, especially power users.
Keeping track of events that affect the computer's stability and performance
is one example. Scheduling jobs that automate maintenance is another.
This chapter covers the maintenance tasks that most power users consider
important. It does not discuss how to manage Microsoft Windows 2000
Professional on networks, however, which is a big job that's better left
to books such as *Inside Windows 2000 Server* (New Riders, 1999).

The most important aspect of managing the computers that are running
Windows 2000 Professional is managing the users. Microsoft Windows 98
users will find this particular aspect of the operating system its most frustrating feature. All users don't share all files on the computer. Instead, users'
settings are in their user profiles, which are separate from all other users'
profiles. Not only does Windows 2000 Professional separate users' files into
different profiles, but users must log on to the computer individually and
an authorization process determines the files they can access, programs they
can run, and so on. The operating system is secure and how you manage
users has a significant impact on your satisfaction with it. As a result, you
should carefully read Chapter 11, "Securing Your Computer," to make sure
you understand how to administer security. This chapter specifically discusses

user profiles and how to best manage them to get around their significant drawbacks that affect power users. For more information about making the switch from Windows 98 to Windows 2000 Professional and for an introduction to user profiles and security, see Appendix B, "Quick Start for Windows 98 Users."

Viewing Events

Windows 98 displays most diagnostic information, warnings, and error messages in simple dialog boxes. Very seldom does it use log files to accumulate information over time. When it does, log files are plain text files, with each application or module creating its own. Microsoft Windows NT introduced a more elegant solution, one that Windows 2000 Professional continues to use, called the *event log*. The operating system still displays a plethora of warnings and error messages in dialog boxes, but it and applications that run on it also stash more detailed information in the event log. Information in the event log is generally more detailed than the error messages you see onscreen.

In fact, entries in the event log are often the most useful tools at your disposal for diagnosing and repairing problems. For example, if the computer is suddenly behaving erratically, check the event log first. Often, you'll see a recent entry that can explain the change in behavior. Also, don't forget to look for relationships between different events in the log. If you see a vague entry in the log, a second entry (usually before or after it) will often shed light on the first entry.

Event Viewer is your window into the event log. And that brings up the fact that there isn't just one log. There are actually three event logs in Event Viewer: application, security, and system. As their names imply, applications log information in the application log. The operating system logs information in the system log. Both log security information in the security log. Of the three event logs, the system log is the most used and the most useful for diagnosing and repairing problems in Windows 2000 Professional. To see these three event logs, open Event Viewer. In Control Panel, double-click the Administrative Tools icon and then double-click the Event Viewer icon. The result is a window similar to what you see in Figure 8.1. Click the event log you want to view: Application Log, Security Log, or System Log. You must log on to the computer as an Administrator in order to view the security log, but power users can view the other two logs.

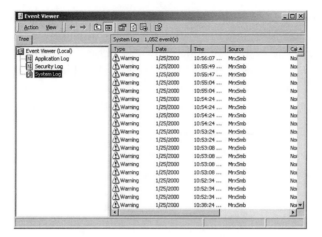

Figure 8.1   You can also view these event logs in Computer Management. In
Control Panel, double-click the Administrative Tools icon, followed
by the Computer Management icon.

Double-click any entry in an event log to view it. There are three types
of events: information, warning, and errors. Their purpose is obvious—based
on their names. Double-click any event to view it. The top portion of the
window shows statistical information about the event, such as its date, source,
user, and so on. The middle portion contains the event's most useful information, text that describes the event. The bottom portion contains the least
useful bits of information: data related to the event that usually requires
technical analysis to figure out what it represents.

Filtering and Searching

Over time, the event log accumulates a huge number of events. This can
make it tough to sort out what led to a particular problem or sort out the
computer's history of errors. Event Viewer provides features to help you sort
all this out, however. First, it supports filtering. With filtering, you see just the
events that interest you. You can limit the display to warnings, for example, or
you can limit the display to errors that a particular component produced. On
the View menu, click Filter. On the Filter tab, shown in Figure 8.2, specify
the events you want to view. When you finish filtering the event log, click
All Records on the View menu.

Second, Event Viewer allows you to search for particular events. On the
View menu, click Find. The dialog box looks similar to the one in Figure
8.2. Specify the events for which you're searching and then click Find Next.
To find the next matching event in the log, click Find Next again. Searching
for events is more useful than filtering events because it allows you to view
events in relation to others that occurred at the same time.

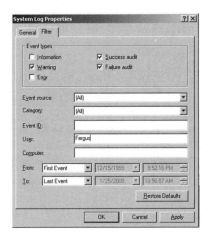

Figure 8.2   Filtering allows you to narrow in on events that a
particular process generated or on certain types of events.

Organizing Event Logs

Much more is behind Event Viewer. It allows you to organize events to suit
your needs. First and foremost, for any of the logs, you can create alternative
views and then filter them however you like. To create an alternative view
of any log, click New Log View on its shortcut menu. After you create
a new log view, filter it as you learned in the previous section, and then
rename it using a name that describes its contents. For example, I like to
create a new view for the system log and then filter it to display only errors.
I call this new view *System Error Log*, so that I can see all system errors at
a glance. You can delete the new log file view by clicking Delete on its
shortcut menu.

When the log files become too big, which happens over time as the
system logs more and more events, you'll start seeing errors that say the log
file is full. Also, the log files can become too big for you to manage. I like
to clear the log files so they show only recent entries. This keeps their sizes
reasonable and ensures that I notice important events when they occur. To

clear any log file, click Clear all events. Before doing this, I suggest that you save a text copy of the log file for future reference, however. When you clear a log file, Event Viewer prompts you to save the current entries to a text file, but you can do so manually: Click Save Log File As on its shortcut menu. If you'd rather not clear the log file, but you want to make sure it doesn't become full, adjust the amount of space that is available to it.

1. Click Properties on the log file's shortcut menu.

2. In Maximum log size, specify the amount of space you want to make available to the log file.

3. In the Log size area, do one of the following:

   - To allow Event Viewer to overwrite events when it runs out of space, click Overwrite events as needed.

   - To allow Event Viewer to overwrite events when they become old, click Overwrite events older than and then specify how old an event must age before Event Viewer overwrites it.

   - To prevent Event Viewer from overwriting events, click Do not overwrite events.

Note

In Windows 2000 Professional, the event log tends to fill with plenty of useless entries, particularly if you still connect to a network that Microsoft Windows NT Server 4.0 manages. One of those entries is due to the fact that the operating system is looking for a timeserver, which Windows 2000 Server provides and Windows NT Server 4.0 doesn't. You can eliminate these entries in the event log by disabling the Windows Time service in Services. Another annoying example is an entry from Oakley, which you'll see if you haven't installed the high-encryption pack.

Examining the System

Windows NT Workstation 4.0 had its diagnostics, Winmsd, which had a tabbed user interface that displayed useful information about the computer and operating system's configuration. Windows 2000 Professional doesn't have this same utility, but it does have Microsoft System Information, a much more useful and much more descriptive utility than Winmsd. Still, users who are in the habit of quickly typing **winmsd** in the Run dialog box will be pleased to know that doing so runs System Information now. The other way to run System Information is by using Control Panel. In Control Panel, double-click Computer Management and then click System Information. Also, you can type **msinfo32** in the Run dialog box.

System Information displays five categories of information, but you can't change any of it using this user interface:

- **System Summary**   Displays basic information about the computer. You know the CPU, amount of memory, BIOS information, and so on.

- **Hardware Resources**   Contains useful information that helps you troubleshoot device conflicts. It displays information about how each device uses computer resources such as I/O ports, IRQs, and memory ranges. Conflicts/Sharing is the node of interest here because it describes any conflicts.

- **Components**   Describes each of the components installed on the computer, including information about the display adapter, ports, modems, network components, storage devices, and printers. Rather than rooting around Device Manager for this type of information, this is the ultimate source.

- **Software Environment**   Contains warm-and-fuzzy information about the applications you installed and the environment in which they run. It describes any processes that are currently running, as well as any DLL files that are loaded.

- **Internet Explorer 5**   Shows the components that Internet Explorer 5 is using, their versions, and how you configured them. This node is rather dull.

Scheduling Tasks

Task scheduling has come a long way in Windows 2000 Professional, particularly over Windows NT Workstation 4.0's AT command, which Windows 2000 Professional continues to support. Task Scheduler started as part of Internet Explorer 4, and it is now included in all of Microsoft's current operating system offerings. It's easy to use and makes automating routing tasks simple. The only problem is that in order to schedule a task to run any particular program, the program must be capable of running with no user interface. That means that the program must have a fairly comprehensive command-line interface. Sadly, many of the utilities in Windows 2000 Professional don't have suitable command-line interfaces and you can't schedule them. You can't schedule Disk Defragmenter to defragment your disks automatically, for example. You can still schedule Windows Backup to automate the backup process, however.

Task Scheduler is in Control Panel. Double-click the Scheduled Task icon. To schedule a task, double-click the Add Scheduled Task icon. Shown in Figure 8.3, the wizard walks you through the entire process, which is rather straightforward. It prompts you for the program you want to schedule, its command-line options, and the schedule. Scheduling options include daily, weekly, or just about any screwball schedule you want to create. For any particular task, you can even create multiple schedules. For example, you can schedule a backup task to run every Friday as well as every other Tuesday. Because scheduled tasks don't give you any feedback, you must use their log file to see their results. Task Scheduler also prompts for credentials and runs the task using those credentials. For example, you can run a task using your Administrator account and password. On the Advanced menu, click View Log. Particularly useful is Task Scheduler's capability to notify you when it misses a task, regardless of the reason. To do that, click Notify Me of Missed Tasks on the Advanced menu.

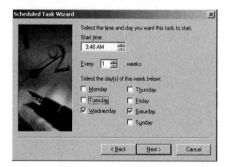

Figure 8.3   The Scheduled Task Wizard is extremely flexible.

Note

Unlike earlier versions of Windows, including Windows 98, Windows 2000 Professional doesn't schedule any default tasks. Therefore, don't automatically assume that the tasks required to keep your computer running well are already scheduled. Also unlike Windows 98, you can't schedule some of the more useful utilities such as Disk Defragmenter. You can schedule many third-party disk defragmenter utilities, however.

Scheduling Backups

Windows Backup has a lot of command-line options—too many for such a simple task, in my opinion. New in Windows 2000 Professional is a user interface for scheduling backup jobs, though, which eliminates the need for you to keep track of all those command-line options. Run Windows Backup:

On the Start menu, point to Programs, point to Accessories, point to System Tools, and then click Backup. Schedule your backup job on the Scheduled Jobs tab. When you schedule a backup job this way, it creates a job file and adds a task to the Scheduled Tasks folder. You can, of course, schedule jobs manually. Windows Backup Help contains a rather complete description of the backup program's command-line options.

All is not well with Windows Backup, however. If you schedule a job, it ignores many options in the job file. For example, it ignores the job file's System State option. Windows Backup always includes the System State because Microsoft considers it to be an essential part of a backup in order for it to be complete. Also, regardless of the settings in the job file, it always backs up protected system files. Again, Microsoft considers it to be an essential part of any backup and doesn't allow you to skip it during a scheduled backup, even if you're just trying to schedule a job that contains a handful of files such as a handful of documents. Not only does Windows Backup ignore some settings in your job files, but the program doesn't have equivalent command-line options for many options you find in the user interface:

- Creating emergency repair disks
- Restoring backup sets
- Backing up mounted drives
- Backing up system-protected files

On the other hand, Windows Backup has command-line options for which you find no equivalent in the user interface. For example, the /um option instructs the backup program to overwrite the first tape in the media pool you specify using the /p option. The purpose of this option is to allow unattended backups with standalone tape libraries.

See also
- Chapter 7, "Managing Disks and Files," for more information about using Windows Backup.

Using the AT Command

Many people continue to use old UNIX-style text editors instead of the modern word processors available. Similarly, old-school Windows NT users will continue to use the AT command, even though Task Scheduler is more robust and has many more capabilities.

The AT command has a simple command-line interface, which you can use from the Run dialog box or at the MS-DOS command prompt:

Syntax: **AT** [*computername*] [[*id*] [**/DELETE**] | **/DELETE** [**/YES**]]
AT [*computername*] *time* [**/INTERACTIVE**]
[**/EVERY:***date*[,...] | **/NEXT:***date*[,...]] *"command"*

Options:

computername	Name of a remote computer. The job is scheduled on the local computer if omitted.
id	Identification number assigned to the job.
/delete	Cancels a job. If you omit id, cancels all jobs.
/yes	Cancels all jobs with no confirmation prompts.
time	Time at which to run job.
/interactive	Allows the job to interact with the current user.
/every:*date*[,...]	Runs the command on the week or month. If omitted, it uses the current day of the month.
/next:*date*[,...]	Runs the command on the next occurrence *date*. If omitted, it assumes the current day of the month.
"command"	Command to be run.

By default, the AT command runs jobs in the context of the System account. In many cases, you might need to run a job in the context of another user, however. For example, you might want to schedule administrative jobs and run them in the context of an Administrator account. To change the service account, click <u>A</u>T Service Account on the Adva<u>n</u>ced menu and provide the credentials of the account in which you want to run scheduled tasks.

Note
Jobs that you schedule using the AT command appear in Task Scheduler. If you edit such a job in the Scheduled Tasks folder, it's no longer available in the AT command. And because Task Scheduler's jobs are so much more complex than the AT command's jobs, jobs that you create in the Scheduled Tasks folder do not appear in the AT command.

Synchronizing Time

If you're using a network-connected computer, time synchronization is becoming a more important issue for you. This is particularly true if you're using roaming user profiles or offline files, which you learn about in Chapter 13, "Using Mobile Computers." Windows 2000 Professional relies on the times that files were modified to determine whether to update them from the network or vice versa. If your computer's clock doesn't match the server's clock, you might end up with the wrong versions of files, or worse.

The easiest way to make sure that your computer's clock matches the server's clock is to use the Net command. Simply add the command **net time** *computer* **/set** to the logon script, where *computer* is the name of the computer to which you want to synchronize your computer's clock. Alternatively, use **net time** *domain* **/set**, where *domain* is the name of the domain to which you want to synchronize your clock.

Windows 2000 Professional and Windows 2000 Server provide a time service that makes this process automatic, though. So, if you're using this combination of software, you don't have to modify your logon script to synchronize your computer's clock with the server. You don't have to do anything at all to enable this time service. If you suspect that it's not working properly, however, double-click in Services to make sure that it's started.

Managing Services

In Control Panel, double-click the Administrative Tools icon and then double-click the Services icon. This is the administrative tool that you use to administer services in Windows 2000 Professional. *Services* are programs that provide some sort of system function. For example, the Windows Time Service updates the computer's clock so that its time matches the server's time. Another example is the RunAs Service, which allows you to run programs in contexts of different user accounts.

Some operating system features require that you start a particular service in order to use them. Still other features you might not want to use, and you can disable them by disabling their corresponding services. You can click Start, Stop, Pause, Resume, or Restart on any service's shortcut menu. This action is temporary, though. When you restart the computer, the service returns to its normal state. You can permanently configure a service by doing the following:

1. In Services, double-click a service.

2. In Startup type, click one of the following:
   - Automatic
   - Disabled
   - Manual

3. In Start parameters, type any command-line options you want to pass to the service (very few services accept command-line options).

4. On the Log On tab, do one of the following:
   - To run the service in the context of the system account, click Local System Account. If you want to allow the service to interact with users, select the Allow service to interact with desktop check box.
   - To run the service in the context of another user's account, click This account and then provide the account's name and password.

5. On the Recovery tab, specify what actions you want Windows 2000 Professional to take when the service fails. In the First failure, Second failure, and Subsequent failures lists, click one of these:
   - Restart the Service
   - Run a File
   - Reboot the Computer
   - Take No Action

Note
Windows 2000 Professional allows you to disable services for certain hardware profiles. This is useful if a service is associated with a device that's not enabled in a particular profile. Although the service shouldn't load if the device isn't enabled, you might still find that you must manually disable the service for that profile. To do this, click the Log On tab on the service's Properties dialog box. Then click the hardware profile in which you want to disable the device and click Disable.

Managing User Profiles

User profiles are folders that contain each user's settings and documents. In Windows 2000 Professional, user profiles are in *SystemDrive*\Documents and Settings. The name of each user profile varies, but it is usually the user name. When users logging on to the computer and creating user profile folders based on their user names would result in duplicate folder names, the operating system appends the name of the computer or domain to the end of the profile folder's name. You'll commonly see two user profile folders after logging on to the computer locally when you normally log on to the domain.

Windows 2000 Professional supports three types of user profiles. *Local user profiles* are the profiles that the operating system creates locally. *Roaming user profiles* are network-based user profiles that the operating system copies to the local computer when you log on to the domain and then copies back to the network when you log off. Roaming user profiles allow you to log on to any computer that's connected to the network and still be able to access your documents and use your own, familiar settings. In short, every computer that's connected to the network has a copy of your settings and documents available. *Mandatory user profiles* are user profiles that administrators create and Windows 2000 Professional downloads from the network. The operating system doesn't copy mandatory user profiles back to the network, however, which means that every time you log on to the domain, you start with the exact same settings. If you don't log on to a network, you're using local user profiles. If you do log on to a network, you might be using roaming user profiles, assuming that the network's administrator enabled them.

Roaming user profiles don't work well with dissimilar computer configurations. If you tend to use computers with screens that have different resolutions, different sets of applications, different directory structures, and so on, your roaming experience won't be very good. The reason is that per-user settings frequently depend on several per-computer settings. The organization of icons on your desktop is one example. If you arrange icons one way on a large monitor and then log on to a lower-resolution display, the operating system will rearrange the desktop so that all the icons fit onscreen. Windows that you might size to fit in one display don't look good in another lower-resolution display. Roaming user profiles are best when both computers have similar configurations so that you're not constantly reorganizing the desktop, resizing windows, and so on. For this reason, roaming user profiles are not a good way to synchronize your settings between a portable and desktop computer. After months of trying, I wasn't pleased with this configuration. Also, synchronizing settings require that you pay attention to the order in which you log on and off each computer.

The last shortcoming with roaming profiles is the actual data that the operating system copies to them. Within each user profile folder is a subfolder called Local Settings. The operating system does not copy this folder to the network when you log off the domain. The problem is that some of the most interesting settings and data are in this folder, and they won't be available on other computers that you use. For example, Microsoft Outlook Express stores its data in Local Settings. Because the operating system doesn't copy this folder to the network, your mail and news files won't be available on other computers you use.

Copying User Profiles

Copying user profiles has two useful purposes. First, when you migrate to Windows 2000 Professional from earlier versions of Windows, the Setup program might create a default user profile for you instead of migrating your existing user profile. If this happens, you can copy your original user profile or your new user profile to preserve your preferences. Second, you can copy a user profile to the Default User user profile in order to establish a template for new users who log on to the computer. For example, after installing the operating system, the first thing I do is configure all my preferences and then copy that user profile to the Default User user profile so each account I create starts with that same basic set of preferences.

Here's how to copy a user profile (you can't copy the profile of the user that's currently logged on, though):

1. In Control Panel, double-click the System icon.

2. On the Users Profile tab, click the user profile that you want to copy and then click Copy To.

3. In Copy profile to, type the path to which you want to copy the user profile.

4. Click Change to pick the user who has permission to use the files in this user profile.

Copying user profiles through the official channels isn't the only solution, though. You can copy files from one user profile folder to another by using Microsoft Windows Explorer. Permissions aren't a problem if you *copy* files from one to another rather than *move* them. When you copy files, they inherit the permissions of the folder into which you copied them. When you move files, they retain their permissions—problematic if you want the user of the target user profile to be able to access them. If your goal is to move files from one profile folder to the other, copy them first and then remove the originals.

Changing Profile Types

If you log on to a domain and the administrator configured your account to use roaming profiles, you can take back control. Roaming profiles are not always the cat's meow when your profile is large, and it takes forever for the operating system to copy it to and from the network. To change a roaming profile back to a local user profile, click Change Type on the User Profiles tab of the System Properties dialog box.

Customizing Consoles

Most of Windows 2000 Professional's management tools are actually Microsoft Management Console (MMC) consoles. The most useful of these are in Computer Management. In Control Panel, double-click the Administrative Tools icon and then double-click the Computer Management icon. Computer Management includes Event Viewer, System Information, Performance Logs and Alerts, Shared Folders, Device Manager, Local Users and Groups, Disk Management, Disk Defragmenter, Logical Drives, Removable Storage, and other tools. All of these and many other tools are available in individually wrapped consoles, however. Run any of them by typing the console filename, including the file extensions, in the Run dialog box:

Certmgr.msc	Certificates
Compmgmt.msc	Computer Management
Devmgmt.msc	Device Manager
Dfrg.msc	Disk Defragmenter
Diskmgmt.msc	Disk Management
Eventvwr.msc	Event Viewer
Faxserv.msc	Fax Service Management
Fsmgmt.msc	Shared Folders
Gpedit.msc	Group Policy
Ntmsmgr.msc	Removable Storage Manager
Perfmon.msc	Performance
Sysmon.msc	System Monitor

Tip

Your computer might have fewer or more MSC files. Thus, search the computer for all files with the .msc file extension to see what consoles are available.

Measuring Performance

For measuring the performance of your computer, Windows 2000 Professional provides Performance, an MMC console that contains the System Monitor and Performance Logs and Alerts snap-ins. In Control Panel, double-click the Administrative Tools icon and then double-click the Performance icon. The differences between these two snap-ins are as follows:

- **System Monitor**   Views real-time information about the computer's performance, including data about memory, disks, processors, and the network. System Monitor displays results in graphs, histograms, and reports.

- **Performance Logs and Alerts**   Records performance information in text files and sets system alerts that notify you when counters are above or below certain values.

System Monitor is more useful for observing your computer's performance while troubleshooting. For example, you can run and close different applications and see their impacts on memory consumption. Performance Logs and Alerts is useful to manage things as exceptions. That is, it notifies you when things aren't right and might require more attention.

System Monitor

In Performance, click System Monitor. You see the results in the right pane. By default, you don't see any counters. You add counters by clicking the Add button in the toolbar, picking the performance object, and clicking the counters you want to add. Other buttons on the toolbar allow you to remove, highlight, freeze, and do other things to counters. Right-click anywhere in the right pane and click Properties to display the System Monitor Properties dialog box, which allows you to further customize it. The following list describes each of its tabs:

- **General**   Change how the counters look. For example, you can display them as graphics, histograms, or remotes. You can display a legend, value bar, and toolbar. Most importantly, you can configure how often Performance updates the display (the default is every second).

- **Source**   By opening a log file, you can display previously logged resources in the right pane. This allows you to save performance data to a log file and view it at a later time. This is particularly useful if you want to show someone else the symptoms of a performance problem without having to create that problem again.

- **Data**   On this tab, add and remove counters, just as you do by clicking the Add button on the toolbar.

- **Graph**   Add a title to the graph, display vertical and horizontal grids, or change the vertical scale.

- **Color**   Change the color of background, foreground, graph lines, and so on.

- **Fonts**   Choose the font to display in the right pane. The default is Tahoma 8.25pt.

I must admit that I seldom use Performance as a troubleshooting tool. For individual users, Performance doesn't tell you anything you don't already know (gee, my computer is running slowly). It doesn't necessarily tell you why. As a troubleshooting tool, it might help you identify applications that are memory hogs and might help you determine if your configuration is the best it can be, but performance alerts are more useful. You learn about those in the next section.

Performance Logs and Alerts

Under Performance Logs and Alerts, click one of the following:

- **Counter Logs**   Log counters to a text file. The counters you log do not have to be the same as those you're displaying in Performance. You can specify a time to begin and a time to stop logging the counters you choose.

- **Trace Logs**   Log events such as process creation and page faults in text files. You can specify a time to begin and a time to stop logging the events.

- **Alerts**   Perform some action when a counter reaches a certain level. This is like receiving pager notification when your favorite stock falls or rises to a certain value. You can log an entry to a log file, send a network message, or a run a particular program.

In all cases, create a log or alert is straightforward. Click New Log Settings or New Alert Settings on any of the folder's shortcut menus. Performance will ask you to name the log or event. It stores log files in *SystemRoot*\PerfLogs.

9

Using Multiple Languages

MOST MEDIUM– AND LARGE–SIZED BUSINESSES COMPETE in a global economy, which puts extra demands on their IT infrasructures. Employees speak different languages in this new world order. Businesses sell goods and services to customers all over the planet. Executives travel to international offices whose local language is not their native tongue, and yet they must still use the offices' computers. Earlier versions of Microsoft Windows failed miserably to keep pace with the shift from national economies to a single global economy; they supported multiple language scenarios poorly. Microsoft Windows 2000 Professional supports the new world order, however, by introducing many new, long–awaited language features.

The most telling change is that all language editions of Windows 2000 Professional are built from the same code. That means that all language editions of the operating system have all the fonts, code pages, keyboard layouts, input method editors, and other files required for reading and writing documents in any language that the operating system supports. The only differences between each language edition are the language resources and help files that ship with them. As a result, supporting Windows 2000 Professional in a multilingual environment costs less. Administrators manage and support only a single edition of the operating system instead of different editions for each language. For example, rather than updating multiple editions of the operating system with multiple service packs, they can update a single edition with a single service pack. Instead of writing multiple scripts to deploy multiple language editions, administrators need to write only a single script.

In addition to the English-language edition of Windows 2000 Professional, Microsoft ships two dozen localized editions. Each localized edition supports the input and output of more than 100 international locales. Regardless of whether users have the English-language edition or any localized edition, they can read and write multilingual documents in any language that the operating system supports. A similar capability was severely limited in earlier versions of Windows. A multilanguage edition of Windows 2000 Professional is also available, and it's the most useful edition of the operating system for large multinational corporations. In addition to creating multilingual documents, users can change the language that the operating system's user interface displays. Users who speak different languages can share computers.

Character Encoding

Clarifying a few terms will help you dive into Windows 2000 Professional's language features. The first is that of a locale. *Locales* are combinations of languages and sub-languages (regions). An example is French as spoken in Canada and France; the language is French, and the sub-languages are French as spoken in Canada and French as spoken in France. Other forms of the word *locale* mean different things, and you learn about those later in this chapter. Two other related concepts are scripts and languages. *Languages* include English, German, Chinese, and Swahili. You're familiar with those. *Scripts* are sets of symbols that represent languages. Latin, Arabic, and Thai are scripts, for example, not languages. One script can represent several languages, too. For example, you write English and German text using a Latin script. In general, operating systems know little about languages; they deal more with scripts instead.

Operating systems use tables to relate numeric values to the alphanumeric characters, numbers, and punctuation in a script. For example, the 65th symbol in most code pages is the letter *A*. The numeric value, or index, is a *code point*. Each code point is thus a particular symbol in the code page. Programs store and exchange text encoded by using code points and then they render that text on the screen using fonts. Who defines code pages? Organizations such as American National Standards Institute (ANSI) define varieties of code pages, and many independent hardware vendors (IHVs) define original equipment manufacturer (OEM) code pages for their computers. Probably the most meaningful way to think of different code pages is in terms of each representing different alphabets, with the index of each character being a code point.

Think back to the days of yore, when computers were text-based and screens were monochrome. Text encoding wasn't much of an issue because most computers used English and therefore relied on Latin scripts. A simple standard for representing Latin text was all that computers required, and that's all they got. ASCII, an acronym for American Standard Code for Interchange of Information, was the original character-encoding scheme. It supported seven-bit encoding (thus, only 128 characters). It supported American English letters, numbers, punctuation, and a handful of control characters. It was primitive. It did not support languages other than English. The nice thing about ASCII is that it was portable, which means that any user using any computer could read and edit ASCII files.

I've alluded to the ASCII encoding scheme's most severe limitation: It's not useful for creating documents in languages other than English. That leads to code pages such as OEM and ANSI code pages, which do provide the support for multiple languages. You learn about them in the following section.

Code Pages

OEM code pages supported text-mode computers and MS-DOS. Again, recall the old days when computers running MS-DOS were connected to monochrome monitors. They did not support graphics, so OEM code pages included line-draw characters that provided a way to draw boxes, text-based window borders, and so on. A lot of interesting games used line-draw characters exclusively. Varieties of OEM code pages were available for different scripts, and they usually have a three-digit label such as 437 or 737. Just because OEM code pages are old doesn't mean that they're not in use anymore. MS-DOS and all versions of Windows still support them. Examples of typical OEM code pages including 720 for Arabic, 737 for Greek, 862 for Hebrew, and 866 for Cyrillic. Code page 437 is the OEM code page used on most computers in the United States.

Windows 3.1 was a graphically oriented operating system, and that fact made line-draw characters obsolete. This freed up the OEM line-draw code points for international characters and punctuation—so the ANSI code pages were born. The first 128 code points of ANSI are always the same as ASCII. The second 128 code points are unique to the script in the code page. Figure 9.1 illustrates this concept. For each of the ANSI code pages that you see in this diagram, the first 128 code points are the same as seven-bit ASCII, and the second 128 code points are unique to the script that the code page represents. Note that a four-digit label usually but not always identifies an ANSI code page. Examples of ANSI code pages are 1250 for Central Europe, 1251 for Cyrillic, 1252 for Latin, and 1255 for Hebrew (see Figure 9.1).

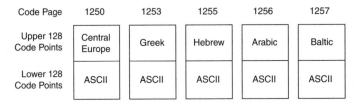

Figure 9.1 The first 128 code points of ANSI code pages are ASCII and the second 128 code pages are unique to the script.

Now, it's time to introduce the concept of single-byte versus multibyte character-encoding schemes. Single-byte encoding schemes use eight bits to represent a maximum of 256 code points. Most single-byte code pages define the first 128 code points as standard ASCII characters, as you already learned, and the remaining code points contain characters required to represent the target script. For example, the first 128 code points of code page 737 are ASCII characters, and the remaining code points are the characters in the Greek script. Windows 2000 Professional supports a wide variety of single-byte code pages other than OEM and ANSI, including EBCDIC, ISO, and Macintosh.

Multibyte character-encoding schemes use between eight and 16 bits to represent a maximum of 65,536 code points. Single-byte code pages are too small to represent scripts used for many languages, such as *Hanzi* for Chinese, *Kanji* for Japanese, and *Hanja* for Korean. These scripts have thousands of characters called *ideographs* and require multibyte code pages to represent them. Complicating matters more is the fact that characters in some multibyte encoding schemes aren't always the same width. Users usually fail to appreciate the complexity that this adds to programmers' tasks. Here are some examples of the scripts that require a multibyte encoding scheme:

- **Hiragana.** A Japanese cursive script that represents phonetic syllables

- **Katakana.** A Japanese script primarily used to spell words borrowed from other languages that represents phonetic syllables

- **Kana.** Japanese hiragana and katakana characters

- **Shift-JIS.** A Japan Industry Standard (JIS) encoding scheme based on the JIS standard X 0208

Note

An *ideographic character* is a character of Asian origin that represents a word or a syllable. They're generally used in more than one Asian language, and people often refer to them erroneously as Chinese characters. *Kanji* is the Japanese name for these characters.

All code page-based, character-encoding schemes have a fundamental weakness. As soon as users start using code points unique to particular code pages, the text is not portable. That is, if a user uses a unique code point in code page 855, users who configured their computers to use different code pages would not see the same characters. This fact is why Unicode is such an exciting character-encoding scheme that makes plain text files portable (important due to the Internet). You learn about Unicode in the following section.

Unicode 2.1

Unicode is a fixed 16-bit character-encoding scheme. It provides code points for 65,536 characters, more than enough to represent most of the scripts used today. At this point, Unicode defines about 39,000 of those code points, and plans are underway to expand Unicode so that it can include millions of code points. In addition to individual scripts, Unicode includes code points for punctuation marks, diacritics, mathematical symbols, technical symbols, arrows, dingbats, and other symbols used in publishing. Windows 2000 Professional uses Unicode 2.1, but version 3 is already available and will include more scripts. Some of the scripts that Unicode includes are Arabic, Chinese, Cyrillic, Greek, Hebrew, Japanese, Korean, Latin, and Thai. Figure 9.2 shows the ranges of scripts that Unicode supports. Many more are in Unicode 2.1 and many more will be in Unicode 3.

With the exception of Microsoft Windows NT, earlier versions of Windows almost exclusively used code page-based, character-encoding schemes to support different scripts. These schemes' limitations know no bounds. Sharing multilingual documents is difficult unless all parties sharing the information have almost identical configurations. Users who speak different languages cannot easily share computers. Networking software must keep track of which code pages each client uses and translate data appropriately, or the data might not make a successful roundtrip. Unicode resolves these issues by providing a single universal character-encoding scheme that includes most of the scripts in common use today.

Another problem that Unicode solves is more of a development issue. In order to allow users to create multilingual documents, a program running on Windows 98 has to tag multilingual text with information about the font and code page. This works only for rich documents (documents that contain formatting information), not for plain text files, which you already learned is an important issue for the Internet. The result is a lot of complicated and often proprietary code to handle these font-tagging schemes. Also, the code usually includes squirrelly pointer arithmetic due to variable-width, double-byte character-encoding schemes. This means that many developers just don't internationalize applications. Unicode addresses these issues as well.

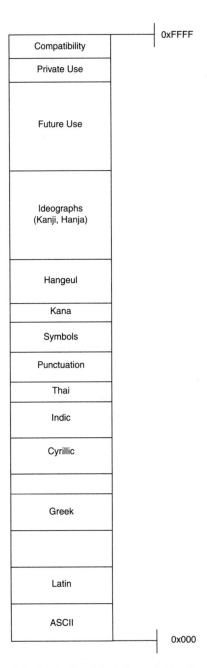

Figure 9.2 Unicode 2.1 includes varieties of scripts.

Unicode is Windows 2000 Professional's base-encoding scheme. Internally, the operating system stores and exchanges strings using Unicode. This includes data that the operating system stores in the registry and keeps in memory. It also uses Unicode for the file system, user interface, and network communication. Unicode helps programmers create multiple language versions of their applications by reducing the complexity involved in the task. Here is a summary of the benefits of Windows 2000 Professional's Unicode implementation:

- Allows plain text files to include multiple scripts, removing the requirements of using rich text files and various font-tagging schemes.

- Provides an environment for Unicode-based applications, which enables users to create documents that contain any mix of scripts.

- Includes translation tables that enable non-Unicode-based applications to work properly.

- Supports Asian languages without the programming hacks required for variable width, multibyte character-encoding schemes.

- Simplifies localization, making it easier for programmers to create multiple language versions of their applications.

- Enables sharing in mixed-language environments.

Conversion tables make it possible for non-Unicode-based applications to work properly. These tables convert Unicode-encoded strings to and from the appropriate code pages. Translation tables are available for Macintosh, EBCDIC, and ISO character-encoding schemes. The operating system also includes translation tables for UTF-7 and UTF-8, which it uses to send Unicode-based data across networks and the Internet. UTF is an acronym for *Unicode Translation Format*. You can enable and disable the varieties of translation tables in the Advanced Regional Options dialog box, shown in Figure 9.3, which you open by clicking Advanced on the General tab of the Regional Options control panel. This option requires you to log on to the computer as an administrator.

Windows 98

Windows 98 and Windows 2000 Professional provide some similar features. Both allow you to switch input locales and support creating multilingual documents. Microsoft ships multiple language versions of each operating system, too. Windows 98's implementation of these features is severely limited, however, when compared to Windows 2000 Professional.

First and foremost, Windows 98 does not use Unicode internally. It does provide functions for handling Unicode strings, but Windows 98 still relies on ANSI code pages for input and output, and programs must translate data to ANSI before calling the system. The result is that sharing data between two computers that are configured with different code pages is more difficult.

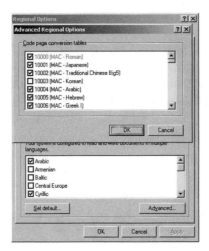

Figure 9.3   Users seldom have a good reason for enabling and
disabling the conversion tables in this dialog box.

Installing Language Groups

Language groups are behind a lot of Windows 2000 Professional's language
features. The operating system includes 17 language groups, which collec-
tively define over 100 international locales.

A language group includes fonts, code pages, and other files that a particular script requires. The terms *language group* and *language setting* are
misnomers, incidentally, because they support particular scripts and not
languages themselves (a Microsoft misnomer caused by trying to oversimplify
the operating system). Cyrillic is an example of a language group, which
includes the files necessary to support various languages that use the Cyrillic
script. Installing a language group doesn't do anything but copy files to the
computer.

Install language groups that support the locales you want to use. If you
have need of the Russian locale, install the Cyrillic language group. If you
have need of the Japanese locale, install the Japanese language group.
Installing a language group does require you to log on to Windows 2000
Professional as Administrator:

1. In Control Panel, double-click the Regional Options icon.

2. In the Language settings for the system area (on the "General" tab
   sheet), do one or both of the following:

   ▪ Select the check boxes corresponding to each language group that you
     want to install.

- Deselect the check boxes corresponding to each language group that you want to remove.

Before running out and installing a bunch of language groups, consider their disk space requirements. Some language groups share common files. Thus, when installing multiple language groups, space requirements will vary slightly, depending on the groups you install. The following list shows the disk space requirements for each language group. The name of the language group is in the first column and the requirements are in the second.

Arabic	1.6 megabytes
Armenian	11.5 megabytes
Baltic	1 megabyte
Central European	1.2 megabytes
Cyrillic	1.2 megabytes
Georgian	5.8 megabytes
Greek	1 megabyte
Hebrew	1.4 megabytes
Indic	.25 megabytes
Japanese	58 megabytes
Korean	29.4 megabytes
Simplified Chinese	32.5 megabytes
Thai	3.9 megabytes
Traditional Chinese	13.5 megabytes
Turkic	.9 megabytes
Vietnamese	.5 megabytes
Western Europe and United States	10.1 megabytes

Note

In most cases, the operating system limits the locales available for most language features to those for which you've installed the appropriate language groups. You won't be able to use the Russian locale until you install the Cyrillic language group, for instance.

Changing the Default System Locale

Even though Windows 2000 Professional uses Unicode, non-Unicode-based applications still work. The operating system can emulate the operating environment of any non-Unicode-based version of Windows, including Windows 98. For example, you can run the French-language edition of a program on the

English-language edition of Windows 2000 Professional. You can run the English-language edition of a program on the Russian-language edition of Windows 2000 Professional. *System locales* make this possible. In order to run any particular language edition of an application, you must change the system locale to match the locale that the application expects. Thus, to run the German-language edition of a program, you must change the system locale to German:

1. In Control Panel, double-click the Regional Options icon.

2. On the General tab, click the Set default button.

3. In the Select the appropriate local list, click the locale you want to use as the default.

The system locale is a per-computer setting, and therefore you must log on to the computer as Administrator in order to change it. Also, changes to this setting don't take effect until after you restart the computer.

You can change the system locale only to those for which you've already installed language groups. Thus, you must first install the language groups you want to use, as you learned in the previous section. When you change the system locale, Windows 2000 Professional changes the default code page for non-Unicode-based applications, and those applications use that code page to display its user interface. This change does not affect the operating system's user interface, nor does it affect Unicode-based applications. Both work as they always did because they don't rely on the system locale for input or output.

The primary limitation of emulating non-Unicode-based operating environments using the system locale is that you can't run, at the same time, two non-Unicode-based applications that rely on two different code pages. The reason is that Windows 2000 Professional has only one system locale and you must restart the computer each time you change it. Thus, you can't run two non-Unicode-based applications, one a French-language edition and another a Spanish-language edition, at the same time. This does not apply to Unicode-based applications; thus, users can run different language editions of different Unicode-based applications while they're running a non-Unicode-based application that's using the system locale.

Note

Developers get the biggest blast from changing the system locale. It enables them to test different localized applications on a single computer without maintaining several different machines with different language editions of the operating system.

Some locales do not have code page support and therefore Windows 2000 Professional supports them only through Unicode. Those include the following:

- Armenian (Armenia)
- Georgian (Georgia)
- Hindi (India)
- Tamil (India)
- Marathi (India)
- Sanskrit (India)
- Konkani (India)

Setting Regional Preferences

A *user locale* contains regional preferences; it is not a language setting, even if the name implies such. It has little to do with languages, scripts, or code pages. It strictly defines cultural conventions for a particular region, such as Canada. In fact, the only language that a user locale controls is the names of days and months. Conventions that a user locale defines include number and currency formatting, date and time formatting, names of days and months, and sorting and searching rules. You change the user locale in Control Panel:

1. In Control Panel, double-click the Regional Options icon.

   You see the Regional Options dialog box. It has six tabs, the first of which is where you change the user locale. Figure 9.4 shows an example of the Regional Options dialog box.

2. In the <u>Y</u>our locale list, click a locale.

   Windows 2000 Professional changes the settings on the dialog box's remaining tabs to reflect the locale's cultural conventions. More information about each tab follows these instructions.

3. In Sorting order, click the sorting algorithm you want applications to use for sorting text.

   Windows 2000 Professional doesn't display this list unless the locale supports it. Also, the options vary, depending on the locale. For example, options for German (Germany) include Dictionary and Phone Book (DIN). Options for Spanish (Spain) include International and Traditional.

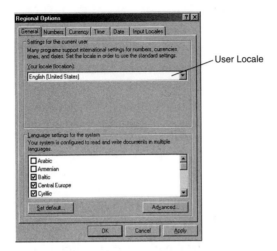

Figure 9.4 Change the user local using the Regional Options
dialog box, and then customize it using each tab.

After changing the user local, Windows 2000 Professional updates the settings
on the remaining tabs of the Regional Options dialog box. For example,
change the user local to English (United States), and the operating system sets
the currency symbol to a dollar sign ($). Change the user local to French
(France), and the operating system changes the currency symbol to Franc (F).
The user can, of course, further customize these settings by changing them on
each of the following tabs:

- **Numbers.** Defines number-formatting conventions. These include
  the decimal, digit grouping, and negative sign symbols. Other
  conventions apply.

- **Currency.** Defines conventions for formatting currency. These include
  the currency symbol, formats, and digit groupings.

- **Time.** Defines how to format times, including the order of hours, minutes, and seconds, as well as the character that separates each part.

- **Date.** Defines how to format dates, including the order of day, date, and
  year, as well as the character that separates each part.

- **Input Locales.** Matches languages to keyboard layouts. You learn more
  about this in the section called "Editing Multilingual Documents."

Changes to the user locale are immediate. You don't have to log off the computer, nor do you have to restart it.

Note

The Date tab has a setting that might be of interest to millennium bashers. It defines the way Windows 2000 Professional and some applications interpret two-digit dates. In the Calendar area, you specify a 100-year range. The operating system assumes that all two-digit dates fall within that range. For example, if the range is 1975 to 2075, '60 is 1960 and '99 is 2099. This setting has no impact on four-digit dates. Not all applications use this setting, however, so it's not necessarily a safeguard against problems with two-digit dates.

Editing Multilingual Documents

Different regions have keyboards with different layouts. French keyboards are different from U.S. keyboards, for example. A French keyboard has additional characters for accented letters and puts keys in different places in relation to a U.S. keyboard (the letter *Z* and letter *W* are reversed). People who type multilingual documents tend to prefer doing so using one keyboard layout for all languages, and thus they configure input locales to enable them to do so. Microsoft has a Web site that illustrates the various keyboard layouts, which you find at `http://www.microsoft.com/globaldev`.

Input locales match locales' languages with a method for inputting them. They're the keys to creating multilingual documents. Input locales can match languages to simple keyboard layouts or to more complex *input method editors* (*IMEs*), which support inputting languages containing thousands of ideographs with a standard keyboard. An example of an input locale is a French locale paired with a U.S. keyboard. French users might prefer to type Spanish, French, and English text by using a single French keyboard layout. They do so by creating three input locales that pair Spanish, French, and English locales with a French keyboard. Locales based on different scripts do require users to change keyboard layouts.

Note

Input method editors (IMEs) translate keystrokes to ideographical characters. They enable users to create thousands of ideographs using a standard keyboard, include a dictionary of common ideographs, and have engines that convert various key combinations into ideographs. In earlier versions of Windows, only the editions that required IMEs provide them, but all language editions of Windows 2000 Professional include all the IMEs necessary for all supported scripts that require them.

Figure 9.5 shows an example of a multilingual document. I wrote this gibberish (not multilingual here) using Microsoft WordPad. It contains Japanese, Cyrillic, Hebrew, and Arabic scripts, all in one document—a feat that was difficult or impossible in earlier versions of Windows, particularly English-language editions. The following sections show you how to create multilingual documents by first creating input locales and then switching between them while editing. Multilingual applications can do more than just input and output multilingual text; at least the smart ones can. For example, they might use a different spell checker or different hyphenation rules for different input locales. Office 2000 is an application that has this feature.

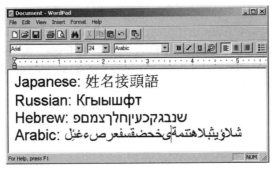

Figure 9.5 Users can easily create multilingual documents.

Creating Input Locales

The locales and keyboard layouts that you can pair up to create input locales depend on the language groups that you've installed. For more information, refer to "Installing Language Groups," earlier in this chapter. Here's how to create an input locale:

1. In Control Panel, double-click the Regional Options icon.

2. On the Input Locales tab, click Add.

   Figure 9.6 shows this tab. The Installed input locales area shows the input locales that you created. The remaining areas allow you to further customize the way the input locales work.

3. In the Input locale list, click a locale.

4. In the Keyboard layout/IME list, click the keyboard layout or input method editor you want to associate with the locale.

Input locales are per-user settings, so users can configure input locales without affecting other users. Also, changes take effect immediately, so you don't have to log off or restart the computer after changing them.

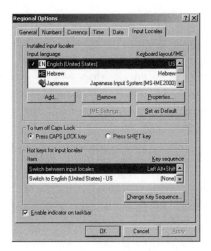

Figure 9.6 The input locales that you can create
depend on the language groups you installed.

You can further customize input locales using other options on the Input
Locales tab:

- To remove an input locale, click the input locale in the list and then
  click <u>R</u>emove.

- To set the default input locale, which applications use when they first
  start, click the input locale and then click <u>S</u>et as Default.

- To configure an input locale's input method editor, click IME Settings and
  then change the input method editor's settings.

- To change the way you toggle the Caps Lock on and off, do one of the
  following:

  - To toggle the Caps Lock by pressing Caps Lock, click Press CAPS
    <u>L</u>OCK key.

  - To toggle the Caps Lock by pressing Shift, click Press SHI<u>F</u>T key.

- To configure key combinations that allow you to quickly switch between
  input locales, click an input locale in the Hot keys for input locales area
  and then click <u>C</u>hange Key Sequence.

- To configure the indicator that shows the current input locale, do one of
  the following:

  - To display the indicator, select the <u>E</u>nable indicator on taskbar check
    box.

  - To remove the indicator, select the <u>E</u>nable indicator on taskbar check
    box.

Editing Documents

You create multilingual documents by switching input locales as you type in a program that supports them. Microsoft Notepad and WordPad both support editing multilingual documents, as does Microsoft Office 2000. While editing a document, type using the current input locale, change input locales, and then continue typing using the new input locale. Switch input locales by doing one of the following:

- Press Left Alt+Shift to switch to the next input locale in the list, using the taskbar indicator to identify the current input locale.

- Press the key combination associated with a specific input locale. If you associated Ctrl+Shift+0 with an input locale, for example, press that key combination.

- Click the taskbar indicator, shown in Figure 9.7, and then click one of the input locales. Table 9.1 shows the different symbols that Windows 2000 Professional uses for different locales.

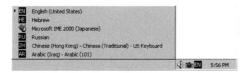

Figure 9.7 The taskbar indicator
shows the current input locale.

While moving the cursor around a document, the current input locale changes to the input locale of the text over which the cursor is pointing. That is, applications change the current input locale to the locale that you used to create text. This makes editing more convenient because you don't have to manually change input locales to change multilingual text. Note, too, that the caret changes to indicate the direction of text, left-to-right or right-to-left. This helps you keep track of where the next character goes when using bidirectional scripts such as Hebrew and Arabic.

When you change input locales, the taskbar indicator shows the current input locale. It displays a two-letter code that reflects the language portion of the input locale. Thus, if you change to a French locale, you'll see *FR* in the taskbar indicator. Table 9.1 shows each indicator. The first column is the two-letter code, and the second column is the language portion of the locale that the code represents.

Table 9.1 **Input Locale Indicators**

Indicator	Language
AF	Afrikaans
AR	Arabic
AZ	Azeri
BE	Belarusian
BG	Bulgarian
CA	Catalan
CS	Czech
DA	Danish
DE	German
EL	Greek
EN	English
ES	Spanish
ET	Estonian
EU	Basque
FA	Farsi
FI	Finnish
FO	Faeroese
FR	French
HE	Hebrew
HI	Hindi
HR	Croatian
HU	Hungarian
HY	Armenian
IN	Indonesian
IS	Icelandic
IT	Italian
KA	Georgian
KK	Kazakh
KN	Konkani
LV	Latvian
MA	Marathi

continues ▶

Table 9.1 **Input Locale Indicators**

Indicator	Language
MK	Macedonian
MS	Malay
NL	Dutch
NO	Norwegian
PL	Polish
PT	Portuguese
RO	Romanian
RU	Russian
SA	Sanskrit
SK	Slovak
SL	Slovenian
SQ	Albanian
SR	Serbian
SV	Swedish
SW	Swahili
TA	Tamil
TH	Thai
TR	Turkish
TT	Tatar
UK	Ukrainians
UR	Urdu
UZ	Uzbek
VI	Vietnamese
ZH	Chinese

You can use a different input locale with each application that is running. When you change input locales, Windows 2000 Professional notifies the current application of the change, not all of them. Thus, you can change the input locale for one application to one based on the Greek script and the input locale for another application to one based on the Cyrillic script. When you switch back and forth between each application, the input locale automatically changes, as indicated in the taskbar. The operating system's desktop and Windows Explorer usually use the default input locale, however.

Core Program Code

Versions of Windows earlier than Windows 2000 Professional had a significant problem that made sharing data and supporting the operating systems in multilingual environments difficult at best: fragmentation. European-language editions used single-byte code pages, whereas Far Eastern-language editions used multibyte code pages. Middle Eastern-language editions used single-byte code pages, but required new code to handle the requirements of bidirectional layout and rendering. Asian and Middle Eastern-language editions were in fact supersets of the core English-language editions, and included additional IMEs and APIs that the other language editions did not include. As a result, many different versions of the operating system floated around the world, some of which were not capable of produce scripts available in other language editions. For example, the English-language edition of Windows 98 doesn't provide the IMEs required to type Japanese text, nor does it handle bidirectional scripts such as Arabic and Hebrew.

A side effect is that multilingual applications are difficult for developers to create, mainly due to the limitations in the operating systems. For example, if developers wanted to create a Chinese-language edition of a program in the old days, they had to run a Chinese-language edition of the operating system and use Chinese-language editions of the programming tools and software development kits (SDKs). The software development tools and SDKs are unified now, making it possible to compile applications on any language edition of Microsoft Windows NT or Windows 2000 Professional, assuming that the appropriate code pages are installed. Still, they had to test their applications on Chinese-language editions of the operating systems. This usually meant that they had a system dedicated to each language edition of the operating system for which they targeted.

Unicode addresses some of these issues. Windows 2000 Professional's single worldwide binary addresses the rest. Microsoft produces every language edition of Windows 2000 Professional from the same core code. The result is that each language edition includes all the files required to produce scripts supported by any other language edition. For example, the English-language edition of the operating system includes the IMEs required to enter Japanese text, and fully supports bidirectional scripts such as Hebrew and Arabic. A few subtle differences exist between each language edition. First, they come with different language resources that include text for the user interface and help files. Second, the default system locale for each language edition is different. Regardless, the result is that creating and sharing multilingual documents is easier because every user can read and edit each language that the operating system supports, regardless of which language edition they're using.

National Language Support

The biggest part of the operating system's international support is through the National Language Support (NLS) APIs. NLS is a set of tables and other files that an application can access through the NLS API. You install these tables and other files when you install language groups, as described in "Installing Language Groups," earlier in this chapter. The types of information that the NLS API provides to applications include the following:

- Information about the user locale, including formatting and localized names of days and months.
- Conversion tables that translate code pages to Unicode, and vice versa. They allow non–Unicode-based applications to work properly.
- Typing information, such as whether a code point is a letter, number, white space, or symbol; and whether a letter is lowercase or uppercase.
- Sorting information, such as the rules for sorting accented characters. NLS supports multiple sorting algorithms for each locale.
- Font information, include the character-encoding schemes, Unicode ranges, and locales it supports.

NLS also includes varieties of functions that help developers create generic code for handling input, storage, and layout of all languages correctly. It has functions for transforming strings, manipulating code pages, manipulating locales, and so on. Programs use NLS functions to convert strings from one character-encoding scheme to Unicode and vice versa. NLS functions also help layout bidirectional text such as Hebrew and Arabic. The resulting code is still complex, but APIs do more of the work. The result is that developers are more likely to localize their applications or make them multilingual. The fact that all language editions of Windows 2000 Professional can produce all supported scripts ensures that a market exists for all their hard work.

Multilanguage Support

Multi-Language (ML) API provides support for handling input locales, including keyboard layouts. It enables applications to handle on-the-fly changes to input locales, all with generic code. It provides functions for handling bidirectional layout. The bottom line is that this boring little API enables transparent support for multilingual documents.

Localizable Resources

Localizable resources are bits of information in a program that change from one language to another. This might be algorithms (sorting, spelling, and so on); but they are usually user interface elements (menus, dialog boxes, and so on), help text, icons, bitmaps, and strings.

In the old days, developers stored localizable resources within executable files. Translating those resources, *localizing the application*, meant that translators had to work with actual program code—thousands of lines of it. Chances were high that translators would introduce errors, and that translators might miss some resources or might not understand the context of other resources. No wonder that so many successful companies sprang into existence for the sole purpose of localizing other company's applications. Microsoft has a better way.

Microsoft's most elegant solution to the problem is to use resource files. *Resource files* are plain text files that have the .rc file extension. The format of the file is fixed, and developers sometimes use a resource editor such as Microsoft Visual Studio to create the file. When developers compile the application, the compiler converts the resource file to a compiled resource file that has the .res file extension. It also embeds the compiled resource file in the executable file, whether it's a .dll, .exe, or other type of executable file. Within the application's code, developers retrieve resources using a resource identifier. The result is that all localizable resources are in a separate file that translators can easily localize. By carefully crafting resource files, developers can also create an application that allows users to change the application's user interface.

Language Editions

As you read in this chapter's introduction, Windows 2000 Professional is available in three flavors: an English-language edition, localized editions, and a multilanguage edition. The English-language edition speaks for itself. It's the most popular edition of the operating system and is available on retail shelves across the U.S.

Microsoft is also shipping 24 fully localized editions of Windows 2000 Professional. Some will ship about six weeks after the English-language edition. The company will ship the remaining language editions in a refresh release about six months later. The initial release will include Chinese, French, German, Japanese, Korean, and Spanish editions. The refresh release will include Arabic, Brazilian, Czech, Danish, Dutch, Finnish, Greek, Hebrew, Hungarian, Italian, Norwegian, Polish, Portuguese, Russian, Swedish, and

Turkish editions. With any language edition of Windows 2000 Professional, users can input, view, and print by using all of the locales that the operating system supports.

Here's some help in choosing which editions are best for your company:

- Companies that conduct most of their business in English and occasionally create multilingual documents should purchase the English-language edition.

- Companies that conduct most of their business in a language other than English and occasionally create multilingual documents should purchase the appropriate localized edition.

- Companies that employ people who speak many different languages or share computers in a multilingual environment should purchase the multilanguage edition.

Localized Editions

The 24 language editions of Windows 2000 Professional are the following:

Arabic	Hebrew
Brazilian	Hungarian
Chinese (Simplified)	Italian
Chinese (Traditional)	Japanese
Czech	Korean
Danish	Norwegian
Dutch	Oikush
English	Portuguese
Finnish	Russian
French	Spanish
German	Swedish
Greek	Turkish

Using any language edition of Windows 2000 Professional, users can read and edit documents in any of the more than 100 locales that Windows 2000 Professional supports. Each language edition sports a fully localized user interface (menus, dialog boxes, help files, folder names, and so on). The operating system's user interface remains in the local language, and users can't change it. Channels for purchasing localized editions of the operating system vary, depending on the registry. Check retail stores or your local Microsoft office.

Multilanguage Edition

Large multinational organizations have users and customers who speak different languages. In many cases, users who share computers don't speak the same languages. When you use most ATM machines, the machine prompts you for which language you want to use. Similarly, Windows 2000 Professional's multilanguage edition allows users to choose the language that the operating system uses to display its user interface, without affecting their data. This is in contrast to the prevailing scenario, in which each computer is dedicated to a single language edition of an operating system: a Russian-language edition of the operating system, running Russian-language edition applications to handle Russian data. Highlights of the multilanguage edition include the following:

- Single worldwide deployment—deploy a single version of Windows 2000 Professional, which costs less than deploying multiple language editions.

- Easier maintenance—apply a single service pack worldwide rather than service packs for each language edition of Windows 2000 Professional. Support and troubleshooting are simpler, too, because there's only one edition to worry about.

- Share computers in multilingual environments—users who speak different languages can share computers. Choice of language for the user interface is a per-user setting, so each user logs on to the computer and immediately gets to work in the language they choose. No longer do companies have to dedicate computers to a single language.

Note

The multilanguage edition doesn't change the user interface that applications display. Some applications offer similar features, though. Office 2000 is an example of an application for which a multilanguage edition is available.

The multilanguage edition has the same features as the English-language or any other language edition of Windows 2000 Professional. Users can edit multilingual documents in any of the more than 100 locales that the operating system supports, for example. The primary difference is that the multilanguage edition ships with the language resources from all localized versions of the operating system.

The only upgrade path to the multilanguage edition of Windows 2000 Professional is from the English-language edition of Windows NT. You must install a new copy of the operating system if you're using any other language edition of Windows NT or if you're using Windows 98. The initial release of the multilanguage edition is within six to eight weeks of the English-language edition. Microsoft will ship a refresh release about six months later, which corresponds to the release dates of the various language editions of the operating system. Note, also, that the multilanguage edition will not be available in retail stores; it's only sold through Microsoft's volume licensing programs, such as these:

- Microsoft Open License program—provides simple volume licensing to small and medium-sized businesses, governments, and educational institutions that have between five to several thousand computers.

- Microsoft Select—a volume software licensing program for businesses, governments, and educational organizations that have more than 1000 computers.

- Microsoft Enterprise Agreements—a licensing agreement for customers who have committed to a fixed number of licenses for Microsoft's platform of products over a three-year period of time.

Installing the multilanguage edition is a two-step process. You first install the language groups necessary to display the user interface, using the scripts you want. Then, you install the multilanguage version files, which provide language content for the user interface and Windows 2000 Professional Help. Here's an overview of installation process:

1. Install Windows 2000 Professional.

2. Install the necessary language groups.

3. Install the Multilanguage Version files.

The multilanguage edition allows you to choose the default language that the operating system uses to display its user interface. The default language applies to all new user accounts. You can always add and remove languages at a later time or change the default language using Muisetup.exe. Each language uses about 45 megabytes of disk space.

10

Making Computers Accessible

MICROSOFT GOES FURTHER THAN MOST COMPANIES to make its software easy to use for people with vision, hearing, and physical impairments. Think back to Windows 95, when it was one of the few operating systems to provide features such as high-contrast color schemes. They document each software product's accessibility features in their print and online documentation. They also fund research into making computers easy for everyone to use, including people with vision, hearing, and physical impairments.

Windows 2000 Professional is the fruit of Microsoft's labors. The operating system has the best of Windows 98's accessibility features, rectifies specific problems with them, and expands them. It provides varieties of ways to enable these features. Controlling them is easy, due to a status indicator that shows the features that are enabled and a wizard that helps users configure them to suit their needs. The operating system provides for virtually every user who needs *assistive technology* to help them. Also, the operating system fixes a usability problem that required users to enable emergency hotkeys in Control Panel before using them. This is a Catch-22 because users who need the accessibility features probably can't navigate Control Panel in the first place.

Most users never need the accessibility features. Nonetheless, they're worth learning for that inevitable moment when you have to teach your elderly aunt how to use Windows 2000 Professional. Administrators have even more impetus to learn them. Administrators must take responsibility for making sure that they know how the operating system's accessibility features work and that they're able to train users how to use them, if required.

And if you need assistive technology to help you use Windows 2000 Professional, you'll find that it's easy to use and will open doors that you might have thought closed.

Accessibility Issues

Most big companies employ people with disabilities, including folks who require computers to perform their jobs. Worldwide, approximately 500 million people have some sort of disability. In the United States alone, about 54 million people have disabilities and more than 30 million of those people have disabilities that might limit their ability to use computers on the job, mostly due to incompetent hardware and software design. Users don't have to have severe disabilities in order to benefit from assistive technology, though. Our aging population, many using computers, is having difficulty seeing the screen and navigating due to mild disabilities such as poor eyesight or an unsteady hand. Have you ever watched an elderly user with a mouse and wished you could help? Table 10.1 shows the percentage of each age group that has disabilities. More importantly, it shows that the number of people with disabilities progressively rises with age.

Table 10.1 **Percentage of Disabilities Within Various Age Groups**

Age Group	Percentage with Disabilities
0 to 21	10%
22 to 44	14.9%
45 to 54	24.5%
55 to 64	36.3%
65 to 79	47.3%
Over 80	71.5%

This data is from the 1994-1995 Survey of Income and Program Participation by the U.S. Census Bureau. (Courtesy of Microsoft Corporation.)

The types of disabilities that affect users' ability to work with computers vary, but fall into the following three categories:

- Visual impairments run the gamut from mild near-sightedness to blindness, and they affect users' ability to see information onscreen. Users with visual impairments need high-contrast color schemes, enlarged fonts, and alternative output, including text-to-speech translators and Braille.

- Users with hearing impairments, ranging from slight hearing loss to deafness, require visual instead of audible cues. A program might flash its title bar when an error occurs, for example, instead of beeping. In general, hearing impairments don't prevent people from using computers, but assistive technology gives them a better experience.

- For people with physical impairments, moving or controlling movements is difficult. These users have difficult using a mouse or keyboard. For example, they might bounce a key, which programs interpret as pressing the key twice, or have trouble controlling the mouse pointer, making it hard to drag objects. Physical impairments range from unsteady hands to people using mouth-sticks.

You aren't unfamiliar with accessibility aids. Ramps help people in wheel-chairs get around stairs. Closed-captioning is useful for more than displaying the play-by-play action in sports bars; it enables people with hearing impairments to watch the premiere of *Frasier* (my favorite show). Large-print books and books-on-tape help bookworms enjoy their latest tome even if they have trouble reading normal print. Notice the verbs in this paragraph and you should pick up on *helps*, *enables*, and *enjoys*; but I prefer to think of it as *empowering* users.

More Help for Users with Disabilities

Microsoft wants to make sure that all users have access to information about the accessibility features in each of its products. In Windows 2000 Professional's help, the topic *Accessibility for Special Needs* describes the operating system's many accessibility features.

People with vision impairments that prevent them from reading help or other printed documentation can order publications from Recording for the Blind. Recording for the Blind distributes publications to members of its distribution service. More than 80,000 titles are available, including Microsoft's product documentation and various books from Microsoft Press. These titles are available on audiocassettes or 3.5-inch disks.

In addition to Recording for the Blind, Trace R&D Center at the University of Wisconsin—Madison publishes information about the products that help people with disabilities use computers. *Trace Resource Book* describes well over 18,000 products. You can get more information by contacting Trace R&D Center at (608)262-6966 or by using a text telephone at (608)263-5408. The organization's Web site is http://www.trace.wisc.edu. Write to Trace R&D Center at the following address:

Trace R&D Center
S-315 Waisman Center
1500 Highland Avenue
Madison, WI 53705-2280

Following through on Microsoft's commitment to support users with disabilities, the company provides product support via text telephone (TT/TTD) devices. In the United States, call (206) 635-4948 between 6 a.m. and 6 p.m. Pacific Time, Monday through Friday, excluding holidays. In Canada, call (905) 568-9641 between 8 a.m. and 8 p.m. Eastern Time, Monday through Friday, excluding holidays.

Microsoft's accessibility features are based on technology developed at the Trace R&D Center at the University of Wisconsin—Madison. These features help users overcome their disabilities and use the full capabilities of Windows 2000 Professional. For more information about Microsoft's efforts, see the company's Web site, http://www.microsoft.com/enable. This Web site describes the company's long-term accessibility strategy, includes product-specific accessibility information, and contains documentation for developers. It also includes an extensive index of numbers of third-party programs and other assistive technologies that help users with disabilities get the most from using their computers.

Emergency Hotkeys in a Pinch

Users with certain disabilities can't always get to Control Panel to turn on the accessibility features they need. By way of experiment, try enabling any accessibility feature with your monitor's brightness and contrast turned down and without using your mouse. Try the same experiment with a single hand. Of course, if you aren't able to try my experiment, you already understand that this task is frustrating and just daunting enough to turn some users away from computers if the computers don't already have the accessibility features enabled.

Emergency hotkeys are a quick and easy way to turn on enough help to allow users to get to Control Panel and refine their settings. Table 10.2 shows each emergency hotkey and the accessibility feature it enables. It doesn't describe each accessibility feature, though. For more information about how to use each accessibility feature, see the appropriate section in this chapter. Each hotkey toggles an accessibility feature on and off and, in general, is squirrelly enough that it won't conflict with most programs. If for some odd reason an emergency hotkey does conflict with a program you use, you can permanently disable it. For instance, to turn on StickyKeys, an accessibility feature that allows users to build key combinations such as Ctrl+Shift+S one keystroke at a time, press Shift five times in a row.

Table 10.2 **Emergency Hotkeys**

Press This . . .	. . . to Turn on this Accessibility Feature
Shift 5 times	StickyKeys
Left Alt+Left Shift+Num Lock	MouseKeys
Hold down right Shift for 8 seconds	FilterKeys with default settings

continues ▶

Press This . . .	. . . to Turn on this Accessibility Feature
Right Shift for 12 seconds	FilterKeys with SlowKeys and RepeatKeys, using conservative settings
Right Shift for 16 seconds	FilterKeys with BounceKeys and RepeatKeys, using conservative settings
Num Lock for 5 seconds	ToggleKeys
Left Alt+Left Shift+Print Screen	High-contrast mode

Tip

Some of the emergency hotkeys require key combinations that are difficult. Enabling MouseKeys by pressing Left Alt+Left Shift+Num Lock is difficult for single-handed typists, for example. In these cases, enable StickyKeys first by pressing Shift five times, and then enable the other accessibility feature by pressing each keystroke in the combination, one at a time. Alternatively, use the On-Screen Keyboard, which you learn about in "On-Screen Keyboard," later in this chapter.

When you press an emergency hotkey, Windows 2000 Professional makes a unique gurgling sound and displays a dialog box similar to the one in Figure 10.1, which confirms that you want to turn on that particular accessibility feature. This dialog box explains the feature that you're enabling so that, if you pressed the hotkey by accident or pressed the wrong hotkey, you can click Cancel to not enable it. Two traits are annoying about this dialog box. First, pressing Esc disables that accessibility feature's emergency hotkey so that you must enable it again in Control Panel. Second, the default button is Cancel, not OK, requiring users who really need the accessibility feature to have enough dexterity to use the keyboard or the mouse. Click Settings to adjust the accessibility feature's configuration, or select Turn off keyboard shortcut for this accessibility feature to permanently disable the emergency hotkey.

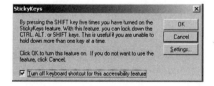

Figure 10.1 Windows 2000 Professional verifies that you want to enable the accessibility feature after pressing its hotkey.

Taking the Accessibility Exam

Versions of Windows prior to Windows 98 required that people use the Accessibility Options icon in Control Panel to enable the accessibility features, and they also required users to know which settings in that dialog box apply to their own circumstances. Considering the obscure names of these features (can Microsoft get any more cute than StickyKeys?), enabling them was difficult. The Accessibility Options icon is still useful for fine-tuning the accessibility features, and you learn more about that later.

Accessibility Wizard is a better way to configure the accessibility features, however. A one-stop shop for configuring users' computers to meet their special needs, it's the Windows 2000 equivalent of an eye exam in which the optometrist asks what looks clearer, A or B. The wizard asks similar questions, such as, "Does text look better this way or that way?" The result is a computer tailored to users' specific needs without complicated settings.

The pages that the Accessibility Wizard displays depend on how you answer its questions. If you indicate that you need extra help seeing the screen, it asks you to choose from the different ways that Windows 2000 Professional can configure the display. If you indicate that you have difficulty using a keyboard, it presents several features that you can enable. If you have a physical impairment that limits your ability to use a keyboard or mouse, consider using the emergency hotkeys, which you learned about in the previous section, to temporarily enable enough help to complete the wizard. The following instructions show how to use Accessibility Wizard to the point that it branches off in different directions, but look to the following sections to learn about additional pages it displays:

1. On the Start menu, point to Programs, point to Accessories, point to Accessibility, and then click *Accessibility Wizard*.

2. On the Welcome to the Accessibility Wizard page, click Next.

3. On the Text Size page, select the smallest text that you can read and then click Next. The current selection is the one with the wide border around it. The wizard adjusts various options to meet your requirements.

4. On the Display Settings page, select the check boxes containing the options you want and then click Next.

   Select the Change the font size check box to make text in title bars and menus bigger (the default), the Switch to lower screen resolution check box to make everything on the screen larger, the Use Microsoft Magnifier check box to magnify portions of the screen, and the Disable personalized menus check box to prevent Windows 2000 Professional from hiding menu items, commands, and shortcuts that you use infrequently. Click Next.

5. On the Set Wizard Options page, select any or all of the following check boxes (see Figure 10.2 for an example of this page) and then click <u>N</u>ext:

- I am b<u>l</u>ind or have difficulty seeing things on screen
- I am <u>d</u>eaf or having difficulty hearing sounds from the computer
- I have difficulty using the <u>k</u>eyboard or mouse
- I want to set <u>a</u>dministrative options

5. Follow the remaining instructions you see onscreen. For more information about completing Accessibility Wizard, see the following sections.

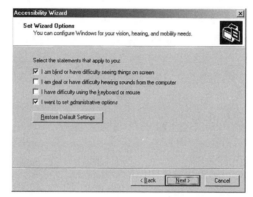

Figure 10.2 Accessibility Wizard displays additional screens based on how you answer these four questions.

> **Note**
> Few settings that Accessibility Wizard changes are in the Accessibility Options dialog box. Most are hidden in Control Panel's Mouse, Display, and Sounds and Multimedia icons.

Visual Impairments

If you selected the I am b<u>l</u>ind or have difficulty seeing things on screen check box on the Set Wizard Options page, Accessibility Wizard presents a series of pages that allow you to make information onscreen easier to see:

- **Scrollbar and Windows Border Size**   This page shows four scrollbars. Click the smallest scrollbar that you can easily see. The size of the window border affects your ability to resize a window, so make sure that you'll be able to grab it with the mouse.

- **Icon Size** This page displays three different icons that are progressively larger. Note that the current icon is the one with the wide border around it. Pick the smallest icon that you can easily see. If you have a large display, consider picking a larger size, ensuring that icon text doesn't wither away into squiggly nothingness.

- **Mouse Cursor** This page presents nine mouse pointers arranged in a three-by-three grid. Top to bottom, the size increases; left to right, the color changes. The sample in the top-left corner is a normal mouse cursor. Click the smallest mouse pointer that's easiest for you to see. Larger mouse pointers are harder to use when accuracy is important, such as when using graphics programs or positioning text in a word processor, but they're terrific when you have difficulty following the pointer onscreen.

- **Display Color Size** This page allows you to choose between various color schemes that Microsoft designed for users with vision impairments. In the Color schemes list, click the color scheme that's easiest for you to see. In the Preview area, you see a sample of the scheme you selected.

You can further adjust the settings you learned about in this section, but not via the Accessibility Options dialog box. Change the sizes of windows, icons, and other objects in the Display Properties dialog box's Appearance tab. Change color schemes in the same dialog box. On the Mouse Properties dialog box's Pointers tab, select from different pointer schemes—some even include animation.

Hearing Impairments

If you selected the I am deaf or having difficulty hearing sounds from the computer check box on the Set Wizard Options dialog box, Accessibility Wizard presents a series of pages that allow you to substitute visual cues for sounds:

- **SoundSentry** This page enables SoundSentry, an accessibility feature that displays visual cues for certain types of sounds. Click Yes to enable SoundSentry.

- **ShowSounds** This page enables ShowSounds, an accessibility feature that causes applications to display captions when they produce speech and sounds. Click Yes to enable ShowSounds.

After configuring either feature using Accessibility Wizard, fine-tune their settings by double-clicking the Accessibility Options icon in Control Panel. "Features for Hearing Impairments," later in this chapter, describes these settings in more detail.

Physical Impairments

If you selected the I have difficulty using the keyboard or mouse check box in the Set Wizard Options dialog box, Accessibility Wizard presents a series of pages that help you enable keyboard-related accessibility features:

- **StickyKeys**   This page enables the StickyKeys feature, which helps if you can't hold down two or more keys together by pressing each keystroke of a key combination, one at a time. Click Yes to enable StickyKeys.

- **BounceKeys**   This page enables the BounceKeys feature, which causes Windows 2000 Professional to ignore repeated keystrokes, a common problem if you have unsteady hands. Click Yes to enable BounceKeys.

- **ToggleKeys**   This page enables the ToggleKeys feature, which helps you track the status of the Caps Lock, Num Lock, and Scroll Lock keys by playing a sound any time you press them. Click Yes to enable ToggleKeys.

- **Extra Keyboard Help**   This page enables a feature that causes programs to provide extra keyboard help if you aren't using a mouse. It usually shows you how to perform mouse-equivalent tasks by using a keyboard. Click Yes to enable extra keyboard help.

- **MouseKeys**   This page enables MouseKeys, a feature that allows you to substitute the numeric keypad for the mouse. If you're using a mobile computer, you must enable the numeric keyboard (see your computer's documentation). Click Yes to enable MouseKeys. To learn what each key on the numeric keyboard does, see "Mouse Troubles" later in this chapter.

- **Mouse Button Settings**   This page switches the mouse buttons for left-handed users. If you're right-handed, click Right-handed. If you're left-handed, click Left-handed.

- **Mouse Cursor**   This page presents nine mouse pointers arranged in a three-by-three grid. Top to bottom, the size increases, and left to right, the color changes. The sample in the top-left corner is a normal mouse cursor. Click the smallest mouse pointer that's easiest for you to see. Larger mouse pointers are harder to use when accuracy is important, such as when using graphics programs or positioning text in a word processor, but they're terrific when you have difficulty following the pointer onscreen.

- **Mouse Speed**   This page adjusts the speed of the mouse pointer. If you have trouble positioning the mouse pointer precisely, slow it down by moving the slider to the left. If you find that you physically pick up and reposition the mouse because you run out of space on the mouse pad, speed it up by moving the slider to the right.

Most of the options you learned about in this section, you can fine-tune using the Accessibility Options dialog box. The options on the Mouse Button Settings and Mouse Speed screens are on the Mouse Properties dialog box.

Administration

If in the Set Wizard Options dialog box you selected the I want to set administrative options check box, Accessibility Wizard presents a series of pages that help you administer the accessibility features:

- **Set Automatic Timeouts** This page allows you to turn off the accessibility features after the computer has been idle for a time. This option is useful if you share a computer with other users. To enable timeouts, click Turn off StickyKeys, FilterKeys, ToggleKeys, and High Contrast features when the computer is idle for N minutes, and then select the number of minutes the computer must remain idle before turning these features off.

- **Default Accessibility Settings** This page determines how the operating system applies the settings you define using Accessibility Wizard. Click Yes to apply the settings to all new users who log on to the computer, or click No to apply the settings only to yourself.

- **Save Settings to File** Click Save Settings and choose the file to which you want to save the settings you define using Accessibility Wizard. You can take the file to any other computer and import its settings by double-clicking it.

Tip

Accessibility Wizard makes deploying accessibility features easy for users who need them. Using the wizard, define the settings you want to deploy and, on the Save Settings to File page, save those settings to a file that has the .acw extension. Place the file on a network share and change each user's login script so that it imports the settings. The command to import the file is this: `%SystemRoot%\System32\Accwiz.exe filename`.

Features for Visual Impairments

Many features that are useful for people with vision impairments aren't actual accessibility features. They're normal means by which users configure their computers:

- Increase the size of anything on the screen using the Display Properties dialog box's Appearance tab. You can also choose from a variety of high-contrast color schemes that make reading text on the screen easier. Figure 10.3 shows this dialog box, which you learn inside and out in Chapter 4, "Personalizing Windows."

- Windows 2000 Professional gives you the choice between using small and large system fonts. Using the Settings tab of the Display Properties dialog box, choose which system font you want to use for displaying information in varieties of places.

- Using the Mouse Properties dialog box, choose from a variety of mouse pointers to make following the mouse on the screen easier. You can also adjust the speed of the mouse and other features that depend on the mouse you're using and its driver.

- Change the blinking rate of the text cursor so that you can see it more easily. I have good vision and still change the blinking rate so that I can see it. Adjust this setting using the Keyboard Properties dialog box.

Sample Area

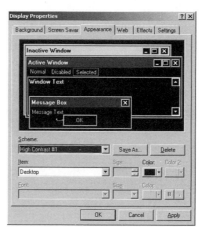

Figure 10.3   The Display Properties dialog box's Appearance tab displays a sample of the current settings at the top.

High Contrast

Although you can change color schemes using the Display Properties dialog box's Appearance tab, using the Accessibility Options dialog box is also easy. It allows you to switch between your normal color scheme and high-contrast color scheme using an emergency hotkey. To toggle the high-contrast accessibility feature using an emergency hotkey, press Left Alt+Left Shift+Print

Screen. The following instructions show you how to enable the high-contrast accessibility feature in Control Panel:

1. In Control Panel, double-click the Accessibility Options icon.

2. On the Display tab, select the Use High Contrast checkbox and then click Settings to choose the color scheme you want to use.

Screen Narration

Microsoft Narrator is an accessibility utility for users with severe vision impairments. It's a text-to-speech converter that reads aloud the contents of menus, dialog boxes, and windows so that users with limited vision can still navigate Windows 2000 Professional. On the Start menu, point to Programs, point to Accessories, point to Accessibility, and then click Narrator. When you start Narrator, it displays a dialog box, which indicates that you might need a more fully functional screen narrator. Prevent this dialog box from opening again by selecting the Do not show this message again check box.

Narrator repeats the names of keys you press. When you press Ctrl, for example, it says "Control" aloud in a scraggly monotone voice. Narrator also describes the foreground dialog box. Its says the title, reads any text on it, reads each option's label, describes each option's current state, and tells you what you must do in order to change each option's state. Narrator can be annoying in Microsoft Windows Explorer because it insists on pronouncing or spelling every item in the window, including icons, file names, and so on.

If you don't like Narrator's default voice, change it (at this writing, a single voice is available but I expect more when Windows 2000 Professional ships):

1. In the Narrator window, click Voice.

2. In the Voice list, click the voice you want to use and configure its speed, volume, and pitch.

Screen Magnifier

Microsoft Magnifier zooms in on portions of the screen to which you point, making fine details in that area easier to see. Figure 10.4 shows an example. Notice how the area enlarged by Magnifier, which you see at the top of the screen, is the area surrounding the mouse pointer on all four sides. Just as you can dock the taskbar to any edge of the screen, with the bottom edge being the default, you can dock Magnifier to any edge of the screen. Just drag the window to the edge you want to dock it to. If you like, leave the window undocked so that you can resize it and it doesn't use as much screen real estate.

On the Start menu, point to Programs, point to Accessories, point to Accessibility, and then click Magnifier. The first time users run Magnifier, it displays a dialog box that says the program provides minimum functionality and they might need a program that's more advanced. Select the Do not show this message again check box to make sure that you don't see it again. It also displays the Magnifier Settings dialog box, also shown in Figure 10.4, which you can minimize to get it out of the way. This dialog box contains several options, which are self-explanatory.

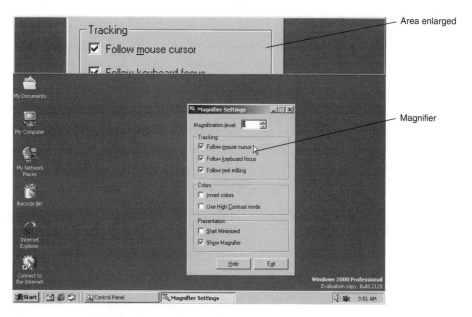

Figure 10.4 Similar to the taskbar, Magnifier moves icons and windows out of its way so they don't overlap with it.

Features for Hearing Impairments

I know this is obvious, but it bears repeating. If you're having trouble hearing sound, adjust the volume. Click the speaker icon in the taskbar, and move the slider up and down to adjust the volume. Also, change the volume in the Sounds and Multimedia Properties dialog box.

SoundSentry and ShowSounds are accessibility features that reflect sounds visibly. SoundSentry helps you know when Windows 2000 Professional is making sounds associated to events such as errors. The operating system gives visual warnings whenever it makes a sound through the internal speaker, ensuring that you don't miss an important message. Choose between flashing the active window's title bar, the active window itself, or the desktop:

1. In Control Panel, double-click the Accessibility Options icon.

2. On the Sound tab, select the Use SoundSentry checkbox and then click Settings to choose the visual cue you want to see when the computer makes a sound:

   - Flash active caption bar
   - Flash active window
   - Flash desktop

Note

SoundSentry works only with sounds that Windows 2000 Professional generates through the computer's internal speaker, not with sounds it generates through the computer's sound card. To use SoundSentry effectively, disable the sound card to force all sounds through the internal speaker.

ShowSounds causes programs to provide audible information visually. A software vendor must provide this capability in its program, and because most don't provide it, don't expect too much from this accessibility feature. Here's how you enable ShowSounds:

1. In Control Panel, double-click the Accessibility Options icon.

2. On the Sound tab, select the Use ShowSounds check box.

Features for Physical Impairments

Windows 2000 Professional has capabilities beyond the accessibility features that are useful for anyone with physical impairments, including people with unsteady hands or who have difficulty using a mouse:

- Using the Keyboard Properties dialog box, change the keyboard's auto-repeat delay and speed. These settings help you type if you have unsteady hands.

- Windows 2000 Professional provides alternate keyboard layouts that make the most frequently used characters more accessible. Chapter 17, "Using Multiple Languages," shows how to change keyboard layouts. Use the Dvorak layout.

- The Mouse Properties dialog box allows you to customize the mouse so that it's easier to use. Swap the left and right buttons, change the mouse's double-click speed, or slow down the pointer.

> **Tip**
>
> Many programs provide additional help for users who rely on the keyboard instead of the mouse. On the **Accessibility Properties** dialog box's **Keyboard** tab, select the **Sho**w **extra keyboard help in programs** check box. Programs that support this feature provide additional information about using the keyboard instead of the mouse.

Key Combinations

Key combinations are common in Windows 2000 Professional, and you see them all over this book. They require you to press and hold down two or more keys at once. Single-handed typists or users who use a mouth-stick have difficulty doing this. StickyKeys enables those users to press each key separately and the operating system pretends that they pressed them simultaneously. To enable StickyKeys, use the following steps:

1. In Control Panel, double-click the Accessibility Options icon.
2. On the Keyboard tab, select the Use StickyKeys check box and then click Settings to configure this accessibility feature further.

> **Note**
>
> StickyKeys treats modifier keys such as Shift and Alt differently, depending on the keyboard layout. On the United States keyboard layout, it treats the left and right modifier keys the same. On non-U.S. keyboard layouts, it treats the left and right Alt keys differently. The left Alt key is normal, but the right Alt key is called AltGr, alt-graphics. Some keyboard layouts use this key for special characters in that language.

Shaky Typists

If you have unsteady hands and tend to accidentally press keys multiple times, enable FilterKeys. FilterKeys causes Windows 2000 Professional to ignore repeated keystrokes. Here's how to configure FilterKeys:

1. In Control Panel, double-click the Accessibility Options icon.
2. On the Keyboard tab, select the Use FilterKeys check box, click Settings to display the Settings for FilterKeys dialog box shown in Figure 10.5, and then do one of the following:

   - To enable the BounceKeys feature, which causes Windows 2000 Professional to ignore keys that you pressed too quickly, select the Ignore repeated keystrokes check box and then click Settings and drag the slider left and right to adjust the amount of time between keystrokes that must elapse before the operating system considers it separate.
   - To enable the SlowKeys feature, which causes Windows 2000 Professional to require that you hold down a key for a certain period of time before accepting it, select the Ignore quick keystrokes and slow

down the repeat rate check box. Then, click S<u>e</u>ttings and drag the bottom slider left and right to adjust the amount of time required for users to hold down a key before the operating system accepts it.

- To enable the RepeatKeys feature, which controls how long you must hold down a key before Windows 2000 Professional starts repeating it, select the Ig<u>n</u>ore quick keystrokes and slow down the repeat rate check box. Then, click S<u>e</u>ttings and drag the first slider left or right.

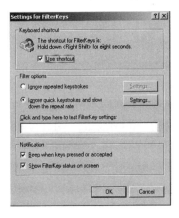

Figure 10.5 Use the Settings for FilterKeys dialog box to enable FilterKeys.

Mouse Troubles

MouseKeys allows you to use the keyboard in lieu of the mouse. You simply move the mouse pointer around the screen by pressing the arrow keys. MouseKeys also provides a clever way to mimic mouse clicks, double-clicks, and even drag-and-drop operations. To use MouseKeys, enable it by using the steps profiled here:

1. In Control Panel, double-click the Accessibility Options icon.

2. On the Mouse tab, select the Use <u>M</u>ouseKeys check box and then click S<u>e</u>ttings to adjust the mouse pointer's speed, acceleration, and other options.

The following list describes the keys on the numeric keypad that control the mouse:

Toggle	Num Lock toggles the numeric keypad between MouseKeys and regular use.
Moving	Move the mouse pointer one pixel at a time by holding down Shift while pressing an arrow key. Move in larger increments by holding down Ctrl while pressing an arrow key.

Clicking	Point to the object you want to click. Then, press divide (/) to select the left mouse button, asterisk (*) to select both, or minus (–) to select the right. After selecting a mouse button by pressing divide, asterisk, or minus, press 5 to single-click or plus (+) to double-click.
Drag-and-drop	Point to an object that you want to drag, and press Insert to start dragging it. Move the pointer to the location where you want to drop it and press Delete.

Tip

Use MouseKeys in conjunction with an actual mouse. For example, when using a graphics program, position the pointer close to the target and then use MouseKeys to position the pointer with pixel-level precision.

Keyboard Status

ToggleKeys provides feedback when you press Caps Lock, Num Lock, or Scroll Lock. The purpose of this feature is to provide audible feedback to users who have difficulty seeing the indicators on the keyboard. When you press one of these keys, you hear a high beep if the key is turned on or a low beep if the key is turned off. Like the other accessibility features, enable ToggleKeys in Control Panel:

1. In Control Panel, double-click the Accessibility Options dialog box.

2. On the Keyboard tab, select the Use ToggleKeys check box.

On-Screen Keyboard

On-Screen Keyboard, provided by Madenta, Inc., is an alternative for users who are restricted to using pointing devices or who have difficulty using a traditional keyboard. On the Start menu, point to Programs, point to Accessories, point to Accessibility, and then click On-Screen Keyboard. Figure 10.6 shows On-Screen Keyboard. Like the other accessibility tools, when you run On-Screen Keyboard, it indicates that many users will require more substantial help. Prevent the dialog box from opening again by selecting the Do not show this message again check box.

   You type using On-Screen Keyboard by clicking the keys you see within its window. To use key combinations such as Ctrl+Shift+S, click Ctrl, click Shift, and click S. If you'd rather not click the mouse, configure On-Screen Keyboard so that you can point at keys instead. On the Settings menu, click Typing Mode. On the Typing Mode dialog box, click Hover to select and then, in Minimum time to hover, select the number of seconds before On-Screen Keyboard selects the key at which you're pointing. On-Screen Keyboard also supports joysticks. In the Typing Mode dialog box, click Joystick or key to select and then select the interval at which the program scans it.

Figure 10.6 On-Screen Keyboard changes the contents of each key when you click Shift in order to reflect its shifted state.

Windows 2000 Professional Shareware?

On-Screen Keyboard is one of Windows 2000 Professional's minor annoyances. Rather than developing a full-blown accessibility utility, Microsoft has foisted a shareware program on users. Isn't *shareware* the term for software that you try before you buy?

On-Screen Keyboard is the shareware version of a Madenta, Inc. product called ScreenDoors98. You're free to use On-Screen Keyboard as long as you tolerate its nags, which it displays after typing 200 keystrokes. Madenta, Inc. prefers to call it a *lite* version. Madenta's Web site indicates that the program quits working after 150 keystrokes, but I haven't found this to be true.

ScreenDoors98 costs $99. The advantages it has over On-Screen Keyboard include word prediction and more control over the window, including the capability to dock the window like the taskbar or space keys further appropriate to reduce typing errors.

The Web site is http://www.madenta.com/sdk2.

Using the Status Indicator

Three of the accessibility features—StickyKeys, FilterKeys, and MouseKeys—provide feedback using small icons that you see in the taskbar. Not only do the icons show the options you enabled, it also shows the keys and mouse buttons you held down using the StickyKeys and MouseKeys features. The taskbar shown in Figure 10.7 shows all three icons (status indicators):

- **Mouse** Enable the MouseKeys accessibility feature, and you see the mouse icon. Windows 2000 Professional dims the left and right buttons to indicate the buttons you selected. Lock the mouse button by pressing Insert, and the operating system fills the appropriate button instead.

- **Stopwatch**   This stopwatch icon indicates that the keyboard's behavior is under the influence of the SlowKeys, BounceKeys, or RepeatKeys features.
- **Keyboard**   Furthest on the right, the keyboard icon has three rectangles that indicate the state of the Shift, Ctrl, and Alt keys. As you hold down each key, Windows 2000 Professional fills the appropriate rectangle. The StickyKeys feature puts this icon in the taskbar.

Although Windows 2000 Professional initially displays the status indicators as icons in the taskbar, you can open it in its own window. Click Show Status Window on any of the status indicator's shortcut menus. Also, configure each accessibility feature by double-clicking its icon.

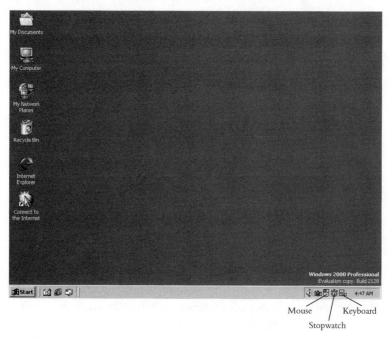

Figure 10.7   The status indicator shows the state of the StickyKeys, MouseKeys, and FilterKeys accessibility features.

Administering Accessibility Features

On computers shared by multiple users, some who need the accessibility features and some who don't, you can set a timeout that turns off accessibility features after the computer is idle for a time. If you don't share your computer with other users and you need the accessibility features, disable the timeout, however. Here's how to change the accessibility timeout:

1. In Control Panel, double-click the Accessibility Options icon.

2. Select the Turn off accessibility features after idle for on the General tab. In the list, select the number of minutes that must pass with the computer idle before Windows 2000 Professional turns off the accessibility features.

Other options on the General tab of the Accessibility Options dialog box control how these features work. Clear the Give warning message when turning a feature on check box if you're familiar with the accessibility features and you don't want the operating system to display its ugly reminders each time you enable them. If all users logging on to the computer have similar needs, select the Apply all settings to defaults for new users to apply your settings to all users when they log on to the computer for the first time. And, if you need the accessibility features in order to log on to the computer, select the Apply all settings to logon desktop check box so that they're available as you type your user name and password.

Managing Accessibility Utilities

Microsoft Utility Manager is the program that administrators use to control Windows 2000 Professional's accessibility utilities such as Magnifier and Narrator. Using Utility Manager, they can start and stop each utility. They can automatically start each utility when Windows 2000 Professional starts or when Utility Manager starts. Figure 10.8 shows Utility Manager with Magnifier and Narrator running.

On the Start menu, point to Programs, point to Accessories, point to Accessibility, and then click Utility Manager. In order to run Utility Manager, you must have administrator rights. Normal users don't have permission to run this program, but they can run it in the context of a different user, such as Administrator, by pressing Shift and clicking Run As on Utility Manager's shortcut menu. To learn more about secondary logon, see Chapter 11, "Securing Your Computer."

Help for Browsing the Web

The Internet grows by leaps and bounds, and the population continues to rely on it as a valuable source of services, information, and entertainment. The Internet promises to level the playing field for everyone, including users with disabilities. They'll never realize the Internet's full potential if nothing is done to make it more accessible to them, however.

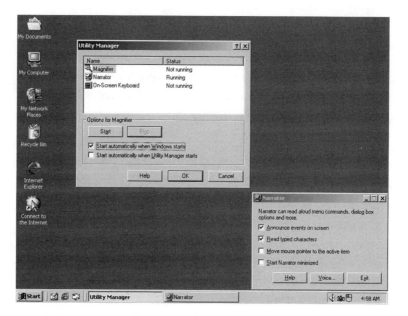

Figure 10.8   Utility Manager shows the status of accessibility
features such as Magnifier and Narrator.

Fortunately, the National Science Foundation and the Department of
Education's National Institute for Disability and Rehabilitation Research
are thinking about this issue. Together, they granted almost $1 million to
the World Wide Web Consortium's Web Accessibility Initiative. For more
information about this program, which is researching the following six areas,
see `http://www.w3.org/WAI`:

- Data formats and protocols
- Guidelines for browsers
- Authoring tools and content generators
- Rating and certification
- Research and advanced development
- Educational outreach

Microsoft Internet Explorer 5 is blazing new trails for users with disabilities by including its Active Accessibility technology. Move the cursor around
the screen by using the arrow keys or voice input, moving from link to link
using the keyboard or a microphone instead of using the mouse. Increase the
size of fonts on a Web page, change colors, or create a custom style sheet that
makes Web pages easier for you to read.

Configuring Accessibility

Listing 10.1 shows a typical style sheet that a Web page might use to format its contents. Style sheets are complicated but you can learn how to create them using a variety of Internet sources—don't waste your money purchasing a book just to create a style sheet. A good source is Microsoft: http://msdn.micrsoft.com/workshop.

More and more Web pages are using style sheets. Often, the style sheets create a presentation that's difficult to read, particularly with vision impairments. You can override these Web pages' style sheets with your own, ensuring that you can read the page:

1. On the Tools menu, click Internet Options.

2. On the General tab, click Accessibility.

3. In the Formatting area, select the check boxes corresponding to the accessibility features you want to use. You can configure Internet Explorer 5 so that it ignores a Web page's colors, font style, font sizes, or any combination.

3. If you want to use your own style sheet, which overrides Web pages' style sheets, select the Format documents using my style sheet check box, and then click Browse to select a style sheet.

Listing 10.1: Sample Style Sheet

```
body { font-size: 16pt }
p { color: blue }
a { font-weight: bold; text-decoration: none}
```

Changing Fonts and Colors

When Web pages don't explicitly specify fonts or colors, Internet Explorer 5 uses the default settings you define:

1. On the Tools menu, click Internet Options.

2. On the General tab, click Colors to configure the colors that Web pages use for links and text when they don't explicitly request certain colors, and then click Fonts to choose the font you want to use for Web pages' text when they don't explicitly use a particular font.

These settings come in handy if you configure Internet Explorer 5 to ignore Web pages' colors, font styles, and font sizes. The previous section showed you how. In that case, the Web browser always uses your settings, regardless of what's in the Web page.

Setting Advanced Options

Internet Explorer 5 has a couple of advanced accessibility features that make using a keyboard to browse the Web easier:

1. On the Tools menu, click Internet Options.

2. On the Advanced tab, select any of the following check boxes:

   - Always expand ALT text for images
   - Move system caret with focus/selection changes

Networking Windows 2000 Professional

11

Securing Your Computer

MOST HOME USERS AND POWER USERS don't worry much about security. In fact, they're used to sharing their computers and files with everyone in the family. With Microsoft Windows 2000 Professional, understanding how security works has a definite impact on how positive your experience with the operating system is, however.

As opposed to Microsoft Windows 98, each user logs on to the computer using their own account name and password. This process is called *authentication*. The operating system uses those credentials to determine what files they have permission to access and what rights they have while using the computer. This is *authorization*. The most notable example is that users can't access files in user profile folders other than their own. Also, with normal and power users' accounts, users can't administer the computer. Those types of accounts don't have enough rights and certainly don't have permission to change the files required to administer the computer. Understanding these concepts will help you go a long way toward living and playing well with Windows 2000 Professional.

Managing Users and Groups

For the average user, managing users and groups is really a simple process. You manage user accounts, which people use to log on to the computer. Also, by giving explicit permission to access an object to a user, you manage the objects that person can use. You can also create groups. *Groups* are collections of user accounts that have a similar purpose. For example, you might have a group for the accounting department or a group for your children. You can give permission to access a particular object to an entire group, too, which is a lot easier to administer than individual permissions given to users.

Two different types of users and groups are important. Local users and groups are those defined on the local computer. No other computer on a network will see those user and group accounts. Domain users and groups are defined on the domain. Those user and group accounts are available to every computer that connects to that domain. When you see a user's name in a security-related dialog box, it's usually in the format *domain\username*, where *domain* is the name of the computer or domain on which the account exists and *username* is the name of the account. If the account is local, *domain* will be the name of the local computer. If it's a domain, it'll be the name of the domain and not the name of the computer managing the domain.

The Easy Way

The easiest way to manage users and groups is by using Users and Passwords. Mind you, you can't use this application to add local users and local groups if the computer is connected to a domain. In that case, all you can do with it is add domain users to local groups, giving them more or fewer capabilities than they have on the local computer. For example, regardless of which groups an account belongs to on a domain, by adding it to the local Administrators group, the user can administer the local computer. I don't recommend that you add regular users to this group, however, because you want to protect administrator access. Consider adding users to the Power Users group so that they can use the computer without too many restrictions. You can also limit domain users local access by adding them to the local Users group, which has very little access to the local computer. Other means are available for preventing users from logging on to the computer altogether, however, and you learn about those later in this chapter.

Using Users and Passwords requires that you log on to the computer as an Administrator. If you didn't, but you do have the name and password of an Administrator, you can type them when Users and Passwords prompts for the name and password of an Administrator. Here's how to use Users and Passwords to manage domain accounts in local groups:

- In Control Panel, double-click the Users and Groups icon.
- Do one or more of the following:
    - To add a domain user to a local group, click Add, type the user's name and domain (or click Browse), click Next, and then select the local group to which you want to add the domain account.

- To remove a domain user from a local group, click the name of the user you want to remove in the Users for this computer list and then click Remove.

- To change an account's name, full name, description, or group membership in the Users for this computer list, click the name of the user you want to change and then click Properties.

- To change your password (you can change your password only), click your account name in the Users for this computer list and then click Set Password.

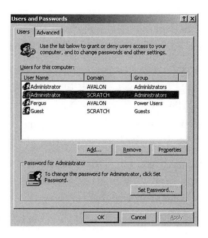

Figure 11.1   Users and Passwords is the easiest way to manage
the local groups in which domain users participate.

Users and Passwords changes just a bit if your computer isn't connected to a domain. Instead of limiting you to adding a domain user to a local group, it prompts you for the information required to add a new local user. That includes the name, description, password, and local group membership. If you still want to add local users, even if you do connect to a domain, see the next section.

The Hard Way

Users and Passwords is the easy way to manage users and groups, but Computer Management isn't that much harder. Additionally, with Computer Management, you can add local users and groups instead of just adding domain users to global groups when you connect your computer to a domain. In Control Panel, double-click the Administrative Tools icon, double-click the Computer Management icon, and then click Local Users and Groups. Underneath the Local Users and Groups snap-in, you see two nodes: Users and Groups. Click Users to manage users and Groups to manage groups.

Here's how to add a new local user:

1. On the Users node's shortcut menu, click New User.

2. In the New User dialog box, type the user's name, full name, description, and password. You must confirm the password in Confirm password.

3. Do any of the following (the options that are available depend on the rights your account has):

   - To force users to change their password the first time they log on to the computer, select the User must change password at next logon check box.

   - To prevent users from ever changing their passwords, select the User cannot change password check box.

   - To prevent user passwords from ever expiring, regardless of Group Policy, select the Password never expires check box.

   - To disable the account, select the Account is disabled check box (administrators often disable an account instead of removing it so that they can reactivate it in the future).

4. Click Create, and repeat steps 3 and 4 for each local user account you want to add.

After creating an account, you can edit it to change its group membership or change any of the options you set in step 3 of the previous instructions. In the Users node, double-click the name of the account that you want to change. Edit the account's name, description, and options on the General tab. Use the Member Of tab to change the account's group membership.

Managing local groups is just as easy as managing local users. On the Groups node's shortcut menu, click New Group. Type a name and description of the new group. You can immediately begin adding users to the group by clicking Add instead of editing individual user accounts to add them to a group. Local Users and Groups displays the Select Users or Groups dialog box shown in Figure 11.2. In the Look in list, click the name of the computer or domain from which you want to add users and then double-click the name of each user you want to add.

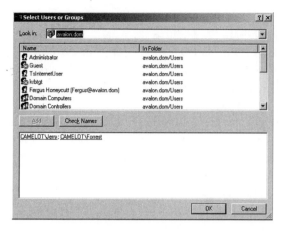

Figure 11.2   Use this dialog box to add users to a group when you first create the group and assign users to this group as required when you create them.

Users or groups, you can rename either by clicking Rename on their shortcut menus. You can remove them by clicking Delete on their shortcut menus.

Should I Use Local Users?

If you log on to a domain, the answer is no. Each domain user has an account on the domain, and if you want to provide that user access to your computer, simply add their domain account to one of your computer's local groups—preferably the Power Users group. Keep in mind that if your computer is on a domain, any domain user can use your computer unless you explicitly prevent them from doing so, which you learn how to do later in this chapter.

If you don't log on to a domain, either you're not using a network-connected computer or your computer is part of a workgroup. Either way, you must use local users to provide each user access to the computer. For example, each member of your family might have an account on the computer, each members of different groups—depending on what you want them to be able to do. In this case, a person can't use the computer unless they know the name and password of a local account.

Logging On as Another User

A hole in security has always been that users tend to log on to the computer as an administrator to perform privileged as well as unprivileged work during the same session. It's just more convenient than logging on to and off the computer, back and forth, depending on which type of work the user is doing. To get this, savvy users add their user accounts to the local Administrators group in order to do away with all problems relating to having enough rights and the appropriate permissions to manage their computer. The problem is that these approaches to the problem open up the computer to Trojan horse attacks. Some viruses are opportunistic, waiting for users to log on to the computer as an administrator in order to do their damage. It's the only way these viruses can damage the configuration. Also, Web sites that contain untrusted code are better able to advertently or inadvertently damage your configuration if you use the computer in an administrator context on a regular basis.

Windows 2000 Professional has a new feature to counteract users' objections to using a normal account for daily work, though. You log on to the computer as a User or Power User and, when you need to administer the computer, you use Secondary Logon to run applications in the context of an administrator. Even as this application is running as an administrator, other applications are not; thus, they don't get the opportunity to do their damage, assuming that they're so inclined. To use Secondary Logon, hold down the Shift key, right-click the program's icon that you want to run, and click Run As. The operating system prompts you for the name, password, and domain of an account you want to use to run the program. For example, if Fergus logs on to his computer using his normal account but discovers that he needs to view the security log quickly, he can click Run As on the Event Viewer icon, type the administrator name, password, and domain, and run Event-Viewer in the context of the administrator. This beats the heck out of logging off the computer, logging on to the computer as an Administrator, running Event Viewer, logging back off of the computer, and logging back on to the computer as Fergus. It also beats the heck out of using the computer as an administrator all day long by preventing damage from untrusted sources.

Secondary Logon has a secondary user interface, too. You can run it from the MS-DOS command prompt or using the Run dialog box. Here are its command-line options:

Syntax: **RUNAS** [**/profile**] [**/env**] [**/netonly**] **/user:***Username program*

Options:

/profile	Specifies whether to load the *Username* user's profile.
/env	Specifies to use the current environment instead of the *Username* user's profile.
/netonly	Specifies to use if the credentials are for remote access only.

/**user:**_Username_	_Username_ is in the form _user@domain_ or _domain\user._
program	Command line to execute.

Preventing Access While Away

One of the biggest security holes for power users, particularly those at home who would rather keep their activities private, is walking away from the computer without protecting it. However, even administrators have a bad habit of going off to lunch while Registry Editor is open on their desktop so that anyone in the organization can walk up to their computer and start hacking network-connected computers.

A few simple precautions can prevent a lot of embarrassment and prevent unauthorized access to your computer. First, use one of the screen savers that come with Windows 2000 Professional and password-protect it so that after a short period of time, the operating system locks the computer until you return. Second, when you're finished with the computer, log off. Many, many users forget to log off their computers, meaning that no one else can use the computer until an administrator unlocks it or the original user comes back to log on to it.

Tip

Any time you walk away from your computer, lock it so that it's protected until you return. Press Ctrl+Alt+Delete and click Lock Computer on the Windows Security dialog box.

Password-Protecting Screen Savers

You can password-protect screen savers so they lock the computer if it's idle for a given period of time. When they lock the computer, you press Ctrl+Alt+Del, and type your user name and password to unlock it. The only people who can unlock a locked computer are the users who locked it and any user who is a member of the local Administrators group. Here's how to configure a screen saver in Windows 2000 Professional so it protects your computer when you wander away from it for too long:

1. In Control Panel, double-click the Display icon and then click the Screen Saver tab.

2. In the Screen Saver list, click the screen saver you want to use (my favorite is Logon Screen Saver).

3. Select the Password protected check box.

Here are some additional notes about screen savers:

- If you start a screen saver manually, which you do by double-clicking the screen saver (SCR) file in Windows Explorer, the screen saver is not password-protected.

- You can force the screen savers to work prior to any user logging on to the computer by adding the REG_SZ value to HKU\.DEFAULT\ Control Panel\Desktop and setting its value to 1. Also, to the same subkey, add the REG_SZ value SCRNSAVE.EXE and set its value to the path and filename of the screen saver you want to use prior to any user logging on to the computer. Last, add the REG_SZ value called ScreenSaveTimeOut and set its value to the time in seconds that the computer must remain idle before the screen saver starts.

Logging Off the Computer

Forgetting to log off the computer when you're finished with it is rude. When your screen saver locks, you'll notice a dialog box that says the computer is locked. It also says that only the user that locked it or an administrator can unlock it. Thus, until you return, anyone else who wants to use the computer is out of luck. To log off the computer, click Shut Down on the Start menu, and then click Log Off *Name*, where *Name* is your user name. Some organizations force users off by using Group Policy. A policy is available that automatically logs users off after a certain idle time.

Setting Object Permissions

You've added users and you've added groups. Permissions is how you specify whether a user or group can access a particular file, folder, or other object. They are rules that define which users can access an object and exactly what they can do with it. Permissions apply to objects, as opposed to rights, which apply to the computer as a whole. When users try to access an object, Windows 2000 Professional determines whether they have permission to do what they're trying to do. This process is called *authorization*. Each object has an access control list (ACL). ACLs contain access control entries (ACEs) that control access to or audit an object. An object's ACL is a list of users and groups that have permission to access the object. The two types of ACLs are discretionary access control lists (DACLs), which give permissions to users and groups; and system access control lists (SACLs), which specify security events that the operating system will audit.

Here's how to edit a file or folder's ACL:

1. On any file or folder's shortcut menu, click Properties and then click the Security tab (see Figure 11.3).

2. Do any of the following:

   - To add a user or group to an ACL, click Add and then double-click the name of each user or group you want to add to the ACL.

   - To remove a user or group from an ACL, click the name of the user or group you want to remove and then click Remove.

3. For each user and group in the Name list, select the Allow check boxes next to the permissions you want to give and select the Deny check boxes next to the permissions you don't. The following list describes what each of these permissions mean:

   - **Full Control**   The user or group has full control of the object, including the ability to change its ACL, take ownership, and so on.

   - **Modify**   The user or group can delete, read, and write the object. If the object is a directory, the user can create subdirectories within it.

   - **Read & Execute**   The user or group can read the object and execute it if it's a program. If the object is a directory, the user or group can list its contents.

   - **Read**   The user or group can read the object, but can't execute it if it's a program. If the object is a directory, the user or group can list its contents.

   - **Write**   The user or group can write to the object, but can't read it. If the object is a directory, the user or group can create subdirectories within it but can't list it.

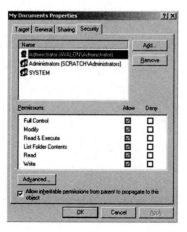

Figure 11.3   The basic features are usually more than adequate for most Windows 2000 Professional users.

You see one last button on the Security tab: Advanced. Click this button to edit a file or folders' ACLs using more advanced features. The primary difference is that the basic features let you set high-level, meta permissions; whereas the advanced features allow you to set specific, low-level permissions. Seldom would any power user have a reason to use the advanced features to edit a file or folder's ACL. The advanced features also allow you to audit objects and also change ownership of an object.

> **Note**
>
> For the most part, Windows 2000 Professional assigns permissions at a high level in the directory hierarchy and allows them to propagate down to subdirectories. For example, the permissions in *SystemDrive*\Documents and Settings\Fergus propagate to all the subdirectories in this directory. When settings propagate from a parent directory, you can't change them. Inherited permissions are gray in the dialog box. You can prevent permissions from propagating, however, by deselecting the Allow inheritable permissions from parent to propagate to this object check box.

Assigning Object Ownership

The user who owns an object has control over assigning permissions to it to other users and groups. The owner of most system files is the administrator. When users create files, they are usually the file's owner (except when an administrator creates a file or folder; then, the Administrators group is usually the owner). Users can transfer ownership of a file and the administrator can take ownership of any file on the computer. The only limitation is that administrators can't transfer ownership of a file to another user. Microsoft states that the purpose of this limitation is to keep administrators accountable, which I interpret to mean that administrators can't cover their tracks.

Here's how to take or transfer ownership of a file or folder:

1. On any file or folder's shortcut menu, click Properties and then click the Security tab.

2. Click Advanced and then click the Owner tab.

3. In the Change owner to list, click the name of the user to which you want to transfer ownership. If you're taking ownership of the object, click your own name.

Auditing Access to Objects

Auditing allows you to watch objects or specific types of objects for access. You can audit unsuccessful attempts to access an object, for example. Although I don't recommend you do so because of the performance penalty, you can audit access to all objects in the file system so that you know exactly what users have been doing. Auditing is a multi-step process:

1. Set the audit policy.

2. Audit a file or folder.

3. View the results.

Set the Audit Policy

Here's how to set the audit policy, which turns on auditing at a system level:

1. In Control Panel, double-click the Administrative Tools icon and then double-click Local Security Policy.

2. Double-click Local Policies and then click Audit Policy.

3. In the details pane, double-click any of the following events you want to audit, and select Success to record audit entries when these events are successful and click Failure to record audit entries when these events fail (to audit file and folder access, enable the Audit object access policy):

- Audit account logon events

- Audit account management

- Audit directory service access

- Audit logon events

- Audit object access

- Audit policy change

- Audit privilege use

- Audit process tracking

- Audit system events

Audit a File or Folder

After enabling auditing of object access, you target specific files and folders that you want to audit and for what types of events you want to audit:

1. On the object's shortcut menu, click Properties, click the Security tab, and then click Advanced.

2. On the Auditing tab of the Access Control Settings dialog box, click Add to add an auditing entry.

3. In the Select User, Computer, or Group dialog box, click the user, computer, or group you want to audit. If you want to audit all access by all users, click Everyone.

4. In the Auditing Entry dialog box, shown in Figure 11.4, select the Successful and Failed check boxes next to each event you want to audit. Here are the types of access you can audit:

- Traverse Folder/Execute File
- List Folder/Read Data
- Read Attributes
- Read Extended Attributes
- Create Files/Write Data
- Write Attributes
- Write Extended Attributes
- Delete Subfolders and Files
- Delete
- Read Permissions
- Change Permissions
- Take Ownership

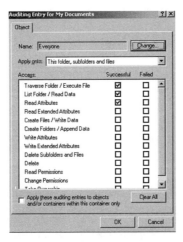

Figure 11.4 Windows 2000 Professional uses this same dialog box to audit other types of objects, including in the registry.

View the Results

When an event that you're auditing occurs, Windows 2000 Professional adds an entry to the security log. You view them in Event Viewer, which you learned about earlier:

1. In Control Panel, double-click the Administrative Tools icon and then click the Event Viewer icon.

2. Click Security Log and then double-click the audit event that you want to view.

The event log entry indicates the date, time, and user that accessed the computer. It also indicates from which computer the user accessed the object, as well as whether that access was a success or failure.

Encrypting Files and Folders

Windows 2000 Professional's Encrypting File System uses public key security to encrypt files so that in the absence of owner's name and password, nobody else can read their files. EFS is a practical way to prevent someone from stealing your hard disk, dropping into another computer, logging on as an administrator, and gaining access to your files by taking ownership of them.

EFS is transparent. It automatically creates an encryption certificate and private key for you. And the first time you log on to the computer, EFS generates a recovery certificate for you that an administrator can use to recover your encrypted files if you lose your encryption certificate. This recovery certificate is your key to gaining access to encrypted files if your original encryption certificate has gone missing. Many other things you should know include the following:

- You don't have to decrypt files before using them because EFS automatically decrypts it when you use it.

- You can't encrypt files in *SystemRoot*.

- You can't encrypt a compressed file, and you can't compress an encrypted file.

- You are the only user who can open a file that you encrypt.

- When you copy a file from an encrypted folder to a folder that's not encrypted, EFS decrypts the file.

- If you move an encrypted file from one folder to another (encrypted or not), the file remains encrypted.

- You can't share encrypted files and folders on the network.

- EFS does not encrypt the file because it's transmitted across the network and because EFS decrypts the file when it loads it from disk.

To encrypt any file or folder, click Properties on its shortcut menu, click Advanced, and then select the Encrypt contents to secure data check box. EFS encrypts the file. However, when you open or use the file, EFS automatically decrypts it for you because your user name and password unlocked your encryption certificate. If, for some reason, you've lost your encryption certificate (maybe you had to reinstall the operating system), you can use your recovery certificate to recover your files.

Windows 2000 Professional provides an alternative method for encrypting files and folders. You can use Cipher.exe, an MS-DOS program. Here are its command-line options:

Syntax: **CIPHER** [/e | /d] [/s:*dir*] [/a] [/i] [/f] [/q] [/h] [/k] [*pathname* [...]]

Options:

/e	Encrypt the specified directory.
/d	Decrypt the specified directory.
/s:*dir*	Specify the directory to encrypt or decrypt using **/e** or **/d.**
/a	Apply operation to files as well as directories.
/i	Don't stop for errors.
/f	Encrypt all directories, even if they are already encrypted.
/h	Display hidden and system files.
/k	Create a new encryption key for the user running Cipher.exe.
/q	Run quietly.
pathname	A patter, file, or directory.

Lose your encryption certificate, and you can use the recovery certificate to gain access to your files. A *recovery agent* is a user who can recover encrypted files using a recovery policy, which contains the recovery certificate. Normal users aren't usually recovery agents, but the local Administrator is a recovery agent. Thus, you'd log on to the computer as an Administrator to decrypt your files.

To protect the recovery certificate, remove the recovery certificate from the Certificate Manager after you export it to a backup file. This prevents unsavory users from gaining access to the recovery certificate and therefore decrypting your files by logging on to the computer as administrator. When you need to use the recovery certificate to recover your files, import the certificate, log on to the computer as Administrator, and recover yourself. Your best bet is to store the recovery certificate in a place that's not obvious, such as on a disk that you store offsite.

Here's how to export and remove the recovery certificate:

1. Log on to the computer as an administrator.

2. In Control Panel, double-click the Users and Passwords icon, click the Advanced tab, and then click <u>C</u>ertificates.

3. Click the certificate that's issued to Administrator with the intended purpose of File Recovery (see the Certificate intended purposes area).

4. Click <u>E</u>xport to export the recovery certificate to a file on a 3.5-inch disk. Follow the Certificate Export Wizard's instructions.

5. Click <u>R</u>emove to remove the recovery certificate from your computer.

With the recovery certificate missing from your computer, no other person can decrypt your files without having your account name and password. If you ever need to recover your files, you can import the recovery certificate back on to the computer, log on to the computer as Administrator, and decrypt the files.

12

Networking Your Computer

In Microsoft Windows 2000 Professional, networking is simplicity itself. Gone are the days of complicated network configurations and strange kluges to make the computer work on networks. Most users, those who use a typical Microsoft network configuration, don't have to change their configurations at all. A typical Microsoft network configuration includes the client for Microsoft networks, TCP/IP, and file and printer sharing. And when users have to change their network configuration, they have one central place to go in order to make them all.

This is all well and good, but what about users who are trying to create a peer-to-peer network at home? Windows 2000 Professional makes this process easy, too, because the operating system automatically handles IP allocation and name resolution. Users aren't stuck using antiquated protocols such as NetBEUI and don't have to set up a server to gain the benefits of networking at home. Because this is the topic that most readers care about most, this chapter has an obvious slant toward that topic. For more information about networking in business environments using Microsoft Windows 2000 Server, see *Inside Windows 2000 Server* (New Riders, 1999).

Installing Network Adapters

Windows 2000 Professional's Setup program automatically recognizes and configures most network adapters it finds when you install the operating system. In fact, the Setup program offers no mechanism for changing the network adapter's configuration during the setup process. Using Device Manager or the Add/Remove Hardware Wizard, you can change the device driver, however. Alternatively, use an unattended answer file to specify the network adapter you want to install.

When you install a new network adapter, Windows 2000 Professional will most likely recognize and configure it. If the operating system can't find a device driver for it, use Device Manager to install its device driver, which presumably came on a disk with the network adapter, or you must get it from the network adapter's vendor. In Device Manager, double-click the network adapter and then click Update Driver on the Driver tab. You can also use the Add/Remove Hardware Wizard to troubleshoot the network adapter: In Control Panel, double-click the Add/Remove Hardware icon, click Next, click Add/Troubleshoot a device, and then follow the instructions you see onscreen. This gives you the opportunity to enable the network adapter by starting the Updated Device Driver Wizard.

If Windows 2000 Professional does not automatically detect and configure a network adapter, and it's not already listed in Device Manager, it's probably a legacy network adapter (there are plenty of those hanging around most boneyards). You must manually install these adapters using the Add/Remove Hardware Wizard. In Control Panel, double-click the Add/Remove Hardware icon and follow the instructions you see onscreen. The wizard displays a list of devices that are installed. Because a legacy network adapter isn't likely to be in this list, however, you want to add a new device and you want to select the network adapter from a list or provide third-party device drivers you have on a disk. The operating system does provide drivers for many legacy adapters and it just might be your only source for them.

Installing a new network adapter or reconfiguring an existing adapter requires that you log on to the computer as an Administrator.

See also
- Chapter 1, "Installing Windows," for more information about installing network adapters using unattended answer files.
- Chapter 3, "Configuring Hardware," to learn more about installing devices such as network adapters.

Configuring Network Connections

In the Network and Dial-up Connections folder is an icon for each network adapter installed in the computer. If the computer contains a single network adapter, you see an icon called Local Area Connection. You might also see icons for additional network adapters or for additional dial-up connections. Of course, the first icon in this folder you see is the Make New Connection icon, which you use to create new dial-up connections. To open this folder, double-click the Network and Dial-up Connections icon in Control Panel. Each local area network icon can have different states:

- **Enabled** The icon is enabled, indicating that the connection is working. If you configured the connection to display its status in the taskbar, you see two computer screens flashing.

- **Disabled** The icon is disabled, or dimmed. This indicates that you disabled the connection, so you don't see an icon in the taskbar.

- **Disconnected cable** The icon is dimmed and you see a red X on it. This indicates that the cable or connection is broken. The icon you see in the taskbar has a red X on it.

In any state, you configure a local area network connection by clicking Properties on its icon. This displays the Local Area Connection Properties dialog box shown in Figure 12.1. For example, if you want to see the connection's status in the taskbar, select the Show icon in taskbar when connected check box on its Local Area Connection Properties dialog box.

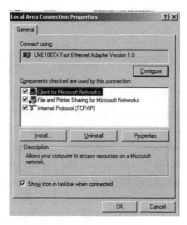

Figure 12.1 Windows 2000 Professional gives you a single centralized location for configuring all network connections.

Installing, removing, and configuring network components works similarly to Microsoft Windows 98. On the Local Area Connection Properties dialog box, do one of the following:

- To install a new client, service, or protocol, click Install.

- To remove a client, service, or protocol, click it in the Components checked are used by this connection list and then click Uninstall.

- To configure a client, service, or protocol, click it in the Components checked are used by this connection list and then click Properties.
- To disable a client, service, or protocol for this connection only, making it available for other connections, clear the check box next to it.

Computer names deserve a special mention because plenty of users still use a mix of Windows 2000 Professional and earlier versions of Windows. Windows 2000 Professional supports DNS names, which look like typical Internet names: jerry.honeycutt.com. Windows 2000 Professional also creates NETBIOS names, which are the old-style names that you used with earlier versions of Microsoft networking. jerry.honeycutt.com and scratch.honeycutt.com have JERRY and SCRATCH NETBIOS names, and these are the names that you use to reference the computers from earlier versions of Windows—not their DNS names.

One last note. You should limit computer names to 15 characters or fewer, even though you can potentially create longer names. This ensures that other computers can see your computer on the network.

Changing Network Identification

As with earlier versions of Windows NT, you can join a computer to a domain or join it to a workgroup. Here are the fundamental differences between the two:

- **Domain**   When you join a computer to a domain, the computer has an account on that domain, and the domain controller authenticates your credentials and authorizes access to network resources. The name of the computer's account and the name of the computer must be the same. Adding a computer to a domain creates a trust relationship with the domain, which means that the computer trusts the domain to authenticate users.

- **Workgroup**   When you join a computer to a workgroup, the local computer is responsible for all of its own security, as opposed to a domain in which the domain takes responsibility for network security. Other computers who happen to be members of the same workgroup can see each other in the workgroup's icon in the My Network Places folder. Just remember that a workgroup is really nothing more than a way to categorize computers.

Unlike Microsoft Windows NT Workstation 4.0, Windows 2000 Professional makes changing computers' identification and domain membership easy. It even provides a wizard for that purpose, which most users really don't need to use:

1. In the Network and Dial-up Connections folder, click <u>N</u>etwork Identification on the Adva<u>n</u>ced menu and then click the Network Identification tab.

2. Click P<u>r</u>operties, type a name for the computer in <u>C</u>omputer name, as shown in Figure 12.2, and then do one of the following:

   - Click <u>D</u>omain and then type the name of the domain to which you want to join the computer. You must have the appropriate credentials on the domain to join a computer to it. Either you must have a domain administrator's name and password or the name and password of a special user account that the administrator set up for this purpose. Many administrators create an account called Installer that has enough permission to join computers to a domain, and that's about all. This is often the most appropriate choice when connecting your computer to a business network.

   - Click <u>W</u>orkgroup and type the name of the workgroup you want to join. If the workgroup doesn't already exist, Windows 2000 Professional will create it. Otherwise, the operating system will add your computer's name to the list with other members. This is often the most appropriate option if your computer isn't on a business network. For example, most peer-to-peer and home networks are actually just workgroup networks.

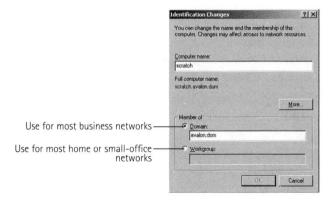

Figure 12.2 In Windows 2000 Professional, changing the computer's name or domain membership isn't as troublesome as it was in earlier versions of Windows.

Logging on to Networks

How you log on to the computer depends on how you connected it to the network and what you want to do. If you joined the computer to a domain, you have two choices. You can log on to the domain or log on to the local computer. In the first case, the domain authenticates your credentials. In the second case, the local computer validates your credentials. If you configured the computer to connect to a workgroup, you must log on to the local computer because no domain is available to authenticate your credentials. The differences are subtle:

- If you log on to a domain, you have access to any network resources to which you have permission. You don't have to have an account on the local computer, but you must have an account on the domain.

- If you log on to the computer locally, you have access to the local computer's resources, but not necessarily the network's resources. You must have an account on the local computer to log on to it, which is not the same as adding your domain account to a local group.

With that out of the way, you log on to Windows 2000 Professional by providing your credentials and then choosing what you want to validate them. When you see the Welcome to Windows dialog box, press Ctrl+Alt+Delete. By forcing users to give the three-finger salute, Windows 2000 Professional prevents Trojan horses from gathering credentials by simulating the logon screen. In User name, type the name of your account and type your password in Password. To choose what you want to log on to, click Options and click the name of the domain or computer you want to log on to in the Log on to list. To log on to the local computer, click the computer's name. In general, if you joined the computer to a domain, you want to log on to the domain. Otherwise, the only choice is logging on to the local computer.

Note

If you used the Network Identification Wizard to configure the computer for home use, you probably configured Windows 2000 Professional to log you on automatically. You won't see the Welcome to Windows dialog box in this case, and it will automatically log you back on again when you log off the operating system. You can cause the operating system to once again prompt for your name and password by running the Network Identification Wizard and clicking Users must enter a user name and password.

See also

- Chapter 8, "Managing the Computer," to learn how logging on to different domains affects local user profiles in Documents and Settings.

Sharing Resources on Networks

Here's how to share a folder on the network:

1. On the folder or printer's shortcut menu, click S<u>h</u>aring.

2. On the Sharing tab, click <u>S</u>hare this folder and then type a name for the share in S<u>h</u>are name.

   The share name doesn't have to be the same as the folder name. Network users never see the actual folder name on the network—all they see is the name of the share.

3. Click <u>P</u>ermissions and specify which users you want to have access to the shared files.

   By default, the Everyone group has access to the share. This is perfectly acceptable if you have limited access to the share's contents using NTFS file permissions. Otherwise, you should set the share's permissions to limit access to it.

4. Click Caching and then do one of the following in the <u>S</u>etting list:

   - To automatically make the share's documents available offline for all network users when they use documents in the share, click Automatic Caching for Documents.

   - To automatically make the share's program files available offline for all network users who use them, click Automatic Caching for Programs.

   - To allow network users to individually determine which files they want to use offline, click Manual Caching for Documents.

   Windows 2000 Professional does not allow you to rename shares. The only way to change a share's name is to actually remove and re-create it.

Caution

Many users, particularly home users, make sharing entire drives a habit. For example, they share all of drive C or all of drive D for convenience. I don't recommend that you do this, however, because it paves the way for human error and virus-propagation by exposing the entire drive on the network. Share specific folders to avoid this problem. Not only does it protect important files, it helps you organize all of your data on the network because each individual share shows up as a separate folder in My Network Places.

Creating Dial-Up Connections

You create dial-up connections in the Network and Dial-up Connections folder. Although the user interface is slightly different, the information it collects is similar to other versions of Windows:

1. In Control Panel, double-click the Network and Dial-up Connections icon and then double-click the Make New Connection icon.

2. Click <u>N</u>ext and then do one of the following:

   - To create a connection to a private network, such as a home or business, click Dial-up to <u>p</u>rivate network.

   - To create a connection to the Internet service provider, click <u>D</u>ial-up to the Internet.

   - To create a virtual private network connection, click Connect to a pri<u>v</u>ate network through the Internet.

   - To configure your computer to accept incoming connections (the other computer would create a connection to a private network), click <u>A</u>ccept incoming connections.

   - To connect your computer to another computer using a serial, parallel, or infrared port, click <u>C</u>onnect directly to another computer. This type of connection is handy and often overlooked when you don't have networking equipment available.

3. See the sections that follow to learn more about each type of connection.

Private Network

A private network connection connects your computer to a business network or even to your Internet service provider (ISP). The host to which you're connecting must use the same protocol, which is usually TCP/IP, and must support one of the connection protocols available in Windows 2000 Professional, which is usually Point-to-Point Protocol (PPP).

The Network Connection Wizard prompts you the phone number. There are two ways you can provide your phone number. You can clear the <u>U</u>se dialing rules check box and type the full phone number in <u>P</u>hone number. Alternatively, you can select the <u>U</u>se dialing rules check box and type the area code in <u>A</u>rea code and the remaining digits in <u>P</u>hone number. You'll want to use dialing rules if you live in an area in which you must use 10-digit dialing, or you must use a credit or calling card. For more information about dialing rules, see Chapter 13, "Using Mobile Computers."

The wizard also asks you whether you want to make the connection available to other users with whom you share the computer or to make the connection available only to yourself. If this is a connection that you don't want other users to see, make sure you keep it to yourself.

You can further refine the connection by clicking Properties on its icon in the Network and Dial-up Connections folder. Figure 12.3 shows the *name* Properties dialog box, and the following list describes the options available on each tab:

- **General**   Choose the modem you want to use and specify the phone number to dial. If you want to see the connection's status in the taskbar, select the Show icon in taskbar when connected check box.

- **Options**   Specify dialing options, such as whether the connection prompts for your name and password each time, how many times it tries to redial, and the amount of time to wait between redial attempts. A useful option that is off by default is the Redial if line is dropped check box, which causes the connection to automatically redial the phone number when you're disconnected.

- **Security**   Specify which authentication protocol you want to use and whether you want to use a logon script or interactive logon. The default authentication is unsecured, so if the host you're calling supports more secure authentication protocols, such as the ones in "Securing Connections," I recommend that you use them.

- **Networking**   Choose the connection protocol you want to use (PPP in most cases, but the default is SLIP for some reason) and which components you want to enable for the connection. For Internet connections, you need to enable only TCP/IP. For connections to business networks, enable the client for Microsoft networks, too.

- **Sharing**   Enable sharing of this connection. If you want other computers on the network to be able to access the Internet through this dial-up connection, select the Enable Internet Connection Sharing for this connection check box. This option enables Internet Connection Sharing and is different from sharing a connection with other users who share the computer.

Internet Connections

If you click Dial-up to the Internet in the Network Connection Wizard, the wizard automatically starts the Internet Connection Wizard. You learn about this wizard in Chapter 14, "Connecting to the Internet." It gives you the option of signing up for a new Internet account, specifying information about an existing account or configuring your Internet connection manually. After you configure the Internet connection, it is exactly the same as any other private network connection, which you learned about in the previous section.

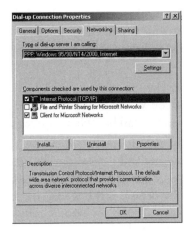

Figure 12.3 In this example, the settings are appropriate for connections to business networks. For an Internet connection, deselect the Client for Microsoft Networks check box.

Virtual Private Network

A *virtual private network (VPN)* is a connection to a private network that you make through the Internet. VPNs are really not as complex as people think. You connect to the Internet using your normal Internet service provider. Then, a tunneling protocol communicates with your private network over the Internet connection, using a secure channel that no one else on the Internet can understand. It's a secure way to communicate with a private network over the Internet, in other words. Here's how to create a VPN:

1. If you want to automatically connect to the Internet when you try opening the VPN, click <u>A</u>utomatically dial this initial connection and then click the name of the connection in the list.

2. In <u>H</u>ost name or IP address, type the name of the remote computer or its IP address.

   The remote computer must be configured to accept VPN connections and must be using one of the tunneling protocols that Windows 2000 Professional supports. This usually requires some cooperation between you and the remote computer's administrator.

3. Do one of the following:

   - To share the connection with other users who use the same computer, click <u>F</u>or all users.

   - To make the connection private so that only you can use it, click <u>O</u>nly for myself.

4. Type a name for the connection.

By default, the connection negotiates the appropriate tunneling protocol with the remote host (most users should leave it this way). You can choose a particular tunneling protocol, however. On the connection's shortcut menu, click Properties. On the Networking tab, in the Type of VPN server I am calling list, click the type of tunneling protocol you want to use, which can be one of the following:

- **Layer 2 Tunneling Protocol (L2TP)** L2TP is supported by Windows 2000 only for client-to-server and server-to-server tunneling. It's more secure than PPTP, but not in common use yet.

- **Point-To-Point Tunneling Protocol (PPTP)** This is the most mature tunneling protocol available today and is used by most versions of Windows. If in doubt, select this protocol.

Incoming Connections

By creating an incoming connection, you allow other computers to connect to your computer using a modem. Creating an incoming connection is easy:

1. Select the check boxes next to the modems you want to accept incoming connections, and click Next.

2. Do one of the following and then click Next:

- To accept virtual private connections, click Allow virtual private connections.

- Otherwise, click Do not allow virtual private connections.

3. Select the users you want to allow access to this connection. By default, the wizard adds all local users to this list (you can't add domain users), but you can add additional users by clicking Add. Click Next.

4. Select the check box next to each networking component you want to use for the connection. You can optionally install additional components or configure each component for this connection without affecting other network connections.

5. Type a name for the connection.

Direct Connections

Direct connections are underutilized. They allow you to connect two computers using ports that most computers already have without requiring you to install networking components that might not be available. For example, if you need a quick way to transfer files from one computer to another, connect the computers by using a serial cable and then use a direct connection. You must configure one of the computers as a host and the other computer as a guest. Here's how:

1. Do one of the following and then click Next:

   - To set up the computer as a host, click Host.

   - To set up the computer as a guest, click Guest.

2. In the Device for this connection list, click the port you want to use for the connection. You can choose any available serial, parallel, or infrared port. Click Next.

3. Do one of the following:

   - If you're configuring the host computer, select the check boxes next to the users you want to allow access. You can add users by clicking Add.

   - If you're configuring the guest computer, choose whether you want to share the connection with other users who use the computer.

4. Type a name for the connection.

After you create the connection icons, connect the computers by using the appropriate cable for the port you selected. Of course, you must configure each connection to use the same type of port, but they don't have to be the exact same port. Open the connection on the host first and then the guest. Note that some ports might require a special cable. For example, connecting two computers via their parallel ports usually requires that you use an appropriate bi-directional parallel cable.

Securing Connections

To change the authentication protocol that a dial-up connection uses, click the Security tab on its *name* Properties dialog box, click Advanced, and then click Settings. Windows 2000 Professional supports numerous authentication protocols that the operating system uses to exchange your credentials with a remote computer when you're connecting via a dial-up connection. They include the following:

- **Password Authentication Protocol (PAP)**   Uses clear-text passwords. It's the simplest authentication protocol. Use this protocol only when the remote connection doesn't support more advanced protocols, which is usually the case when connecting to an Internet server provider.

- **Challenge Handshake Authentication Protocol (CHAP)**
Negotiates secure authentication. This proves to the remote computer that you know your password without actually sending the password across the connection. It uses the Message Digest 5 (MD5) hashing scheme. Most Point-to-Point Protocol (PPP) servers support CHAP and MD5.

- **Microsoft CHAP (MSCHAP)**   Similar to CHAP, but for Microsoft products, MSCHAP version 2 is the latest version.

- **Extensible Authentication Protocol (EAP)**   An extension of the Point-to-Point Protocol (PPP), it provides remote authentication using third-party security devices such as Smart Cards, retina scan, voiceprint, and others.

Creating Peer-to-Peer Networks

Home networking is all the rage these days. Microsoft announced its new initiative, called Universal Plug and Play. The goal of Universal Plug and Play is to enable users to build home networks for communication, entertainment, home automation, and so on. It will support intelligent appliances and allow you to connect all of the computers in the household and share resources. In fact, with a home network, all of your computers can share a single Internet connection. For more information, see `http://www.microsoft.com/homenet`.

With regard to Windows 2000 Professional, home networking is nothing more than a plain old workgroup or peer-to-peer network. What makes Windows 2000 Professional suited for this purpose is a new feature that prevents you from having to configure complicated DHCP and WINS servers while you still have all the advantages of TCP/IP. Microsoft Automatic Private IP Addressing (APIPA) makes creating workgroup networks easy. It automatically assigns unique IP addresses to network-connected computers. Because it assigns IP addresses without any work on your part, it eliminates the need for you to assign static IP addresses or manage IP addresses using the Dynamic Host Configuration Protocol (DHCP) or a Domain Name System (DNS) server. APIPA does for workgroup networking what Plug and Play did for device management. Globally unique IP addresses aren't required on private networks. As a result, APIPA uses IP addresses that the Internet reserves for private networks (169.254.0.0 through 169.254.255.254 with the subnet mask 255.255.0.0). APIPA automatically assigns these reserved IP addresses to computers on private networks. It also prevents hosts from having duplicate IP addresses.

Note

The IP addresses that APIPA assigns aren't globally unique beyond the workgroup network, so computers on the Internet can't connect them. Still, with Internet Connection Sharing or a proxy server, you can share a single Internet connection with all the computers on the workgroup network.

Windows 2000 Professional also handles name resolution automatically. Combine APIPA and automatic name resolution, and you'll find that building a home network is no harder than installing network adapters in each computer and connecting each computer to a hub. The default network configuration works in almost every case.

13
Using Mobile Computers

Users with mobile computers have special needs, assuming they actually travel with their computers. Their biggest need is access to files when they're not connected to the network. Just because they're not connected to the network doesn't mean they don't need access to their files. Microsoft Windows 2000 Professional helps out in two ways. First, offline files make taking network files with you easy. Second, Briefcase, a feature that Windows 95 introduced, fills the voids left by offline files.

A bigger need is good power management, though. If you're traveling with a mobile computer, power is not always available and you want the battery to last as long as possible. For that matter, if you were curled up with your mobile computer in front of a good movie, you'd like to hope that the battery lasts long enough to make it all the way to the movie's credits. Windows 2000 Professional makes substantial improvements to power management that will conserve battery power. Many of these improvements rely on Advanced Configuration and Power Interface (ACPI), which is still relatively rare for moderately priced mobile computers, but the operating system also supports computers with Advanced Power Management (APM).

This chapter describes Windows 2000 Professional's features that are specifically designed for mobile users. Whether you're traveling or not, these features help mobile computer users get more out of their computers.

Taking Files with You

Offline Files is a new feature that's similar to Briefcase, a feature that all recent versions of Windows support. There are some big differences, though. In particular, using Offline Files is a no-brainer when compared to using Briefcase. Specify that you want to use a file offline and when you disconnect from the network, that file is still available. Better yet, you access the file in the same place as you did when you were connected to the network. That means that you don't have to root around in a briefcase when you want to access the file. If the file is in \\camelot\public\letters, it'll appear in that same place when you disconnect from the network. Still, Briefcase has its appropriate uses and you learn about them in "Briefcase." In particular, Offline Files doesn't work well when you log on to two computers at the same time and want to share files between those two computers. The feature gets too confused and requires you to pay careful attention to the order in which you log off and on each computer, so Briefcase is better here.

To make any network folder or file available offline, click Make Available Offline on its shortcut menu. Windows 2000 Professional copies those files to the local computer's offline files cache. Unlike Briefcase, users can make the root of a shared folder available offline, a source of frustration for Briefcase users. Offline files and folders remain in their original places, whether the computer is offline or not. Thus, you find your offline files in My Network Places, just as if you're still connected to the network. Note that many more files might be available on the network when you're connected to it, but you won't see those files in My Network Places unless you make them available offline. You can easily tell which files are available for offline usage because Windows Explorer puts an overlay in the bottom-left corner of each icon. Offline folders get a bit fuzzy when users add files to the network folder, so rely on this icon to tell whether you're really going to have an offline copy of the file or not.

The first time you make a file available offline, Windows 2000 Professional starts a wizard to explain how the feature works and allows you to customize it a bit. You can choose to display reminders in the taskbar whenever network connections' statuses change. Also, you can configure offline files to automatically synchronize with the network each time you log on or off the computer. All these options are on the Offline Files tab of the Folder Options dialog box:

1. On the Tools menu, click Folder Options and then click the Offline Files tab (see Figure 13.1).

2. Select any of the following options:

- **Enable Offline Files**   Select this check box to enable offline files; otherwise, deselect this check box.

- **Synchronize all offline files before logging off**   Select this check box if you want to synchronize all offline files every time you log off the computer; otherwise, deselect this check box.

- **Enable reminders**   Select this check box if you want offline files to remind you when you offline files need to be synchronized or when you are working offline.

3. Drag the slider to the left to reduce the amount of disk space available for temporary offline files or drag the slider to the right to increase the amount of disk space available to them.

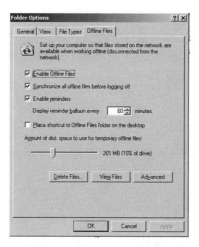

Figure 13.1   In most cases, you'll have few reasons to change these options because the default settings are most appropriate.

Temporary offline files are those that the operating system, in its infinite wisdom, makes available offline. Any time you create a file or use a file on the network, the operating system automatically makes an offline copy of that file available. You didn't ask to make these files available offline, but the operating system assumed that you'd want them to be available. Sounds great, but temporary offline files can use a lot of disk space, so you should limit the amount of space that's available to them. Periodically, you might want to delete all the temporary offline files, which you do by clicking Delete Files on the Offline Files tab of the Folder Options dialog box.

Disconnecting

When the Windows 2000 Professional loses the network connection, it notifies you by displaying a ToolTip next to the Offline Files button in the taskbar. It tells you that the computer isn't connected to the network, but you can work offline. By default, the operating system displays this information every 60 minutes, but you can configure how often it displays this information, as you learned in the previous section. Double-click the Offline Files button in the taskbar to display more information about the status of offline files.

You can continue working normally, even if you're no longer connected to the network and even if you're editing a network file. Offline files will prompt you to synchronize your changes with the network once the network becomes available again.

Note
Offline Files has an annoying problem with long filenames. If you're missing files that you're certain you specified you wanted to be available offline, the first thing you should suspect is that long filenames are causing problems. The only solution is to shorten the filenames.

Synchronizing

By default, Windows 2000 Professional synchronizes offline files each time you log on and off a network connection. You can synchronize anytime, though: On Microsoft Windows Explorer's Tools menu, click Synchronize, and then click Synchronize. The Items to Synchronize dialog box displays a list of each shared folder that contains offline files. Deselect the check boxes next to each shared folder that you don't want to synchronize.

You can configure when Windows 2000 Professional synchronizes offline files. For example, create schedules that are appropriate for individual shared folders. On the Items to Synchronize dialog box, click Setup to display the Synchronization Settings dialog box. For each of the following tabs, you can schedule each shared folder to synchronize:

- **Logon/Logoff**   The operating system synchronizes each shared folder you select on this tab when you log on and off the network connection that you click in the When I am using this network connection list. By default, Windows 2000 Professional configures all offline shared folders to synchronize when you log on or off a network connection. This is the most practical way to synchronize offline files.

- **On Idle**   The operating system synchronizes each shared folder you select on this tab when you haven't used the computer in a specified amount of time. These settings apply to the network connection you click in the <u>W</u>hen I am using this network connection list. To specify how long the computer must be idle before the operating system synchronizes, click A<u>d</u>vanced.

- **Scheduled** This tab is a bit more complicated than the others. You add individual scheduled items to the list on it. Click A<u>d</u>d and follow the Scheduled Synchronization Wizard's instructions to select the shared folders you want to synchronize and the schedule you want to use for them. The scheduling options are somewhat flexible, allowing you to synchronize daily, on weekdays, or every-however-many days.

Exactly what Offline Files does when it synchronizes offline files and folders deserves more attention:

- If you add files to an offline folder, Offline Files copies those files to the network when it synchronizes the folder. It also copies files added to the network to the local computer.

- If you delete a file from an offline folder, Offline Files does not remove the file from the network folder when it synchronizes the folder.

- Offline Files does not support subfile-level synchronization; it only supports file-level synchronization. If both copies of a file change, you can choose to preserve the network version, the local version, or both. If you want to keep both copies, you must rename the local version, and both copies will exist in both locations.

- If you make a folder available offline and it contains shortcuts to documents on the network that you didn't make available offline, Offline Files goes ahead and makes the documents that the shortcuts point to available offline. This does not apply to folder shortcuts, however.

- Offline Files maintains files' and folders' permissions as if you were still connected to the network; thus, this isn't a good way to get around NTFS file permissions.

Using Briefcase

Use Briefcase to synchronize files and folders that you copy from another computer on the network. This is similar to Offline Files, except that the process is completely manual and you have to access the offline versions of those files in the briefcase, not in their normal namespace. Briefcase is the method of choice if you're sharing files between two computers that you use at the same time. For example, I log on to my network with a desktop and mobile computer at the same time using the same account. Offline Files breaks down in this situation, but Briefcase doesn't.

Before using a briefcase, you must create one. On any folder's shortcut menu, click <u>N</u>ew and then click Briefcase. Rename the briefcase. I tend to give them meaningful names that describe what they contain. I also tend to create multiple briefcases, one for different sets of files. After you create a briefcase, you specify which files you want in it by dragging them to the briefcase. The first time you copy files or folders to a new briefcase, Windows 2000 Professional displays a brief bit of information about briefcases and how they work.

A *briefcase* is nothing more than a folder, which you can browse with Windows Explorer. What makes it a briefcase are the Desktop.ini file and briefcase database files stored in the folder. Desktop.ini points Windows 2000 Professional to the shell extension that adds the Briefcase features to the folder. The briefcase database contains information about the origin of each file and folder in the briefcase.

Like Offline Files, Briefcase performs file-level synchronization. In general, Briefcase doesn't know how to handle the situation in which both versions of a file change, so it simply prompts you for direction. Independent software vendors (ISVs) can publish reconciliation handlers, such as Microsoft did for Microsoft Office 2000, but most don't. Here's how to synchronize a briefcase:

1. On the briefcase's shortcut menu, click Update All.

2. For each item in the list, verify the action that Windows 2000 Professional proposes for each file.

   You can change the action by right-clicking the arrow and picking a different one. The operating system might report that it's skipping a file because the file has changed in both locations. If you're certain that you want to replace either version of the file, do so by changing the action.

3. Click Update, and Windows 2000 Professional synchronizes the briefcase.

At any time, you can stop synchronizing a file by splitting it from the original. In the briefcase, click <u>P</u>roperties on the file's shortcut menu and then click Split From Original.

Securing Mobile Computers

Beyond security measures that you normally use, additional security for mobile computers is a concern only if you actually travel with your computer. I'd anticipate that extra security isn't necessary if the farthest you go with your mobile computer is the backyard. However, if you take your computer to school, to work, or on road trips, consider taking these extra precautions:

- Use the computer's BIOS to password-protect access to the computer. You can require a password in order to start the computer, for example. This is not a reliable security measure, however, because determined hackers can find information on the Internet about getting around BIOS passwords.

- Use the encrypting file system. This is the strongest measure you can take. Even if someone steals your computer, removes its hard disk, and mounts the hard disk on another computer, the hacker will not gain access to your files unless they know your name and password.

- Use third-party products to protect your mobile computer from theft. Some products can even contact you via the Internet the first time an unauthorized user tries using it.

Understanding Hardware Profiles

As most versions of Windows do, Windows 2000 Professional supports docking stations and port replicators. These are particularly useful for mobile computer users, giving them the combination of a portal and desktop computer with one box. Some companies are turning to mobile computers and docking stations to replace traditional desktop computers. The biggest benefit is that you can insert PC Card devices and plug monitors and keyboards in to a docking station. When you're ready to pack up and go, you simply eject the computer from the docking station without having to remove PC Card devices or unplug the keyboard, mouse, and monitor.

Hardware profiles make docking stations work. In fact, docking stations are the primary reason that hardware profiles exist at all. A hardware profile tells Windows 2000 Professional which devices to use and how to configure them. For mobile computers, the operating system creates two hardware profiles by default: docked, for times when you connect the computer to the docking station, and undocked. The operating system uses the docked profile when you're connected to the docking station. This profile would include the keyboard, mouse, monitor, and any PC Card devices in the docking station. The undocked profile wouldn't have any of these devices. For the most part, you don't have to do anything to manage hardware profiles. The operating system handles them automatically. Still, here's how to configure hardware profiles:

1. In Control Panel, double-click the System icon, click the Hardware tab, and then click Hardware Profiles (see Figure 13.2).

2. Do one of the following:

   - To specify whether a profile belongs to a docked or undocked configuration, in Available hardware profiles, click a profile and then click Properties.

   - To copy a hardware profile, in Available hardware profiles, click a profile and then click Copy.

   - To rename a hardware profile, in Available hardware profiles, click a profile and then click Rename.

   - To remove a hardware profile, in Available hardware profiles, click a profile and then click Delete.

3. In the Hardware profiles selection area, do one of the following:

   - To cause the boot loader to always prompt you for the profile you want to use when you start Windows 2000 Professional, click Wait until I select a hardware profile.

   - To cause the boot loader to use the first hardware profile as a default if you don't choose one within a certain period of time, click Select the first profile listed if I don't select a profile in, and then type the number of seconds you want the boot loader to wait before choosing the default profile.

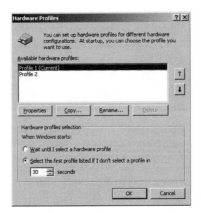

Figure 13.2 Configure hardware profiles only when Windows 2000 Professional doesn't automatically configure them.

You use Device Manager to determine which devices are in each hardware profile. Double-click a device and then select the hardware profiles in which you want to use the device. If you disable a device in a hardware profile and then start the computer with that profile, Windows 2000 Professional does not load the device's drivers when you're using that hardware profile.

A Day in the Life

Most analysts expect Windows 2000 Professional to roll out slowly—except when it comes to mobile computer users. Analysts all agree that the operating system is an outstanding platform for mobile computers and this brief case study shows you why.

Fergus is going on a week-long business trip. Before he leaves for the airport, he figures out which files he needs to take with him and then makes them available offline. He also decides to make his favorite news and business sites available offline to read on the airplane. After he boards the plane, he powers up his computer. He doesn't have to change his hardware profile or reconfigure power management because the operating system takes care of both automatically. The operating system recognizes the change in configuration and also recognizes that he's using the computer on battery power and thus adjusts to preserve as much battery power as possible. After he arrives at his destination, he creates a new dialing location so he can connect to the office using his calling card and doesn't even have to worry about how it happens.

The list of features for mobile users is lengthy and the best part is that they work automatically without requiring a lot of intervention by the user. Beyond working better with mobile computers, particularly those with ACPI BIOSes, the operating system makes taking your work with you much easier. It also helps make your batteries last longer, which is the number one request of most mobile users.

Creating Dial-Up Connections

You create dial-up connections in the Network and Dial-up Connections folder. Though the user interface is slightly different, the information it collects is similar to other versions of Windows:

1. In Control Panel, double-click the Network and Dial-up Connections icon and then double-click the Make New Connection icon.

2. Click <u>N</u>ext and then do one of the following:

   - To create a connection to a private network, such as a home or business, click Dial-up to <u>p</u>rivate network.

   - To create a connection to the Internet service provider, click <u>D</u>ial-up to the Internet.

   - To create a virtual private network connection, click Connect to a pri<u>v</u>ate network through the Internet.

   - To configure your computer to accept incoming connections (the other computer would create a connection to a private network), click <u>A</u>ccept incoming connections.

- To connect your computer to another computer using a serial, parallel, or infrared port, click Connect directly to another computer. This type of connection is handy and often overlooked when you don't have networking equipment available.

3. Follow the instructions you see onscreen. For more information about each type of connection, see Chapter 12, "Networking Your Computer."

See also

- Chapter 12, "Networking Your Computer," to learn more about dial-up connections.

Configuring Modem Options

The most frustrating part of traveling with a mobile computer is figuring out how to dial dial-up connections from various locations. In Control Panel, double-click the Phone and Modem Options icon to configure each modem and describe how you want the operating system to dial different telephone numbers.

Install modems using the Modems tab; click the Add button. Windows 2000 Professional automatically detects most modems, however, so you seldom ever have to manually install a modem.

Set dialing rules on the Dialing Rules tab. These set rules that determine how Windows 2000 Professional dials telephone numbers, depending on the location from which you're calling. For example, I require the operating system to dial the area code when calling from 972 to 214, and I require it to use 1+ dialing when calling 817 (even if all of these area codes are part of the same D/FW metroplex). In the past, these 10-digit dialing schemes were difficult to configure, requiring you to disable dialing locations altogether so you could manually configure phone numbers each time you call. Dialing rules alleviate the problems, however. Here's how to create a dialing rule:

1. Do one of the following:
   - To edit an existing location, in the Locations list, click the location you want to edit and click Edit.
   - To create a new location, click New.

2. On the General tab, type a name of the location; then, in Area code, type the location's area code.

3. On the Area Code Rules dialog box, do one of the following:
   - To create a new dialing rule, click New.
   - To edit an existing dialing rule, click the rule you want to edit in the Area code rules list and then click Edit.

- To remove a dialing rule, click the rule you want to remove in the Area code rules list and then click <u>D</u>elete.

4. On the Calling Card tab, click the calling card you want to use in the Card <u>T</u>ypes list and then provide details for it in the spaces provided. You can create new calling cards by clicking <u>N</u>ew.

Troubleshooting Power Management

Windows 2000 Professional supports two types of power management. Support for Advanced Power and Configuration Interface (ACPI) delivers the latest power-management features when you combine Windows 2000 Professional with mobile computers that have ACPI BIOSes. ACPI gives the operating system complete control over the computer's power management. For more information about ACPI BIOSes, see Chapter 3, "Configuring Hardware." Windows 2000 Professional also includes support for legacy mobile computers that don't have ACPI BIOSes. It supports hibernation, suspend and resume via the APM BIOS, and basic battery-level reporting via the APM BIOS.

Configure battery-management policy and other power-management features in the Power Options Properties dialog box (see Figure 13.3). To open this dialog box, double-click the Power Options icon in Control Panel. Here's a description of each tab:

- **Power Schemes** Choose or create power schemes that determine how long the computer must remain idle before changing the monitor or hard disk's power state, and before the operating system suspends the computer.

- **Advanced** Select whether to display the power status on the taskbar and whether the operating system prompts you for a password when the computer resumes.

- **Hibernate** Enable or disable hibernation. When the computer hibernates, it stores everything in memory to disk and then shuts down. When you turn on the computer, the computer restores its previous state. This feature requires an amount of disk space equivalent to the amount of RAM to be available.

- **APM** If you don't have a computer with an ACPI BIOS, make sure you enable support for APM, which will provide some of the power-management functions that ACPI provides. Enabling APM allows the operating system to suspend the computer.

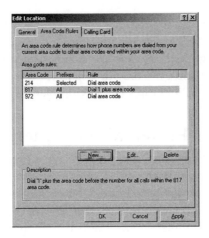

Figure 13.3 Power schemes allow you to adjust your computer's power configuration for different scenarios.

14

Connecting
to the Internet

MICROSOFT WINDOWS 2000 PROFESSIONAL COMES WITH MICROSOFT Internet Explorer 5, and you're already familiar with this Web browser. Because it's been around awhile and you're already familiar with it, I'm not going to cover any of its features in this chapter. This chapter deals with issues that you might not be aware of, as well as how to connect your computer to the Internet. In particular, Windows 2000 Professional's dial-up networking features have significantly different user interfaces than Microsoft Windows 98 or Microsoft Windows NT Workstation 4.0. The result is easier connections.

You can connect to the Internet via a dial-up connection or a network connection, which are more popular these days due to the proliferation of cable modems and DSL. Most power users, particularly home users, aren't terribly familiar with how to connect their computers to a network, so they rely on their installers to do the task for them. This isn't always a good idea because the installers tend to want to install their own software on your computer, and very often they make a mess out of your settings. You don't always know whether they've done the job right or not, but the first time a different Web browser pops up, you type a URL in the Run dialog box, or when you notice that your connection isn't *quite* as fast as a neighbor's, you'll immediately suspect that the installer messed up.

Another problem the knowledge in this chapter helps to solve is when you want to connect multiple computers to the Internet via a single cable modem or DSL. Most services, including the cable modem service that I use, prohibit using a proxy server to connect multiple computers to the Internet via a single cable modem. They see unrealized revenues. This chapter does show you how to get around this problem, but don't tell anyone I told you.

Creating Connections

To create an Internet connection, use the Internet Properties dialog box. Double-click the Internet Options icon in Control Panel to open it and then click the Connections tab. Also, you can click Internet Options on Internet Explorer's Tools menu or click Properties on the Internet Explorer icon you see on the desktop. Figure 14.1 shows what the Connections tab looks like. You configure dial-up connections in the top portion and network connections in the bottom portion.

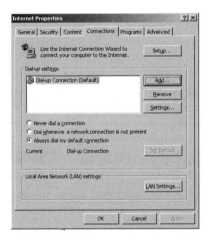

Figure 14.1   Manage your Internet connections via the Connections tab of the Internet Options dialog box.

The simplest way to create a dial-up connection is by using Internet Connection Wizard. The first time you start Internet Explorer, Outlook Express, or any other Internet tool that comes with Windows 2000 Professional, the operating system automatically starts Internet Connection Wizard. You can start the wizard yourself by clicking Setup on the Internet Properties dialog box's Connections tab. After you start the wizard, do one of the following:

- To sign up for new Internet service, click I want to sign up for a new Internet account.

- To use an existing dial-up connection, click I want to transfer my existing Internet account to this computer. You will require the information that your Internet service provider gave you, including the telephone number, domain name server addresses, your IP address (if any), and so on.

- To configure your account yourself, as when you're connecting to the Internet via a network, click I want to set up my Internet connection manually. Using this option, you must configure each aspect of your Internet connection, including the address of your proxy server if you're using one.

The wizard closes by asking you if you want to create an e-mail account in Microsoft Outlook Express. If you don't want to use Outlook Express, click No when it asks if you want to set one up.

Dial-up Settings

In the middle of the Internet Properties dialog box is the Dial-up settings area. The connections you see in this area are the same connections you see in the Network and Dial-Up Connections folder, except for the Local Area Connection icons. Clicking Add displays first, third, and fifth options of Network Connection Wizard: Dial-up to private network, Connect to a private network through the Internet, and Connect directly to another computer. What's missing, oddly enough, is Dial-up to the Internet, but you can create Internet connections using Dial-up to private network.

Here's how to manually create an Internet connection:

1. In Control Panel, double-click the Internet Options icon and then click the Connections tab.

2. In the Dial-up settings area, click Add, click Dial-up to private network, and then click Next.

3. To use dialing rules, which allow you to control the way Windows 2000 Professional treats different area codes and prefixes, select the Use dialing rules check box. In Area code, type your ISP's area code; in Phone number, type its phone number. If you don't use dialing rules, type the phone number you want to dial, including the area code if necessary, in Phone Number.

4. Click Next, and do one of the following:

   - To share this connection with all users, click For all users.

   - To keep this connection to yourself, click Only for myself.

5. Click Next and type a name for this connection. This is the name that you'll see in the Network and Dial-up Connections folder and the Connections tab of the Internet Options dialog box.

6. Click Finish and then customize your connection in the Dial-up Connection Settings dialog box (the information required varies between ISPs):

   - When connecting to an ISP via a dial-up connection, you should have no reason to configure a proxy server. Therefore, for this type of connection, leave the settings in the Automatic configuration and Proxy server areas alone.

   - In the Dial-up settings area, type the credentials required to log on to the ISP. In most cases, you don't provide a domain.

   - Click Properties to choose the modem you want to use, edit dialing rules, configure the connections security options, and set up Internet Connection Sharing, which you learn about later in this chapter.

See also

- Chapter 13, "Using Mobile Computers," for more information about connecting to a private network over the Internet (virtual private networking).

Network Settings

If your network is already connected to the Internet, you can access the Internet through that network. There are two ways to do this:

- Install a proxy client, which you must do if you want the largest variety of Internet programs to work properly. Many different proxy servers are available on the market, so the instructions for installing each are a bit different. If you suspect that your network is using Microsoft Proxy Server, look for a share called Proxy on the server. This share usually contains the installation point for the proxy client.

- Configure Windows 2000 Professional to use a proxy server using Control Panel, which allows Internet Explorer and Outlook Express to work via a proxy server without requiring you to first install a proxy client, but some applications won't. Although this is the simplest way to connect to the Internet through a proxy server, it is also the least flexible.

Here's how to configure Internet Explorer to connect to the Internet through a proxy server:

1. In Control Panel, double-click the Internet Options icon and then click the Connections tab.

2. Click <u>L</u>AN Settings, and you see the dialog box shown in Figure 14.2.

3. Do one of the following:

   - To allow Internet Explorer to automatically detect your proxy server and configure itself appropriately, select the <u>A</u>utomatically detect settings check box. Note that selecting this check box causes Internet Explorer to take a bit longer to load Web pages than using a manual configuration.

   - To manually configure your proxy settings, select the Use a pro<u>x</u>y server check box and then type the address of the proxy server, either a name or an IP address, in Add<u>r</u>ess; and type the proxy server's port number in Po<u>r</u>t. If you want to configure a different address for each protocol (HTTP, Secure, FTP, Gopher, and Socks) or if you want to specify addresses for which you don't want Internet Explorer to use a proxy server, click Advan<u>c</u>ed.

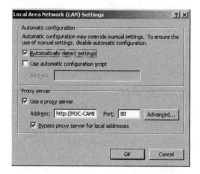

Figure 14.2   If you don't know your proxy server's address for certain, just select the <u>A</u>utomatically detect settings check box.

See also

- Chapter 12, "Networking Your Computer," for more information about connecting to networks.

Using Cable Modems

When using a cable modem, you install a network adapter, as described in Chapter 12, "Networking Your Computer." Actually, in most cases, your service provider installs the adapter for you. Windows 2000 Professional installs the basic networking components required for connecting to a Microsoft network or the Internet. The components it installs are the Client for Microsoft Network, File and Printer Sharing for Microsoft Networks, and Internet Protocol (TCP/IP). In actuality, the only component that you must have to connect your computer to the Internet is Internet Protocol (TCP/IP). And you must make sure that it's configured correctly:

1. In Control Panel, double-click the Network and Dial-up Connections icon and then click Properties on the icon corresponding to the network adapter's shortcut menu you use to connect to the ISP.

2. In the Local Area Connection Properties dialog box, deselect the Client for Microsoft Networks check box and the File and Printer Sharing for Microsoft Networks check box, unless your ISP tells you to do otherwise.

3. Double-click Internet Protocol (TCP/IP), click Use the following IP address, click Use the following DNS server addresses, and then click Advanced.

4. On the IP Settings tab, click Add to add the IP address and subnet mask that your ISP assigned to you, and click Add (in the Default gateways area) to add the default gateway that your ISP gave you. Not all cable modem or DSL providers give you a gateway, but most do.

5. On the DNS tab, click Add to add the DNS server addresses that your cable modem or DSL provider gave you. You should have two addresses. Also, cable modem providers usually give you a domain suffix, which is nothing more than a suffix that TCP/IP adds to the end of addresses when it can't find the address in the DNS database. Click Append these DNS suffixes, click Add, and type the suffix that your cable modem provider gave you.

After you properly configure your TCP/IP connection and restart your computer, if required, you should be able to open a Web page in your browser. The next section, "Sharing Connections," shows you how to use Internet Connection Sharing to do just that.

Sharing Connections

Internet Connection Sharing, a new feature in Windows 2000 Professional, helps you share Internet connections on a small peer-to-peer network. You can use it to share a regular dial-up connection, however. This assumes that you have a properly configured network and you want to share one of the computer's Internet connections with the other computers on that network:

1. In Control Panel, double-click the Network and Dial-Up Connections icon, click Properties on the connection's icon that you want to share, and then click the Sharing tab.

2. On the Sharing tab, shown in Figure 14.3, select the Enable Internet Connection Sharing for this connection check box and make sure you select the Enable on-demand dialing check box if you want it to automatically dial any time a client tries to access the Internet using that connection.

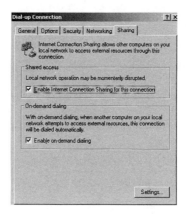

Figure 14.3   Internet Explorer and Outlook Express work properly with Internet Connection Sharing with changing other settings.

Here are some additional notes about using Internet Connection Sharing:

- You must log on to the computer as an Administrator to share a connection.

- Don't use Internet Connection Sharing on any network that uses static IP addresses. Each computer must use dynamic IP addresses. In Windows 2000 Professional, here's how you configure TCP/IP to use dynamic IP addresses:

  1. In Control Panel, double-click the Network and Dial-up Connections icon and then click Properties on the Local Area Connection icon's shortcut menu.

  2. Double-click Internet Protocol (TCP/IP) and then click Obtain an IP address automatically.

- Internet Connection Sharing uses a block of private IP addresses that begins with 192.168.0.1; thus, make sure that you haven't assigned this address as a static address to any client.

- Some programs won't work properly until you add them. On the Sharing tab of the connection's dialog box, click Settings. Add the ports that an application requires by clicking Add on the Internet Connection Sharing Settings dialog box's Applications tab.

- Other network clients can't access the Internet while you're using a virtual private network connection on the computer that's sharing the connection.

- You can't change the network configuration that Internet Connection Sharing uses. For example, you can't change the range of IP addresses that it uses, enable or disable DNS, or change mappings.

IV

Appendixes

A
Glossary

A

access control entry (ACE) In discretionary access control lists, specifies the permissions given to a single user or group to access an object. In system access control lists, specifies security events the operating system will audit for a user or group.

access control list (ACL) Contains access control entries (ACEs) that administrators use to control access to or audit an object. An object's ACL is a list of users and groups that have permission to access the object. The two types of ACLs are discretionary access control lists (DACLs), which give permissions to users and groups; and system access control lists (SACLs), which specify security events that the operating system will audit.

Active Directory The directory service in Microsoft Windows 2000 Server. A directory service stores information about objects on the network—much like a telephone book—in an intuitive hierarchical organization and provides both users and administrators access to this information. Users easily locate network resources, and administrators have a single interface to administer network resources.

administrator A user who is usually a member of the Administrators group and has full control of a computer or network domain. *Local administrators* manage the local computer and *network administrators* manage the domain.

administrative account A user account that includes membership in the local Administrators group on a computer or in a domain, providing administrative access to services and resources.

Advanced Configuration and Power Interface (ACPI)   A specification that defines power management for a wide range of computers (mobile, desktop, and server) and peripherals. In Microsoft Windows 2000 Professional, ACPI is the heart of power management and Plug and Play. Your computer must be ACPI-compliant to take full advantage of either feature. If you're not sure whether your computer is compliant, check its documentation. Note that some computers require a BIOS upgrade to work properly with Windows 2000 Professional.

American Standard Code for Information Interchange (ASCII)   A standard for a single-byte, character-encoding scheme that represents text on a computer. Standard 7-bit ASCII allows 128 characters, including uppercase and lowercase letters, numbers, punctuation marks, and other control characters. Extended 8-bit ASCII allows 256 characters and includes some foreign-language letters and symbols.

Application Programming Interface (API)   Predefined functions, usually packaged as dynamic link libraries, which provide services to applications.

asymmetric encryption   Encryption that uses two encryption keys that are mathematically related—one private and one public. The private key is confidential, whereas the public key is given to anyone with to which whom you correspond. Only the private key can decrypt data encrypted by the public key. The public key can verify data that's digitally signed by the private key. Another name for asymmetric encryption is *public key encryption*.

asynchronous communication   Communication that occurs without regard for timing, one character at a time. Analog modems are asynchronous devices that send and receive data at irregular intervals.

asynchronous transfer mode (ATM)   A high-speed, connection-oriented protocol for transporting different types of traffic on a network. ATM is an up-and-coming standard that will be in more common use in the future.

auditing   A process that records selected security events in the security log. The audit policy determines which events the operating system records.

authentication   The process of validating users' credentials, their names, and passwords. After authenticating their credentials, the operating system gives users access to the computer per the rights and permissions assigned to their accounts and the groups they belong to. When users log on to the local computer, Windows 2000 Professional authenticates their credentials. When they log on to a domain, a server in that domain validates their credentials.

authorizaton   The process of verifying users' rights or permissions to access a resource locally or in a domain. Each time users open a file, for example, the operating system authorizes the user by checking its ACL for the permissions given to the user.

API   Application Programming Interface; a set of predefined routines that a programmer can use to accomplish low-level tasks.

B

backup operator   A local or global group with rights to back up and restore files and folders, regardless of ownership, permissions, encryption, or audit settings.

Bandwidth Allocation Control Protocol (BACP)   A protocol that manages the use of multiple linked lines. Bandwidth Allocation Protocol (BAP) allocates lines when they're required, thus eliminating wasted bandwidth.

bandwidth   The rate a connection can transmit data. Bandwidth is usually expressed as bits per second (bps).

basic disk   A disk containing primary partitions, extended partitions, and logical drives. In Windows 2000 Professional, basic disks can contain spanned, mirrored, striped, and RAID-5 volumes created by using Microsoft Windows NT 4.0 or earlier. (Basic disks are what you used in MS-DOS.)

Basic Input/Output System (BIOS)   The BIOS contains instructions for testing the hardware when the computer starts, starting the operating system, and communicating with devices. It is stored in read-only memory (ROM) and executed when you turn on the computer. You must upgrade the BIOS on many computers in order for Windows 2000 Professional to work properly; check with the computer's manufacturer.

basic volume   Any volume on a basic disk. Basic disks are primary partitions, extended partitions, and logical drives. Basic volumes can also be spanned, mirrored, or striped. They can be RAID-5 volumes created with Windows NT 4.0 or earlier, but not with Windows 2000 Professional.

baud rate   A modem's communication speed. Baud rate does not necessarily equal bits per second because as it is the number of times the line condition changes. If one signal corresponds to one bit, however, they're equal.

bits per second (bps)   The number of bits a device transmits each second. Bits per second is the typical measure of a communication device's speed.

boot loader   Defines the information necessary to boot the operating system, such as the location of the operating system files.

browser   The software that makes it possible to view pages presented on the Internet, predominantly in HTML. Both Microsoft's Internet Explorer and Netscape's Navigator are examples of this type of software.

boot partition   The partition that contains Windows 2000 Professional's system and other files. The boot partition is often the same as the system partition, but this configuration is not required.

boot volume   A volume on a dynamic disk that contains Windows 2000 Professional's system and related files. The boot volume is often the same as the system volume, but this configuration is not required.

built-in groups   The groups that Windows 2000 Professional provides by default. Built-in groups have useful purposes, such as Power Users, Backup Operators, and Administrators. The best way to give users the rights they need is to assign their user account to the appropriate group. For daily use, assigning a user's account to the Administrators group is not a good idea because it opens the door for viruses that require that level of access to inflict their damage.

C

C2-level security   A standard defined by the US Government for secure computing systems.

cache   Memory or disk space in which the operating system or a program stores recently-used data to make accessing it quicker. Caches are effective when access to the cache is faster than access to the data's original source, as in the case of caching Web pages to memory instead of reading them from the Web again.

certificate authority (CA)   An organization that grants public keys to users and other certificate authorities; it also vouches for a public key's authenticity.

certificate   Data that authenticates and secures information on nonsecured networks. Certificates associate public keys with the person holding the private key. Certificate authors digitally sign certificates, allowing the authenticity of those certificates to be verified. ITU-T X.509 defines the most popular format for certificates.

Challenge Handshake Authentication Protocol (CHAP)   An authentication protocol used for remote access. It allows clients to securely send credentials to servers.

code page   Provides support for the character sets and keyboard layouts of different countries. It's a table that translates keystrokes to character codes and character codes to characters on the display.

computer account   A special account that uniquely identifies the computer in the domain. Computer accounts allow secure communication between two computers.

console tree   Microsoft Management Console's let pane, which displays items in the console tree; a hierarchy of nodes that have different capabilities.

credentials   Users' names, passwords, and other information required to authenticate and authorize them.

CryptoAPI (CAPI)   An API that allows applications to encrypt or digitally sign data in order to protect users' data. Independent cryptographic service providers (CSPs) provide cryptographic operations.

D

default user   The user profile that Windows 2000 Professional copies to create new users' profiles.

directory service   Both directory information and the services that provide access to that information. Users can search for objects using their attributes.

disk duplexing   Using a second disk with its own controller to create a complete copy of the disk to ensure data security.

disk mirroring   Using a second disk or partition to create a complete copy of the contents of a disk or partition in order to provide fault tolerance.

domain   A collection of computers in a Windows NT network that share a security account database.

domain   A logical group of networked computers that share a common directory. The name of each domain is unique, and administrators manage domains as a unit.

domain controller   A computer that's running Windows 2000 Server in a domain and manages users' access to the network's resources. Domain controllers log users on, authenticate their credentials, and authorize access to objects in the directory and shared resources.

domain name   In a domain managed by Windows 2000 Server, the name of the domain on the network.

Domain Name System (DNS)   A name service for TCP/IP hosts that translates host names to IP addresses.

dual boot   A configuration that allows you to start two different operating systems on the same computer.

dynamic disk   A physical disk that Disk Management manages. Dynamic disks can contain only dynamic volumes, not basic volumes, such as partitions or logical drives. MS-DOS cannot access dynamic volumes.

Dynamic Host Configuration Protocol (DHCP)   A service that dynamically allocates IP addresses and distributes other TCP/IP parameters as required. DHCP manages the IP addresses on a network, preventing conflicts and the hassles involved with statically assigned addresses.

dynamic link library (DLL)   An executable file that contains functions used by other programs. Programs load DLL files when they need the functions they contain.

dynamic volume   A volume that Disk Management creates. Dynamic volumes can be simple, spanned, striped, mirrored, or RAID-5. You can create dynamic volumes on dynamic disks only. MS-DOS can't read dynamic volumes.

E

emergency repair disk (ERD)   A disk containing enough information to repair Windows 2000 Professional if it fails. You create an emergency repair disk by using Microsoft Windows Backup.

Encrypting File System (EFS)   A file system feature that allows you to encrypt files and folders on NTFS volumes, preventing unauthorized access to them.

expanded memory   Defined by the Expanded Memory Specification (EMS). Supports memory boards that contain RAM, which software can enable or disable.

extended memory   Memory beyond one megabyte.

Extensible Authentication Protocol (EAP)   Extensions to the Point-to-Point Protocol (PPP) that supports remote authentication using miscellaneous security devices, including token cards, dial-up, Kerberos V5, one-time passwords, and certificates. Remote access, PPTP, and L2TP support EAP as an authentication protocol.

F

file allocation table (FAT)   The data table used in the FAT file system to maintain the list of disk clusters and their allocation states.

file transfer protocol (ftp)   Program used to transfer files across a TCP/IP connection.

G

global group   A group that can be used in both its own domain and in trusting domains. Global groups allow you to create groups within a domain that can be used within it and trusting domains. Global groups apply only to Windows 2000 Server.

group   A collection of objects—including users, computers, and other groups—that are used to grant access to resources or create e-mail distribution lists.

group account   A collection of user accounts, each of which has all the permissions given to the group.

H

hardware compatibility list (HCL)   A list of computers and devices that Windows 2000 Professional and other versions of windows supports. You find a copy of the list on the Windows 2000 Professional CD-ROM in Support. See `http://www.microsoft.com/hwtest/hcl` for a more current hardware compatibility list.

hive   A part of the registry that Windows 2000 Professional stores on the disk. The operating system stores hive files in *SystemRoot*\System32\Config and in *UserProfile*. You edit the registry using Registry Editor, and you can copy hive files only when they're not in use.

home directory   A folder on the network in which a user can store documents and programs. Using Active Directory Users and Computers, administrators can assign home directories to a user or a group of users.

host name   The DNS name of the computer on the network. Finding a computer on the network requires that its name be in the Lmhosts file or in the DNS namespace.

Hosts files   A text file that translates the names of computers to IP addresses. On the local computer, *SystemRoot*\System32\Drivers\Etc is where you find this file. Using Hosts is common on networks that aren't using WINS or DNS to resolve host names.

I

IEEE 1394   A recent standard for high-speed serial devices, particularly digital video and audio.

input locale   Describes the language in which you want to type. Adding an input locale usually adds a corresponding keyboard layout.

input method editor (IME)   A small program that allows users to enter characters written in Asian languages. It contains an engine that translates keystrokes to phonetic and ideographic characters as well as to a dictionary of common ideographic words. An IME makes it possible to enter thousands of different characters using a standard 101-key keyboard.

Internet   The series of networks that create a global information resource.

Internet Control Message Protocol (ICMP)   A protocol, required in every implementation of TCP/IP, which helps two nodes share status and error information.

Internet Protocol (IP)   The part of TCP/IP that addresses and forwards packets on a network such as the Internet. IP does not guarantee delivery.

Internetwork Packet Exchange (IPX)   A Novell NetWare protocol that's similar to IP in that it controls packet addressing and routing. Like IP, it doesn't guarantee delivery. It does route between networks.

IPX/SPX   Novell NetWare transport protocol that's similar to TCP/IP. Windows 2000's implementation of IPX/SPX is through NWLink.

J

junction point   A folder on a disk that points to data in another location on the disk or to another disk. You create junction points by mounting a disk on a folder.

K

Kerberos V5   An open, Internet standard protocol for authenticating users and computers. It encrypts passwords instead of sending them as plain text, and improves authentication and authorization performance.

keyboard layout   A table that maps keys on the keyboard to the characters you see on the screen. Keyboard layouts accommodate the special characters and symbols that different languages require. Note that with some layouts, the characters you see on the screen might not correlate to the characters printed on the keys.

L

Layer 2 Tunneling Protocol (L2TP)   An industry-standard tunneling protocol based on Layer 2 Forwarding (L2F) and PPTP that does not require IP connectivity between the client and server computers. L2TP does require a packet-oriented, point-to-point connection. L2TP provides the same features as PPTP, but you can use it over ATM, Frame Relay, and X.25.

Lmhosts file   A text file that translates the names of computers outside the current subnet to IP addresses. The text file is in *SystemRoot*\System32\Drivers\Etc on the local computer. Using Lmhosts is common on networks that aren't using WINS or DNS to resolve host names.

local area network (LAN)   A group of computers and other devices connected together to share resources.

local computer   The computer that you logged on to using the keyboard, as opposed to a remote computer, which you access via a communications device such as a network adapter or modem. Local programs, local users, local groups, and so on refer to those objects that reside physically on the computer you're using.

local group   On computers running Windows 2000 Professional and Windows 2000 Server as a member server, a group that has rights and permissions on the local computer. On computers that participate in a domain, user accounts and global groups in that domain and trusted domains are *local groups*.

local user profile   The user profile that Windows 2000 Professional or Windows 2000 Server creates for users the first time they log on to the computer. By default, user profiles are in the Documents and Settings folder.

logon script   Script files (usually batch files) that an administrator associates with a user account. The operating system runs the logon script each time the user logs on to the network. Typical uses for a logon script are to configure the environment, map network drives, run programs, and more. No capability exists to assign logon scripts to groups.

M

mandatory user profile   A user profile that users can't permanently change. Windows 2000 Professional downloads the profile from the network each time they log on to the domain, but it never updates the network copy of the profile. Members of the Administrators group are the only users that can update mandatory profiles.

master boot record (MBR)   The first sector on a disk. The MBR contains the code necessary to start the computer and also contains the partition table, which describes primary and extended partitions on the disk. A disk's MBR is frequently a target of viruses, but the BIOS in most computers allows you to protect it.

master file table (MFT)   A system file on NTFS volumes that contains information about each file and folder. The MFT is always the first file on the volume.

member server   A computer running Windows 2000 Server that is not a domain controller. Member servers, which are usually resource servers, don't have a copy of the directory. Administrators can grant permissions to local and domain users and groups.

Message Digest 5 (MD5)   Developed by RSA Data Security, Inc., an industry-standard 128-bit hashing algorithm for encrypting authentication data. This one-way scheme transforms data into a unique hash value that can't be transformed back into the original data. CHAP is an authentication protocol that uses MD5 to transmit users' credentials without actually sending their passwords.

Microsoft Management Console (MMC)   A framework that hosts one or more administrative tools, each of which is a console. A console can contain a variety of objects, including utilities, folders, Web pages, and so on. Consoles form a hierarchical structure that is in the left pane of MMC and is called the *console tree*. MMC has two different modes: In authoring mode, MMC provides features for authoring consoles; in user mode, MMC hides the authoring features and possibly the console itself.

mirror   An identical copy of a disk that's kept on a separate disk. If one of the disks fails, you can still access the volume's data on the other disk.

mounted drive   A drive mounted to an empty folder. Instead of assigning a letter to the drive, you can assign a name and then access that drive as part of the path to which you mounted it. You must be a member of the Administrators group to mount a drive on a folder or to assign a letter to it using Disk Management.

multihomed computer   A computer that contains two or more network adapters—each of which has a unique IP address—or a computer with a single network card that has multiple IP addresses.

multilink   Two or more physical communications links combined to create a single logical link that increases the bandwidth available for remote access. In Windows 2000, Multilink is based on RFC 1990, a standard defined by the Internet Engineering Task Force (IETF). Multilink combines analog, digital, or both types of connections.

N

namespace   The set of unique names within a specific scope. In Microsoft Windows Explorer, the namespace contains the names in the left pane of the window. In Microsoft Management Console (MMC), the namespace is the console tree. In Domain Name System, the structure of the domain name tree is its namespace.

Network Basic Input/Output System (NetBIOS)   An application programming interface (API) that programs use for low-level services such as managing names, conducting sessions, and sending datagrams between network nodes.

node   On a network, a node is a computer that's connected to the network. In a Microsoft Management Console, a node is any item in a snap-in's console tree.

nonpaged memory   Memory that the operating system can't page to disk, ensuring that it's always available.

NT File System (NTFS) -   File system designed for and implemented in Windows NT to provide increased security and other features beyond the standard FAT file system. This is the most secure file system in Windows NT.

O

object   Any entity that has an access control list and possibly other attributes. Objects are files, folders, printers, or entities in Active Directory.

owner   The user who owns an object and can grant other users permission to access it. Each object has an owner, which is usually the user who created the object.

P–Q

page fault   An interrupt that the CPU generates when a program tries to read from or write to a virtual memory location that is paged to disk and is thus not present.

paged memory   Virtual memory that can be paged to disk. Paging is the process of moving less frequently used parts of memory to another storage device, such as a disk, making more memory available to programs that the computer has available physically.

paging file   The file to which Windows 2000 writes memory that it pages to disk. The file is hidden. The paging file and the computer's physical memory represent the computer's total virtual memory. The operating system pages less-frequently-used memory to disk to make room for new data, logically providing more memory than is actually installed on the computer. Another more common name for a paging file is a *swap file*.

permission   A rule that defines which users can access an object and exactly what they can do with it. Permissions apply to objects, as opposed to rights, which apply to the computer as a whole.

Point-to-Point Protocol (PPP)   A set of industry-standard framing and authentication protocols, part of Windows 2000 remote access, which ensures interoperability with other remote access software. PPP negotiates configuration parameters for networking protocols such as TCP/IP, IPX, and AppleTalk. Point-to-Point Protocol is also called *PPP*.

Point-to-Point Tunneling Protocol (PPTP)   An industry-standard tunneling protocol that enables users to create a private, secure network connection through public, unsecure network connections such as the Internet. PPTP can tunnel IP, IPX, or NetBEUI inside IP packets.

policy   The feature that administrators use to automatically configure client computers when users log on to the network. With Windows 2000, policy refers to Group Policy or a setting in a Group Policy object; with Windows NT 4.0, it refers to policies set using System Policy Editor.

private key   One of the two keys used with public key encryption. The private key is secret and is used to decrypt data that's encrypted with the public key or to digitally sign data. The public key verifies data signed with the public key.

process identifier   A number that uniquely identifies a process as it runs. You can view each process' process identifiers (PIDs) in Task Manager.

Public Key Cryptography Standard (PKCS)   Public key cryptographic standards that include certificate request syntax, cryptographic message syntax, Diffie-Hellman key agreement, extended-syntax, password-based encryption, private key information syntax, and RSA encryption. RSA Data Security, Inc. owns and maintains PKCS.

public key   One of the two keys used with public key encryption. The public key is nonsecret and is used to encrypt data that the only the private key can decrypt. It can also verify data that's digitally signed by the private key.

R

recovery agent   An administrator who can recover data that's encrypted by Encrypting File System (EFS). The recovery agent uses a public key certificate.

Recovery Console   A command-line interface that provides limited access to the computer without actually starting Windows 2000. Recovery Console provides a limited number of commands and provides limited access to the file system. Administrators can use it to start and stop services, read and write data in *SystemRoot*, repair the master boot record (MBR), format drives, and more. Start Recovery Console from the setup disks or by running setup with the /cmdcons command-line option.

registry size limit (RSL)   The maximum size of the registry. Setting a cap on the size of the registry prevents applications from using up the paged pool with registry data. Adjust the registry size limit by double-clicking the System icon in Control Panel and then clicking Performance Options on the Advanced tab.

remote procedure call (RPC)   A mechanism that allows distributed applications to call services on other computers on the network. Registry Editor and other remote administration tools use RPC.

Request for Comments (RFC)   Documents created by the Internet Engineering Task Force (IETF) that define protocols such as TCP/IP and PPP. IETF identifies RFCs by number. For example, RFC 2284 defines Extensible Authentication Protocol (EAP). You can obtain any RFC from the RFC Web site, `http://www.rfc-editor.org`.

roaming user profile   A user profile that's stored on a server and downloaded to the local computer when the user logs on to the computer. Windows 2000 Professional updates the network copy of the profile when the user logs off the computer. Roaming user profiles are available on any computer running Windows 2000 Professional or Windows 2000 Server when the user logs on to the domain containing the profile. If the local user profile is more current than the network copy, the operating system uses the local user profile instead.

S

secret key encryption   Also called *shared secret encryption* or *symmetric encryption*, an encryption algorithm that uses the same secret key to encrypt and decrypt data. Symmetric encryption is faster than asymmetric encryption and is thus frequently used to encrypt large amounts of data.

Secure Hash Algorithm (SHA-1)   A 160-bit, one-way hashing scheme that's used to create digital signatures with the Digital Signature Standard's (DSS's) Digital Signature Algorithm (DSA).

Secure Multipurpose Internet Mail Extensions (S/MIME)   A protocol for sending secure e-mail over the Internet. Both the clients must support S/MIME.

Secure Sockets Layer (SSL)   A protocol that uses public and secret key technologies to create secure network connections. SSL is common on the Internet.

security ID (SID)   A unique number that looks similar to S-1-5-21-553393301-1521681255-927750060-1004, plus or minus a few digits; and uniquely identifies a user, group, or computer account. Every account has a unique SID; although the name of the account might change, the SID never changes. Internally, Windows 2000 Professional and Windows 2000 Server refer to an account by its SID and never by its name.

simple volume   A volume on a dynamic disk that consists of space allocated on a single disk. The space can be contiguous or can contain multiple discontinuous regions that are linked together. You can extend a simple volume on the disk, or you can extend a simple volume onto another disk, creating a spanned volume. You can mirror simple volumes, but they are not fault-tolerant.

single sign-on   A mechanism that allows users with a domain user account to log on to the network one time and access any computer in the domain. Users can log on with a password or a smart card.

Small Computer Systems Interface   Defines a bus standard by which multiple devices can be connected to a computer.

smart card   A device that looks similar to a credit or debit card that securely stores public and private keys, passwords, and other personal information. A Smart card requires a smart card reader attached to the computer and a PIN number that unlocks the data on the card. Windows 2000 supports single sign-on with smart cards.

snap-in   A tool that you can add to a Microsoft Management Console (MMC) console. Add stand-alone snap-ins by themselves. You can only add extension snap-ins to extend the capabilities of other snap-ins.

spanned volume   A volume on a dynamic disk that uses space on more than one physical disk. You can further extend a spanned volume at any time. Spanned volumes are not fault-tolerant and you can't mirror them.

special access permissions   Custom permissions that you define by selecting individual parts that make up the standard permissions. For example, *Read Attributes* is a permission that's automatically selected when you select *Read & Execute* permission.

STOP error   Also known as the Blue Screen of Death (BSOD), a significant error that causes Windows 2000 Professional and Windows 2000 Server to stop rather than continuing and causing data loss. STOP errors are characterized by the white text on a blue background.

striped volume   A volume on a dynamic disk that stripes data onto two or more physical disks. The operating system alternates data evenly between each disk. Striped volumes are not fault-tolerant, and you can't mirror or extend them. The primary benefit of striped volumes is that they improve disk performance.

subkey   Any key in the registry that's contained within another key. *Subkey* is also the common term for a path in the registry.

symmetric encryption   An encryption algorithm that uses a shared secret for encryption and decryption. Other names for symmetric encryption are *secret key* and *shared secret encryption*.

system access control list (SACL)   Contains access control entries that defines which events the operating system will audit and for which users and groups.

systemdrive   The drive on which you installed Windows 2000 Professional. The default is C. This book uses *SystemDrive* to represent this drive. Windows 2000 Professional and Windows 2000 Server define this as an environment variable that you can expand in scripts and other places using %SYSTEMDRIVE%.

systemroot   The folder in which you installed Windows 2000 Professional. The default is C:\Winnt. This book uses *SystemRoot* to represent this folder. Windows 2000 Professional and Windows 2000 Server define this as an environment variable that you can expand in scripts and other places using %SYSTEMROOT%.

system partition   The partition that contains the files, such as the boot loader, required to start the computer and load Windows 2000 Professional. Although the system and boot partitions are often the same, they don't have to be.

system volume   The volume on a dynamic disk that contains the files, including the boot loader, required to start the computer and load Windows 2000 Professional. The system and boot volumes are often the same, but that is not a requirement.

SYSVOL   A directory shared on the server that contains the domain's public files. SYSVOL is replicated across all domain controllers in the domain.

T

Transmission Control Protocol/Internet Protocol (TCP/IP)   The protocol suite used on the Internet. TCP/IP defines how to connect networks and route traffic to and through them.

trust relationship   A relationship between two domains, in which one domain trusts another's authentications. The first is the *trusting* domain and the second is the *trusted* domain. You can give accounts on a trusted domain rights and permissions on the trusting domain, even though the accounts don't exist on the latter.

U

Unicode   A standard for a 16-bit, character-encoding scheme that uses two bytes to represent each character. Unicode can represent almost all written languages because 65,536 character codes are available. Currently, 39,000 character codes have been used, with about 21,000 of them used for Chinese ideographs. Unicode was developed by the Unicode Consortium and is the character-encoding scheme used by Windows 2000 Professional and Windows 2000 Server.

Universal Naming Convention (UNC)   The fully-qualified name of any resource on a network. The format of a UNC name is *servername**sharename*\ *directory**filename*. *Servername* is the name of the server sharing the resource, *sharename* is the name of the share, *directory* is an optional path, and *filename* is an optional file name. UNC allows users to access network resources without physically mapping them to drive letters.

universal serial bus (USB)   A recent hardware standard for a bus that supports Plug and Play and allows users to connect up to 127 devices to a single USB port. USB makes up for a flaw in the PC-compatible architecture that limits the number of devices users can install in a computer due to the finite resources available.

user account   A record that defines a user. Each user account includes the user's name, password, group membership, rights, and permissions. On Windows 2000 Professional and Windows 2000 Server member servers, administrators manage user accounts with Local Users and Groups. On Windows 2000 Server domain controllers, administrators manage user accounts with Active Directory Users and Computers.

user profile   The folders and files that define a user's environment. A user's profile includes their settings and a variety of application files, and stores their documents and Internet shortcuts.

user rights   Tasks that users can perform on a computer or on a domain. Rights apply to the computer as a whole and not to individual objects. They include backing up files and folders, logging on to the computer locally, and profiling the computer's performance. You can assign rights to individual users or groups of users.

userprofile   The folder under *SystemDrive*\Documents and Settings that contains the current user's profile.

V

value   A value contained within a subkey in the registry. Values have names, types, and data. Values are commonly called *value entries*.

virtual memory   Available memory as it appears to the operating system and to programs. Virtual memory is the computer's physical memory combined with the temporary storage to which the operating system swaps out less less-frequently-used memory, the paging file. A computer with four gigabytes of virtual memory might only have only 128 megabytes of physical memory, with the remaining memory stored in a paging file.

virtual private network (VPN)   A secured connection to a private network through unsecured public networks. VPNs provide remote access to private networks through the Internet.

volume   Any part of a physical disk that appears logically as a separate disk. In Windows 2000 Professional, each volume has its own drive letter.

W–Z

Windows Task Manager   A program that displays information about the tasks and processes running on the computer and high-level information about the computer's performance. Using Windows Task Manager, you can end processes, create and end new tasks, and observe real-time information about the computer's performance. To open Windows Task Manager, press Ctrl+Shift+Esc.

workgroup   A group of users who work on a common project or in the same department, and who share resources with each other. Each computer in a workgroup is responsible for providing its own security, as opposed to a domain in which a domain server provides security.

B

Quick Start for
Windows 98 Users

I KNOW MANY MICROSOFT WINDOWS 98 USERS WHO were crying fifteen
minutes after installing Microsoft Windows 2000 Professional. They were
mostly novice users who didn't appreciate the business benefits of this new
operating system. Somehow, people tend to get very attached to their
favorite hardware and software. They almost always shed their tears because
their favorite programs and favorite hardware didn't work. They didn't like
having to deal with security so tight that they couldn't install what they
wanted to install when they wanted to install it. They also didn't like going
from a zippy operating system to what they described as a dog.

Education is part of a solution. It's a fact that all the hardware and software that's compatible with Windows 98 will not be equally compatible
with Windows 2000 Professional. It's a fact that Windows 98 was not a
secure operating system and Windows 2000 Professional is a secure operating system. It's a fact that Windows 98 is faster at some tasks than Windows
2000 Professional. It's equally a fact that Windows 2000 Professional isn't the
right operating system for novice users who are attached to hardware and
software that doesn't work in Windows 2000 Professional or for novice users
who can't yet deal with the intricacies of a complex operating system.
Finally, it's a fact that you're reading this book and are probably more than
able to deal with Windows 2000 Professional, so this appendix is your diving
board into it.

Windows 2000 Professional is not as forgiving as Windows 98. Forgiveness? Yes. Windows 98 overlooks varieties of problems that Windows 2000 Professional does not overlook. Here's an example: After plugging a new keyboard into my computer and using an incompatible device driver, Windows 2000 Professional failed to recognize any keyboard whatsoever. The result was that I could no longer log on to the computer; the quickest solution to the problem was to start the computer and edit its configuration from another computer over the network. This same human error did not break Windows 98, which recovered quite easily from it. Part of the problem stems from the fact that if you're using Windows 2000 Professional to its full potential, you'll convert the file system to NTFS. After doing so, you have no ability to troubleshoot using MS-DOS because this basic, command-line-oriented operating system can't read NTFS volumes. The bottom line, and a new concept for Windows 98 users, is that every configuration change is risky business.

New Concepts

Security, user profiles, file systems, and the hardware compatibility list are just some of the concepts about which most Windows 98 users need to learn. Because this appendix is "Quick Start for Windows 98 Users," I'll keep these introductions gentle and brief, and refer you to other portions of this book that contain more information.

This book's glossary is another good place for Windows 98 users to check new concepts and terms. It defines terms such as *user*, *group*, and *access control list*. You find a similar glossary in Windows 2000 Help and you can print the glossary and keep it by your side while reading this book. In Windows 2000 Help, print the Glossary topic, and click Print the selected heading and all subtopics in the Print Topics dialog box. The list is long, but it's a valuable resource when learning this operating system.

Security

Windows 98 is not a secure operating system. It doesn't maintain any sort of security information about files, their owners, or users' rights to access those files. It doesn't maintain any sort of security to anything except password lists, each of which contains credentials for a user's access to network resources. None of this means that the operating system does not provide features for secure communications and secure storage of sensitive information, but they protect computers from the Internet and not from users themselves. The implications are many. Users can do anything they like on a computer running Windows 98. They can install hardware and software, administer the computer, delete files, snoop into other users' files, and so on. This type of open-door policy is not acceptable in a business environment and is one of the reasons why businesses turn to operating systems such as Windows 2000 Professional.

Windows 2000 Professional is a secure operating system. It's one of the primary benefits that Microsoft touts any time you read about the operating system's major strengths: reliability, stability, security, and so on. At the heart of it all are users and groups. Each person logging on to a computer that's running Windows 2000 Professional has a *user account*. It identifies the user, and that's about all. *Credentials* are combinations of users' names and passwords. *Groups* are collections of users that have something in common. For example, the Administrators group contains administrators' user names, and an Accounting group might contain user names from the accounting department. Groups provide a way to apply the same security settings to groups of related users. To make matters a bit more complicated, realize that the operating system uses two types of accounts and groups:

- **Local Users and Groups**   On the local computer, the computer in front of which you're sitting, Window 2000 Professional keeps its own accounts database. In that database are *local users* and *local groups*. Users can use the accounts in the local account database only to log on to and use resources on the local computer, not to any other computer on the network.

- **Domain Users and Groups**   The network keeps its own accounts database, too. The way it stores accounts depends on the type of server that's managing the network. When logging on to a network that a Microsoft server operating system is managing, you're logging on to a *domain. Domain users* and *domain groups* are therefore accounts and groups on the network, not on the local computer. You can still log on to Windows 2000 Professional using a domain account, however. In fact, by using a domain account, you can log on to any computer that's connected to the same domain.

When users log on to a computer running Windows 2000 Professional, one of two things happens. When users log on to the computer, they choose to log on to the local computer or they choose to log on to a domain. If they log on locally, the operating system authenticates their credentials against the local computer's security database. Logging on locally gives users access to the resources on the local computer only. If they log on to a domain, the operating system passes on their credentials to the server that's managing the domain, and the server authenticates their credentials. After approving their credentials, the operating system provides access to the computer by displaying the desktop, Start menu, etc. The important things to remember are that if you log on locally, the local computer authenticates your credentials and you have access to local resources; if you log on to the domain, the domain server authenticates your credentials and you have access to resources on the local computer and on the network.

User accounts do more than just give you access to the computer and network. Things get more granular. In Windows 2000 Professional, each and every object has an *access control list* (ACL) that describes the users and groups that can access that object. Objects include files and folders. An object's ACL gives permission to users in one of two ways. First, an object's ACL might have an *access control entry* (ACE) for specific users, and each ACE describes the user's permissions: read, write, delete, and so on. Second, an object's ACL might have an ACE that does the same thing for specific groups, only the permissions in the ACE apply to users who are members of that group. This is where the importance of groups comes into play because administrators can assign permissions to entire groups of users instead of individual users.

Note

Domain user accounts aren't the only type of account; *computer accounts* are also important. Each computer running Windows 2000 Professional has a computer account in the domain. This account sets up secure communication between the client computer and the server computer. In a strange sort of way, computers must log on to the network before users can log on to the network using those computers. Users assign names to their computers when they install the operating system. Optionally, administrators can assign names in advance using answer files. In order to *join a computer to a domain*, users installing the operating system must have access to credentials that have administrator rights on the server managing the domain. If you're installing the operating system, you can get these credentials from the administrator.

Such pervasive and strict security has implications of which Windows 98 users must be aware:

- You can't bypass the logon process to gain access to the computer. You have to type your user name and password every time you want to access the computer. Chapter 11, "Securing Your Computer," does describe a way to log on to the computer automatically, but you should do this only if the computer isn't on a business network.

- You're used to administering the computer as you see fit, but administering a computer that's running Windows 2000 Professional often requires administrative rights. You must log on to the computer as an administrator to do things such as install new hardware and software, run varieties of utilities, or change certain settings. If you have the password for the Administrator account, you're all set.

- When logging on to the computer as a normal user, not as an administrator, the system is a bit harder to damage than otherwise. That's because security prevents you from doing certain tasks that might not be in the computer's best interests. If you go the route of always logging on to the computer as Administrator, however, you have no protection.

- You won't have access to all the files on the computer. These include other users' files, if you're sharing the computer with other users, and some system files. In some cases, you'll see the file in Microsoft Windows Explorer, but you won't be able to open, copy, or remove the file.

- Some applications just won't work if you log on to the computer as a normal user. This saddens me because the applications are not well-behaved. One example is Microsoft Money 99, which requires that you log on to the computer as Administrator in order to keep the program from displaying error messages.

See also:

- Chapter 3, "Configuration Hardware," for more information about the rights you must have to install, remove, and configure hardware.

- Chapter 5, "Installing Applications," to learn how security affects your ability to install, remove, and use applications.

- Chapter 11, "Securing Your Computer," for more information about security in Windows 2000 Professional, including in-depth analyses of key concepts and how to administer security.

User Profiles

Most users never have to deal with user profiles in Windows 98. By default, Windows 98 doesn't enable user profiles, and novice users don't understand their benefit. Although enlightened administrators deployed Windows 98 with user profiles enabled, most administrators didn't because doing so was too much work.

So what's the big deal with user profiles? First, they're beneficial if users share a single computer. Windows 2000 Professional keeps users' settings separately, so that their settings and documents are theirs. Fergus can customize his desktop without changing another user's settings. Fergus can access his documents, but he can't access any other user's documents. The operating system puts user profiles in *SystemDrive*\Documents and Settings. Users have their own folders under this directory, which I indicate with the placeholder *UserProfile*. Thus, *SystemDrive*\Documents and Settings\Fergus is Fergus's user profile folder. The second benefit is *roaming user profiles*, which follow users to any computer they use. The operating system stores roaming user profiles on the network and, when users log on to a computer, the operating system copies their user profile folders to the local computer.

User profiles work similarly in both Windows 98 and Windows 2000 Professional. There are two differences, though. First, Windows 98 stores user profile folders in the system directory, *SystemRoot*\Profiles, whereas Windows 2000 Professional doesn't. The way that Windows 2000 Professional stores them is superior, keeping users out of the system directory altogether. The second difference is the amount of information that each operating system puts in user profile folders. Windows 98 puts limited types of information in user profile folders, whereas Windows 2000 Professional puts just about all per-user settings and files in user profile folders. The implication is that although many settings in Windows 98 were shared among all users, even those with user profiles, most settings are not shared between users in Windows 2000 Professional. Again, Windows 2000 Professional's way is preferable because it better separates users.

Note

Windows 98 and Windows 2000 Professional user profiles are not compatible. Not even a little bit. If you're using roaming user profiles, don't log on to the network using the same user name in both Windows 98 and Windows 2000. The result is a mix of incompatible settings that aren't easily repaired.

Like security, user profiles have special implications for users who never used them before:

- You can't access other users' files unless they give you permission. An exception is if you log on to the computer as Administrator.

- Get used to saving documents and other files in your user profile folder. In particular, save them in My Documents. Doing this makes backing up your documents and administration easier. This is a change for users who commonly save documents in the directory containing the application that created them or save them in other places.

- After any user installed an application in Windows 98, anyone using the machine saw it on the Start menu. This isn't the case in Windows 2000 Professional. Some applications require each user to install the application if they want to use it. An example is Microsoft Office 2000. You can get around this situation, however, as discussed in Chapter 5.

- If you walk up to an unattended computer that's already in use, anything you do affects the user who is currently logged on to it. This might seem obvious, but I see users lose documents time and time again because of this. For example, if Fergus is using a computer but leaves it unattended for a minute, and then I use the computer to create a document, chances are good that the document is in Fergus's user profile folder. The next time I go looking for the document, I don't find it because it's not in my user profile folder.

See also

- Chapter 4, "Personalizing Windows," for more information about personalizing your settings.

- Chapter 11, "Securing Your Computer," to learn how to give other users permission to access files in your user profile folder.

- Chapter 8, "Managing the Computer," for more information about managing user profiles.

File Systems

Windows 98 supports a single type of file system: FAT. Two different flavors of this file system are FAT16 and FAT32. They're both similar except for the disk and file sizes that they support. FAT is limited. It's a file system that began with the original version of MS-DOS and has aged beyond its useful years. The primary problems with this file system are that it's not very efficient and it doesn't provide any sort of security whatsoever.

Windows 2000 Professional offers an additional file system: NTFS. You *should* use NTFS. It provides security. It handles bigger disks and is more efficient. As discussed in Chapter 7, "Managing Disks and Files," it has many more features that make it undeniable. The only reason that you wouldn't use NTFS is that some operating systems can't read files on it (Windows 98 and MS-DOS). Thus, if you want to use Windows 2000 Professional in conjunction with one of these other operating systems, a *dual-boot configuration*, you must use FAT if you want to access your files from both operating systems. If you want to be able to troubleshoot by starting the computer with an MS-DOS disk, you must use FAT. If neither of these scenarios applies to you, go ahead and use NTFS.

The question you're asking now is probably this: How do I make this choice? In Windows 2000 Professional, a file system isn't just something that happens to you. The setup program asks you which file system you want to use as you're installing the operating system. You can convert to NTFS later, too, using a utility you learn about in Chapter 7. After you convert a partition to NTFS, you can't restore it unless you back up and reformat the partition using FAT.

See also

- Chapter 7, "Managing Disks and Files," for a technical description of the differences between FAT and NTFS. This chapter also describes various tools that you can use to manage files and disks.

- Chapter 11, "Securing Your Computer," to learn how to work with NTFS security, including permissions.

Hardware

Windows 2000 Professional does a reasonable job of making hardware installation and removal similar to Windows 98. After all, Microsoft likes to position Windows 2000 Professional as having the best features of Windows 98, including Plug and Play.

What you're not going to like is that some devices aren't compatible with Windows 2000 Professional. Few users have installed the operating system and had it properly recognize and configure every device on their computers. You can almost always work around these issues with a bit of careful detective work, however:

- Get used to checking the hardware compatibility list before purchasing new hardware. Microsoft maintains this list to indicate which devices work with its operating systems. The company certifies some devices and indicates whether other devices are known to work or not. The address of this list is `http://www.microsoft.com/hcl`.

- Windows 2000 Professional might only partially support some hardware. For example, it might not support all the buttons on your mouse. Check with the manufacturer to find a new device driver.

- If you already own a device and the operating system doesn't include drivers for it, start poking around the Web to find new drivers. For popular devices, you can always find new device drivers this way. Search by using your favorite portal or go directly to independent hardware vendor's (IHV's) Web site if you know the address. Two unrelated Web sites are good sources for updated drivers:

    - `http://www.betaos.com/drivers`

    - `http://www.worldowindows.com/win2000.asp`

Note

Some computers won't work properly until you update their BIOSs. For example, I had to update my IBM Thinkpad and Compaq Presario's BIOSs before I could restart Windows 2000 Professional properly. ACPI-enabled computers might also require a BIOS upgrade to work properly with Windows 2000 Professional. Because IHVs implemented ACPI well before Windows 2000 Professional shipped, many of these computers were untested with the operating system. For more information about updating your computer's BIOS, see Chapter 3, "Configuring Hardware."

Professional Upgrade

Two methods you can use to install Windows 2000 Professional are upgrading from a previous version of Windows and installing a new copy of the operating system. Upgrade if you want to replace your Windows 98 with

Windows 2000 Professional and you want to keep your existing files and preferences. Install a new copy of Windows 2000 Professional if you don't want to keep existing files and preferences or if you want to use both Windows 98 and Windows 2000 Professional. The differences between each method are distinct:

- **Upgrade**   The setup program installs Windows 2000 Professional in the same folder as Windows 98, replacing its files but preserving as many of its settings as possible.

- **New Install**   The setup program installs Windows 2000 Professional in a new folder, doesn't replace Windows 98's files, and doesn't use the existing settings. You must reinstall each application that you want to use in Windows 2000 Professional.

Note

You can't install Windows 2000 Professional on a computer that already has two operating systems. In other words, if you already installed Windows 98 and Windows NT Workstation 4.0 in a dual-boot configuration, Windows 2000 Professional's setup program will complain about it and not let you install it. The only solution is to remove one of the operating systems. The setup program won't even let you upgrade one of the other operating systems.

See also

- Chapter 1, "Installing Windows," for more information about installing Windows 2000 Professional. In addition to describing how to upgrade from Windows 98, this chapter also describes how to use both Windows 98 and Windows 2000 Professional at the same time.

Preparation

Windows 2000 Professional's setup program can generate an upgrade report without putting you through the actual upgrade process. This report is applicable only when upgrading from an earlier version of Windows. It lists the software that will not work, as well as the software that requires upgrade packs in order to work properly. It also reports any 32-bit device drivers that won't work in Windows 2000 Professional, which is handy information if you're upgrading from Windows 98. At the MS-DOS command prompt or in the Run dialog box, type **winnt32/checkupgradeonly** to generate an upgrade report. After generating the report, do one of the following and then follow the report's instructions to upgrade your software:

Before upgrading to Windows 2000 Professional, record your computer's hardware configuration. The information will come in handy if you run into problems later. This is particularly true if you're using a legacy device that no Plug and Play operating system can configure. These might be network interface cards that you manually configured by setting jumpers or switches. Windows 98 has an easy way to record your computer's configuration. Use Device Manager to print the computer's configuration, including the resources that each device uses. You can also use System Information to print similar information that also includes the network configuration.

Gather the following network settings before starting Windows 2000 Professional's setup program:

- Computer name
- Domain or workgroup name
- IP address, if using static IP addresses
- WINS or DNS server IP address
- Other network settings, as required

These settings are in the Network Properties dialog box, but they might not reflect the settings you must use to connect Windows 2000 Professional to the network. For example, although Windows 98 certainly does have a computer name, it might not reflect the name of the computer account that the administrator created for you. Checking these settings with the administrator before installing Windows 2000 Professional is a good idea.

The most important thing you can do before installing Windows 2000 Professional is to back up the computer. Do a full backup, if possible, so that you can easily restore the computer if something goes awry. As much as I'd like to tell you that installing the operating system is always successful, it just isn't so. On a number of occasions, I had to give up and restore the previous configuration because the hardware just wasn't compatible with the new operating system. On the Start menu, choose Programs, point to Accessories, point to System Tools, and then click Backup.

Just prior to starting Windows 2000 Professional's setup program, clean up the computer to make sure that the setup program doesn't fail. On more than one occasion, I've had to restart the setup program because I forgot the items on this list:

- Decompress your disks. You can't install Windows 2000 Professional on a compressed disk because the operating system doesn't support any compression technologies other than its own.

- Disconnect the UPS (uninterruptible power supply) from the computer's serial port. The setup program's hardware-detection process probes each serial port. Not only does this start the UPS beeping like a smoke detector on a low battery, it also confuses the operating system by incorrectly reporting information about the serial port.

- Disable BIOS virus protection and shut down any virus scanners such as Norton Antivirus. Both prevent the setup program from working properly and virus scanners that vendors designed for earlier versions of Windows will not work in Windows 2000 Professional.

- Disable third-party network clients and services, particularly those that might interfere with the setup program. The exception is network clients and services required to install Windows 2000 Professional from the network, of course.

- Shut down applications that are not essential to run the setup program. These include Microsoft Windows Explorer or any other program that might interfere with the setup program.

After cleaning the computer by minimizing the trouble spots, double-check the computer's settings, making sure that everything works properly. Check everything. In Windows 98's Device Manager, make sure you don't see any little yellow or red icons and, if you do, fix the problem. Make sure that your network connections are working properly and that you have access to the resources that you expect. Windows 2000 Professional's setup program migrates your settings from the operating system you're upgrading. By getting these settings right in an environment with which you are already familiar, you don't have to struggle to fix problems in a somewhat alien environment. In other words, pay a little now or a lot later.

Note
After upgrading from Windows 98 to Windows 2000 Professional, you can't go back. You can't uninstall Windows 2000 Professional and you can't upgrade Windows 98 over it.

Step-by-Step

To start the setup program, you need either the Windows 2000 Professional CD-ROM or access to a network share that contains the source files. Insert the CD-ROM. If the setup program doesn't start automatically, run it yourself: on the Start menu, click <u>R</u>un, and then type **d:\i386\winnt32.exe**, where *d* is the driver containing the Windows 2000 Professional CD-ROM. If installing from a network share, **type\\server\share\i386\winnt32.exe** in the Run dialog box, where *server* is the name of the server and *share* is the name of the share. No matter how you start the setup program, the following instructions walk you step-by-step through the remainder of the process:

1. Click Yes to confirm that you're upgrading.

2. On the Welcome to the Windows 2000 Setup Wizard screen, click Upgrade to Windows 2000 (Recommended), and then click Next.

3. On the License Agreement screen, read the license agreement, click I accept this agreement, and then click Next.

4. On the Preparing to Upgrade to Windows 2000 screen, read the steps that the setup program will perform, and then click Next.

5. On the Domain Logon screen, do one of the following:

   - Click Yes to continue logging on to the domain configured in Windows 98 and then click Next. The setup program asks you to create a new computer account or to locate an existing computer account. Follow the instructions you see on the screen for doing this.

   - Click No to install Windows 2000 Professional without connecting to a domain and then click Next.

6. On the Provide Upgrade Packs screen, do one of the following:

   - Click Yes, I have upgrade packs to provide upgrade packs that make already-installed programs work in Windows 2000 Professional. Follow the instructions you see in the Provide Upgrade Packs screen.

   - Click No, I don't have any upgrade packs if you don't have any upgrade packs.

7. On the Upgrading to the Windows 2000 NTFS File System screen, do one of the following:

   - Click Yes, upgrade my drive to convert the volume to which you're installing Windows 2000 Professional to the NTFS file system.

   - Click No, do not upgrade my drive if you don't want to convert any drives to NTFS.

8. On the Upgrade Report screen, read the upgrade report and then click Next.

   If any item in the upgrade report indicates that you should address the issue before continuing, click Cancel to stop the setup program. Likewise, use your intuition and make sure that everything in the upgrade report sits well with you before going any further with the setup process.

9. On the Ready to Install Windows 2000 screen, read the description of the remaining steps and then click Next to continue.

After this point, the setup process is automatic. The setup program won't ask you any more questions, and the next time you touch the keyboard will be to log on to Windows 2000 Professional for the first time.

10. On the Password Creation dialog box, type the password for Administrator in <u>N</u>ew Password and in <u>C</u>onfirm New Password.

See also

- Chapter 1, "Installing Windows," for a plethora of more advanced setup options. It describes the setup program's command-line options as well as other setup techniques.

First Logon

Unlike Windows 98, you can't bypass the Log On to Windows dialog box. You must provide a user name and password. Initially, Windows 2000 Professional fills <u>U</u>ser name with Administrator but, if you're logging on to a domain and have an account on that domain, you can type over Administrator with your actual user name:

1. In <u>U</u>ser name, type your user name.

2. In <u>P</u>assword, type the password that matches the user name you typed in step 1.

If you want more than a few minutes to log on to the computer, the Log On to Windows dialog box goes away and you see the Welcome to Windows window. This window instructs you to press Ctrl+Alt+Del to log on to Windows 2000 Professional. This requirement is for your own protection. It prevents a clever user from creating a Trojan horse that collects your credentials by simulating the Log On to Windows dialog box.

Note

After upgrading from Windows 98 to Windows 2000 Professional, you'll notice minor changes in the logon process. Your existing logon scripts work fine. In fact, because Windows 2000 Professional supports more options in MS-DOS commands, you can create even more advanced logon scripts. The operating system won't load policies from the network the same way that Windows 98 loaded them. It doesn't look for the file called Config.pol in the Netlogon share. However, Windows 98 *tattoos* the registry with policies and those settings still exist in the registry. Windows 98 policies might still affect what you do, even after upgrading to Windows 2000 Professional.

See also

- Chapter 12, "Networking Your Computer," for more information about how to use network resources in Windows 2000 Professional.

- Chapter 11, "Securing Your Computer," to learn more about the logon process and more about how Windows 2000 Professional uses security.

Common Tasks

The remainder of this chapter helps you find things that have moved. For example, if you want to add a printer, where do you do that now? Where is the Folder Options dialog box hiding now? Although these sections get you started, you must still see the appropriate chapters in this book to learn about these tasks in detail:

- "Administration" contains tasks such as using system tools or adding printers. For more information, see Chapter 8, "Managing the Computer."

- "Communications" contains tasks such as connecting to the Internet or configuring modems. For more information, see Chapter 14, "Connecting to the Internet."

- "Disk Management" contains tasks that you'd do with disks, such as formatting system disks. For more information, see Chapter 7, "Managing Disks and Files."

- "Files and Folders" contains tasks that you'd normally do in Windows Explorer. For more information, see Chapter 7, "Managing Disks and Files."

- "Hardware" contains tasks such as configuring hardware or changing a device's settings. For more information, see Chapter 3, "Configuring Hardware."

- "MS-DOS Prompt" contains tasks related to the MS-DOS command prompt, including opening it. For more information, see Chapter 5, "Installing Applications."

- "Networking" contains tasks related to connecting to and using network connections. For more information, see Chapter 12, "Networking Your Computer."

Administration

Changes to the way you administer your computer include the following:

- Printers is now in Control Panel. In Control Panel, double-click the Printers icon.

- The Regional Settings icon is now the Regional Options icon. Settings in both dialog boxes are roughly the same, however.

- Scheduled Tasks is now in Control Panel. In Control Panel, double-click the Schedule Tasks icon. Other than new capabilities, adding tasks works similarly in both operating systems.

- The Users icon is now the Users and Passwords icon. Rather than changing users' profiles, the purposes of both are similar.
- Most of the remaining administrative tools are now in Control Panel. In Control Panel, double-click the Administrative Tools icon and then double-click the Computer Management icon.
- Windows 2000 Professional doesn't have an equivalent of Registry Checker, but you can back up the registry using Microsoft Windows Backup.

Communications

Changes to the way you communicate include these:

- By default, Favorites isn't on the Start menu. To add it, click Properties on the taskbar's shortcut menu. On the Advanced tab's Start Menu Settings list, select Display Favorites.
- On the Start menu, the Find menu is now the Search menu. The commands on this menu are similar, but they open Windows Explorer, not the Find dialog box as they did in Windows 98.
- The Internet icon is now the Internet Options icon. The settings in the Internet Options dialog box are similar in both resulting dialog boxes.
- The Modems icon is now the Modem Options icon.

Disk Management

Changes to disk management include the following:

- In Windows 2000 Professional, Disk Defragmenter is part of Computer Management. In Control Panel, double-click the Administrative Tools icon and then double-click the Computer Management icon. In Computer Management's tree pane, click Disk Defragmenter. Using both tools is similar.
- Windows 2000 Professional provides no way to format a 3.5-inch disk and transfer system files to it in order to make a bootable disk. Thus, if you want to create an MS-DOS bootable disk, you must use another operating system such as Windows 98.
- Compression Agent doesn't exist in Windows 2000 Professional and the operating system doesn't support DriveSpace or DoubleSpace disk compression. To compress a disk, click Properties on the disk's shortcut menu and then select the Compress drive to save disk space check box.

Files and Folders

Changes to the way you work with files and folder include the following:

- Windows Explorer has a new location on the Start menu. Point to Programs, point to Accessories, and then click Windows Explorer.

- In Windows 2000 Professional, you configure Active Desktop using the Folder Options dialog box.

- In Windows 2000 Professional, open the Folder Options dialog box by clicking Folder Options on the Tools menu.

Hardware

Changes to the way you configure hardware include the following:

- The Power Management icon is now the Power Options icon. The options in both resulting dialog boxes are similar, but Windows 2000 Professional adds support for uninterrupted power supplies.

- Device Manager has a new location. In Control Panel, double-click the Administrative Tools icon and then double-click the Computer Management icon. In Computer Management's tree pane, click Device Manager.

- The System Properties dialog box is different. In Windows 2000 Professional, it has the following tabs: General, Network Identification, Hardware, User Profiles, and Advanced. Most of the settings in this dialog box require administrative rights.

- Windows 2000 Professional combines the Sounds and Multimedia icons into a single Sounds and Multimedia icon. The options are similar, however.

MS-DOS Prompt

Changes to MS-DOS that you'll notice include the following:

- The command prompt has a new name on the Start menu. On the Start menu, point to Programs, point to Accessories, and click Command Prompt.

- Instead of starting a command prompt by typing **command** in the Run dialog box, you start a command prompt by typing **cmd** in the same dialog box.

- Almost all MS-DOS commands have more options in Windows 2000. Professional than they do in Windows 98. To learn more about a command's option, type **command /?** at the command prompt.

Networking

Changes to networking that you should know about include the following:

- To change settings that were in the Configuration tab of the Network dialog box, double-click the Network and Dial-up Connections icon in Control Panel and then double-click the Local Area Connection icon.

- To change settings that were in the Identification tab of the Network dialog box, double-click the System icon in Control Panel and then click the Network Identification tab.

- The settings that were in the Access Control tab of the Network dialog box don't exist in Windows 2000 Professional. The operating system always uses user-level access control, never share-level access control.

- Network Neighborhood is now My Network Places. The organization of My Network Places is different, too. The first folder is Entire Network, followed by the name of the client, followed by each domain or workgroup on the network. Within each domain or workgroup is a list of each computer on it.

- Dial-Up Networking is now Network and Dial-Up Connections. In Control Panel, double-click the Network and Dial-up Connections icon. To add a new networking connection, double-click the Make New Connection icon.

- By default, Logoff isn't on the Start menu. To add it, click Properties on the taskbar's shortcut menu. On the Advanced tab's Start Menu Settings list, select Display Logoff.

- To change your password, press Ctrl+Alt+Del. This won't restart the computer. Click Change Password.

C

Quick Start for Windows NT 4.0 Users

Aᴌᴛʜᴏᴜɢʜ Mɪᴄʀᴏsᴏғᴛ Wɪɴᴅᴏᴡs 98 ᴜsᴇʀs ʜᴀᴠᴇ a steep learning curve when they upgrade to Microsoft Windows 2000 Professional, Microsoft NT Workstation 4.0 users do not. They're already familiar with the concepts that take a bit of work for users to understand, including security, NTFS, and user profiles. For that reason, this appendix is briefer than Appendix B.

What you learn in this appendix is how to quickly upgrade your computer so that it's running Windows 2000 Professional. The upgrade instructions are very similar to upgrading from Windows 98. This appendix also helps you locate familiar utilities and Control Panel icons that are in different places in Windows 2000 Professional. This alone will be the greatest source of frustration for users who upgrade because experienced Windows NT Workstation 4.0 users will find Windows 2000 Professional a joy to work with.

Life Gets Better

My tone in Appendix B, "Quick Start for Windows 98 Users," might have lead you to believe that I'm down on Windows 2000 Professional. Far from the truth—Windows 2000 Professional is going to be a stretch for many Windows 98 users, but Windows NT Workstation 4.0 users are going to be in hog heaven. Here are the reasons why:

- Windows 2000 Professional supports almost all the devices that Windows NT Workstation 4.0 supports (with the exception of devices that are retired) and many more devices. In fact, Windows 2000 Professional supports whole classes of devices that Windows NT Workstation 4.0 never supported, including USB and IEEE 1394 (Firewire) devices.

- Windows 2000 Professional supports almost any program that Windows NT Workstation 4.0 supports, and many more. Some programs that only worked in Windows 98 and whole new breeds of programs all work in Windows 2000 Professional.

- Windows 2000 Professional supports DirectX 7, which means that many more games are going to be available for Windows 2000 Professional.

- Varieties of user interface enhancements make Windows 200 Professional easier to use than ever before. Some features are long in coming, such as the new Open With menu that makes opening unknown types of files in applications easier. Others make finding documents quicker.

- Administrative tools are better consolidated in Control Panel. Rather than looking in several different places, you find them in one place. Although some users find this frustrating because they have to go digging around to find an administrative tool, after you get used to their new locations, they're easier to access.

- Configuration is easier. For example, configuring network connections is almost a no-brainer because the default settings work on most Microsoft networks. Configuring hardware is easy now that Windows 2000 Professional is Plug and Play-capable.

- Windows 2000 Professional is more stable and stays up-and-running longer. For example, Windows 2000 Professional doesn't require that you restart the computer after seemingly trivial configuration changes. Also, features such as System File Protection prevent setup programs from errantly overwriting system files and damaging the system's stability.

- Windows 2000 Professional performs better than Windows NT Workstation 4.0. The performance gains are slight but noticeable.

Yes, I'm very bullish on Windows 2000 Professional for users of Windows NT Workstation 4.0. It has all the traditional strengths of the NT technologies and many more features that make it a better operating system.

Professional Upgrade

Two methods you can use to install Windows 2000 Professional are upgrading from a previous version of Windows and installing a new copy of the operating system. Upgrade if you want to replace your Windows NT Workstation 4.0 with Windows 2000 Professional and you want to keep your existing files and preferences. Install a new copy of Windows 2000 Professional if you don't want to keep existing files and preferences or you want to use both Windows NT Workstation 4.0 and Windows 2000 Professional. The differences between each method are distinct, as follows:

- **Upgrade** The setup program installs Windows 2000 Professional in the same folder as Windows NT Workstation 4.0, replacing its files but preserving as many of its settings as possible.

- **New Install** The setup program installs Windows 2000 Professional in a new folder, doesn't replace Windows NT Workstation 4.0's files, and doesn't use the existing settings. You must reinstall each application you want to use in Windows 2000 Professional.

Note

You can't install Windows 2000 Professional on a computer that already has two operating systems. In other words, if you already installed Windows 98 and Windows NT Workstation 4.0 in a dual-boot configuration, Windows 2000 Professional's setup program will complain about it and not let you install it. The only solution is to remove one of the operating systems. The setup program won't even let you upgrade one of the other operating systems.

See also

- Chapter 1, "Installing Windows," for more information about installing Windows 2000 Professional. In addition to describing how to upgrade from Windows NT Workstation 4.0, this chapter also describes how to use both operating systems at the same time.

Preparation

Windows 2000 Professional's setup program can generate an upgrade report without putting you through the actual upgrade process. This report is applicable only when upgrading from an earlier version of Windows. It lists the software that will not work as well as the software that requires upgrade packs in order to work properly. It also reports any 32-bit device drivers that won't work in Windows 2000 Professional. At the MS-DOS command prompt or in the Run dialog box, type **winnt32 /checkupgradeonly** to generate an upgrade report.

Before upgrading to Windows 2000 Professional, record your computer's hardware configuration. The information will come in handy if you run into problems later. This is particularly true if you're using legacy device that no Plug and Play operating system can configure. These might be network interface cards that you manually configured by setting jumpers or switches. Windows NT Workstation 4.0 has an easy way to record your computer's configuration. Use Microsoft Windows Diagnostics to print the computer's configuration, including the resources that each device uses.

Gather the following network settings before starting Windows 2000 Professional's setup program:

- Computer name
- Domain or workgroup name
- IP address, if using static IP addresses
- WINS or DNS server IP address
- Other network settings, as required

These settings are in the Network Properties dialog box and probably won't change for Windows 2000 Professional. Check with the administrator, however, to make sure you don't need to use a different computer name, domain name, etc.

The most important thing you can do before installing Windows 2000 Professional is back up the computer. Do a full backup, if possible, so that you can easily restore the computer if something goes awry. As much as I'd like to tell you that installing the operating system is always successful, it just isn't so. On a number of occasions, I had to give up and restore the previous configuration because the hardware just wasn't compatible with the new operating system. On Windows NT Workstation 4.0's Start menu, choose Programs, followed by Administrative Tools (Common), and then click Backup.

Just prior to starting Windows 2000 Professional's setup program, clean up the computer to make sure the setup program doesn't fail. On more than one occasion, I've had to restart the setup program because I forgot the items on this list:

- Disconnect the UPS (uninterruptible power supply) from the computer's serial port. The setup program's hardware-detection process probes each serial port. Not only does this start the UPS beeping like a smoke detector on a low battery, it confuses the operating system by incorrectly reporting information about the serial port.

- Disable BIOS virus protection and shut down any virus scanners such as Norton Antivirus. Both prevent the setup program from working properly, and virus scanners that vendors designed for earlier versions of Windows will not work in Windows 2000 Professional.

- Disable third-party network clients and services, particularly those that might interfere with the setup program. The exception are the network clients and services required to install Windows 2000 Professional from the network, of course.

- Shut down applications that are not essential to run the setup program. These include Microsoft Windows Explorer or any other program that might interfere with the setup program.

After cleaning the computer by minimizing the trouble spots, double-check the computer's settings, making sure everything works properly. Check everything. Make sure your network connections are working properly and that you have access to the resources that you expect. Windows 2000 Professional's setup program migrates your settings from the operating system you're upgrading. By getting these settings right in an environment with which you are already familiar, you don't have to struggle to fix problems in a somewhat alien environment. In other words, pay a little now or a lot later.

Note

After upgrading from Windows NT Workstation 4.0 to Windows 2000 Professional, you can't go back. You can't uninstall Windows 2000 Professional and you can't install Windows NT Workstation 4.0 over it.

Step-by-Step

To start the setup program, you need either the Windows 2000 Professional CD-ROM or access to a network share that contains the source files. Insert the CD-ROM. If the setup program doesn't start automatically, run it yourself: On the Start menu, click <u>R</u>un, and then type **d:\i386\winnt32.exe**, where *d* is the driving containing the Windows 2000 Professional CD-ROM. If installing from a network share, type ***server\\share*\\i386\\winnt32.exe** in the Run dialog box, where *server* is the name of the server and *share* is the name of the share. No matter how you start the setup program, the following instructions walk you step-by-step through the remainder of the process:

1. Click <u>Y</u>es to confirm you're upgrading.

2. On the Welcome to the Windows 2000 Setup Wizard screen, click <u>U</u>pgrade to Windows 2000 (Recommended) and then click <u>N</u>ext.

3. On the License Agreement screen, read the license agreement, click I <u>a</u>ccept this agreement, and then click <u>N</u>ext.

4. On the Preparing to Upgrade to Windows 2000 screen, read the steps that the setup program will perform and then click <u>N</u>ext.

5. On the Domain Logon screen, do one of the following:

   - Click <u>Y</u>es to continue logging on to the domain configured in Windows NT Workstation 4.0 and then click <u>N</u>ext.

The setup program asks you to create a new computer account or to locate an existing computer account. Follow the instructions you see onscreen for doing this.

- Click <u>N</u>o to install Windows 2000 Professional without connecting to a domain and then click <u>N</u>ext.

6. On the Provide Upgrade Packs screen, do one of the following:

- Click <u>Y</u>es, I have upgrade packs to provide upgrade packs that make already-installed programs work in Windows 2000 Professional.

  Follow the instructions you see in the Provide Upgrade Packs screen.

- Click No, I don't have any upgrade packs if you don't have any upgrade packs.

7. On the Upgrading to the Windows 2000 NTFS File System screen, do one of the following:

- Click <u>Y</u>es, upgrade my drive to convert the volume to which you're installing Windows 2000 Professional to the NTFS file system.

- Click <u>N</u>o, do not upgrade my drive if you don't want to convert any drives to NTFS.

8. On the Upgrade Report screen, read the upgrade report and then click <u>N</u>ext.

   If any item in the upgrade report indicates that you should address the issue before continuing, click Cancel to stop the setup program. Likewise, use your intuition and make sure everything in the upgrade report sits well with you before going any further with the setup process.

9. On the Ready to Install Windows 2000 screen, read the description of the remaining steps and then click <u>N</u>ext to continue.

   After this point, the setup process is automatic. The setup program won't ask you any more questions and the next time you touch the keyboard will be to log on to Windows 2000 Professional for the first time.

10. On the Password Creation dialog box, type the password for Administrator in <u>N</u>ew Password and in <u>C</u>onfirm New Password.

Note

After upgrading from Windows NT Workstation 4.0 to Windows 2000 Professional, you'll notice minor changes in the logon process. Your existing logon scripts work fine. The operating system won't load policies from the network the same way that Windows NT Workstation 4.0 loaded them. It doesn't look for the file called Ntonfig.pol in the Netlogon share. However, Windows NT Workstation 4.0 *tattoos* the registry with policies and those settings still exist in the registry. Windows NT Workstation 4.0 policies might still affect what you do, even after upgrading to Windows 2000 Professional.

See also

- Chapter 1, "Installing Windows," describes a plethora of more advanced setup options. It describes the setup program's command-line options as well as other setup techniques.

- Chapter 12, "Networking Your Computer," for more information about how to use network resources in Windows 2000 Professional.

- Chapter 11, "Securing Your Computer," to learn more about the logon process and more about how Windows 2000 Professional uses security.

Common Tasks

The remainder of this chapter helps you find things that have moved. For example, if you want to add a printer, where do you do that now? Where is the Folder Options dialog box hiding now? Although these sections get you started, you must still see the appropriate chapters in this book to learn about these tasks in detail:

- "Administration" contains tasks such as using system tools or adding printers. For more information, see Chapter 8, "Managing the Computer."

- "Communications" contains tasks such as connecting to the Internet or configuring modems. For more information, see Chapter 14, "Connecting to the Internet."

- "Disk Management" contains tasks that you do with disks, such as formatting system disks. For more information, see Chapter 7, "Managing Disks and Files."

- "Files and Folders" contains tasks that you normally do in Windows Explorer. For more information, see Chapter 7, "Managing Disks and Files."

- "Hardware" contains tasks such as configuring hardware or changing a device's settings. For more information, see Chapter 3, "Configuring Hardware."

- "MS-DOS Prompt" contains tasks related to the MS-DOS command prompt, including opening it. For more information, see Chapter 5, "Installing Applications."

- "Networking" contains tasks related to connecting to and using network connections. For more information, see Chapter 12, "Networking Your Computer."

Administration

Changes to the way you administer your computer include the following:

- Most of the tools on the Administrative Tools (Common) menu are now in Control Panel. In Control Panel, double-click the Administrative Tools icon.

- Printers is now in Control Panel. In Control Panel, double-click the Printers icon.

- The Regional Settings icon is now the Regional Options icon. Settings in both dialog boxes are roughly the same, however.

- Scheduled Tasks is now in Control Panel. In Control Panel, double-click the Schedule Tasks icon. Other than new capabilities, adding tasks works similarly in both operating systems.

- The Services icon is missing from Control Panel. To configure services, double-click the Administrative Tools icon in Control Panel and then double-click the Computer Management icon. In Computer Management's tree pane, click Services.

- Event Viewer is in Computer Management. In Control Panel, double-click the Administrative Tools icon and then double-click the Computer Management icon. In Computer Management's tree pane, click Event Viewer.

- Performance Monitor is now System Monitor. In Control Panel, double-click Administrative Tools and then click Performance.

- Windows NT Diagnostics doesn't exist in Windows 2000 Professional. Use System Information to collect the same types of information and more. In Control Panel, double-click the Administrative Tools icon and then double-click the Computer Management icon. In Computer Management's tree pane, click System Information.

- Windows 2000 Professional doesn't have Rdisk, the tool you used to create emergency repair disks, but you can create the disks by using Microsoft Windows Backup.

Communications

Changes to the way you communicate include the following:

- Remote Access Admin is now built into the Network and Dial-up Connections folder. In Control Panel, double-click the Network and Dial-up Connections icon. To create a new connection, double-click the Make New Connection icon.

- By default, Favorites isn't on the Start menu. To add it, click Properties on the taskbar's shortcut menu. On the Advanced tab's Start Menu Settings list, select Display Favorites.

- On the Start menu, the Find menu is now the Search menu. The commands on this menu are similar, but they open Windows Explorer, not the Find dialog box as they did in Windows 98.
- The Modems icon is now the Modem Options icon.

Consoles

Changes to the way you configure and use consoles include the following:

- The Console icon is missing from Control Panel. You configure consoles by clicking Properties on a console window's system menu.
- Most MS-DOS commands that you can use in a console have new command-line options available.

Disk Management

Changes to disk management include the following:

- Disk Manager is now called Disk Management and is part of Disk Management. In Control Panel, double-click the Administrative Tools icon and then double-click the Computer Management icon. In Computer Management's tree pane, click Disk Management.

Files and Folders

Changes to the way you work with files and folder include:

- Windows Explorer has a new location on the Start menu. Point to Programs, point to Accessories, and then click Windows Explorer.
- In Windows 2000 Professional, you configure Active Desktop using the Folder Options dialog box.
- In Windows 2000 Professional, open the Folder Options dialog box by clicking Folder Options on the Tools menu.

Hardware

Changes to the way you configure hardware include the following:

- The PC Card (PCMCIA) icon is missing from Control Panel. Configure PC Card devices using Device Manager. Double-click the Administrative Tools icon in Control Panel and then double-click the Computer Management icon. In Computer Management's tree pane, click Device Manager.

- The Ports icon is missing from Control Panel. Configure ports using Device Manager. Double-click the Administrative Tools icon in Control Panel and then double-click the Computer Management icon. In Computer Management's tree pane, click Device Manager.

- The SCSI Adapters icon is missing from Control Panel. Configure SCSI adapters using Device Manager. Double-click the Administrative Tools icon in Control Panel and then double-click the Computer Management icon. In Computer Management's tree pane, click Device Manager.

- The Tape Devices icon is missing from Control Panel. Configure tape devices using Device Manager. Double-click the Administrative Tools icon in Control Panel and then double-click the Computer Management icon. In Computer Management's tree pane, click Device Manager.

- The Devices icon is missing from Control Panel. Add new hardware by double-clicking the Add/Remove Hardware icon in Control Panel. Configure hardware by double-clicking the Administrative Tools icon and then double-click the Computer Management icon. In Computer Management's tree pane, click Device Manager.

- Windows 2000 Professional combines the Sounds and Multimedia icons into a single Sounds and Multimedia icon. The options are similar, however.

Networking

Changes to networking that you should know about include the following:

- The Dial-Up Monitor icon is missing from Control Panel. To monitor dial-up and local area network connections, double-click the Network and Dial-up Connections folder in Control Panel.

- To change settings that were in the Identification tab of the Network dialog box, double-click the System icon in Control Panel and then click the Network Identification tab.

- To change settings that were in the Services tab of the Network dialog box, double-click the Network and Dial-up Connections icon in Control Panel and then double-click the Local Area Connection icon.

- To change settings that were in the Protocols tab of the Network dialog box, double-click the Network and Dial-up Connections icon in Control Panel and then double-click the Local Area Connection icon.

- To change settings that were in the Adapters tab of the Network dialog box, double-click the Administrative Tools icon and then double-click the Computer Management icon. In Computer Management's tree pane, click Device Manager.

- To change settings that were in the Bindings tab of the Network dialog box, double-click Network and Dial-up Connections icon in Control Panel and then double-click the Local Area Connection icon.

- Network Neighborhood is now My Network Places. The organization of My Network Places is different, too. The first folder is Entire Network, followed by the name of the client, followed by each domain or workgroup on the network. Within each domain or workgroup is a list of each computer on it.

- By default, Logoff isn't on the Start menu. To add it, click Properties on the taskbar's shortcut menu. On the Advanced tab's Start Menu Settings list, select Display Logoff.

D

Frequently Asked Questions

THIS APPENDIX CONTAINS A LIST OF FREQUENTLY asked questions (FAQs) and my answers to them. In most cases, each answer contains a reference to a chapter in this book that contains more information. Many of these questions I mined from the beta newsgroups, particularly the questions that I thought might interest new users.

The topics that I cover in this appendix include the following:

- General
- Hardware
- Applications
- Installation
- Networking
- Administration
- User Interface

General Questions

Is Windows 2000 Professional stable enough to use?   I feel good about recommending Windows 2000 Professional to anyone. It has many more useful features than any previous version of Windows. It also crashes less and stays up-and-running as long or longer than Windows NT Workstation 4.0. My answer is *yes*.

What does history say about the initial release of Windows 2000 Professional?   The closest thing to the release of Windows 2000 Professional was the release of Windows 95. Learning from previous experience, the initial release will come with somewhat poor device support and with a number of bugs that haven't yet been addressed. Microsoft will quickly follow up to address issues that didn't get addressed in the initial release. None of these issues should deter most users from upgrading to Windows 2000 Professional, but some organizations will likely wait until the first few service releases before adopting this new operating system.

Why did Microsoft change the name from Windows NT Workstation 5.0 to Windows 2000 Professional?   Microsoft's marketing department had too much time on their hands. They feel like that any confusion that the name change will cause is worth communicating the vision that this is an operating system for a new millennium. A key position that they want to enforce is that this operating system isn't just for high-end workstations such as graphics and CAD. It is for everyday business use.

Installation Questions

What's the most important thing to do before installing Windows 2000 Professional?   There are actually three important things you should do. First, back up all the files on your computer. Second, record your computer's configuration, including the resources used by each device. Third, create an upgrade report so you'll know in advance about any potential compatibility problems and how to resolve them. For information about all these tasks, see Chapter 1, "Installing Windows."

What different methods can I use for installing Windows 2000 Professional?   Two methods are available. First, you can upgrade your existing operating system to Windows 2000 Professional. Upgrade paths are available from Windows 95, Windows 98, Windows NT Workstation 3.51, and Windows NT Workstation 4.0. The second method is to install a new copy of the operating system. You can install on a freshly formatted hard disk or you can install on another disk and share the computer with two different operating systems. For more information about either method, see Chapter 1, "Installing Windows."

For novice users, what's the best way to install Windows 2000 Professional?   Installing and configuring a new operating system is beyond the capabilities of most novice users. These users should consider upgrading their existing operating system so that Windows 2000 Professional's setup program can use the existing operating system's settings. See Chapter 1, "Installing Windows."

For technically savvy users, what's the best way to install Windows 2000 Professional? Technical users will appreciate getting a fresh start by removing all the artifacts from their computers. These users are also capable of installing and configuring a new operating system. For best results, I recommend that they back up important files, format the hard disk, and install Windows 2000 Professional after starting the computer with an MS–DOS boot disk.

Can I use Windows 98 and Windows 2000 Professional on the same computer? Yes. If you install Windows 2000 Professional on a different disk from the disk Windows 98 is already installed on, you have a dual-boot configuration. The only caveat is that the active partition must be a FAT volume, not NTFS. Also, don't try installing both operating systems on the same volume because the result is an unpredictably unstable system that's likely to choke in the future.

Can I use Windows NT Workstation 4.0 and Windows 2000 Professional on the same computer? Yes. See the previous FAQ—the same rules apply. Do note that Windows NT Workstation 4.0s can't read NTFS volumes that Windows 2000 Professional creates without the appropriate device drivers. See Chapter 1, "Installing Windows," to learn how to update Windows NT Workstation 4.0 so that it can read NTFS 5 volumes.

Hardware Questions

Will my current hardware work in Windows 2000 Professional? Common hardware will work in Windows 2000 Professional. Many hundreds of device drivers are included on the Windows 2000 Professional CD-ROM (some devices the operating system doesn't fully support). The operating system doesn't support less-common devices at all. The problem almost always stems from not having a device driver that's compatible with Windows 2000 Professional. To help test whether your devices are compatible and learn how to overcome problems, see Chapter 3, "Configuring Hardware."

How do I know whether a device is compatible with Windows 2000 Professional before purchasing it? Check Microsoft's hardware-compatibility list. The address is `http://www.microsoft.com/hcl`.

What are the minimum requirements for installing Windows 2000 Professional? My recommendations differ from Microsoft's—they're less optimistic. You must have a Pentium II or compatible processor with at least 96 megabytes of memory and a disk with 650 megabytes of free disk space. The desktop gets cluttered with anything but a 17-inch monitor attached to an SVGA video adapter. Last, using Windows 2000 Professional without a mouse is frustrating.

What are the differences between ACPI and APM power management?
A computer's BIOS is responsible for APM power management and the operating system has very little control over it. Thus, managing the power of individual devices is difficult with APM. ACPI moves control of power management to the operating system, which gives it more control over individual devices. Some of the key benefits to ACPI is the *always on* computer that actually goes to sleep when you turn it off and comes up instantly when you turn it on. For more information, see Chapter 3, "Configuring Hardware."

What's the big deal with USB devices? USB devices overcome a few limitations in the Intel architecture. First, Intel-based computers have a limit on the number of devices you can install in them because only a limited number of resources are available. You can chain many different USB devices together, however, all of which share the same resources in the computer. Another limitation is cost. USB devices are reasonably priced as opposed to devices that use more proprietary technology. Examples of low-cost USB devices include video cameras, speakers, keyboards, and mice. The last limitation is that USB devices are not only Plug and Play-capable, but they're also hot-pluggable, which means that you can insert and remove USB devices while the computer is running. If possible, and you own a computer with USB ports, purchase USB devices. For more information, see Chapter 3, "Configuring Hardware."

Does Windows 2000 Professional support DirectX version 7? Yes. For more information, see Chapter 3, "Configuring Hardware."

How does Windows 2000 Professional's mobile support compare with Windows 98? Windows 98 and Windows 2000 Professional have many mobile-computing features in common. Both support Briefcase. Both support Plug and Play, docking and undocking, and power-management features that stretch out batteries' lives. Windows 2000 Professional has more advanced features that make disconnecting from the network and taking your work with you a better experience. Offline Files and Folders is the most notable new feature for mobile users. For more information about this feature, see Chapter 13, "Using Mobile Computers."

Do I need to configure hardware profiles if I'm using a portable computer? No. In general, Windows 2000 Professional automatically configures hardware profiles for your docked and undocked configurations. For more information, see Chapter 13, "Using Mobile Computers," and Chapter 3, "Configuring Hardware."

Applications Questions

What's the hubbub about System File Protection? System File Protection prevents hardware and software setup programs from overwriting system files that Windows 2000 Professional protects. System File Protection creates more work for developers, but it makes the operating system more stable by preventing errant changes. Chapter 7, "Managing Disks and Files," contains more information about this feature.

Does Windows 2000 Professional have a boot menu like Windows 98's boot menu? Advanced Options menu, the boot menu, is one of many useful features that Windows 2000 Professional inherits from Windows 98. This menu helps you troubleshoot computers that aren't working properly. You learn more about the boot menu in Chapter 2, "Troubleshooting Setup."

How can I get control of my computer back quickly after a program crashes? Each time an application crashes or generates an application error, Dr. Watson stores information about the event in a log file and makes a snapshot of memory. The purpose of these two items is to help technicians diagnose the problem. Even on fast computers, the process is frustrating because it takes so long and prevents you from getting back to work. In order to disable this troubleshooting feature, type *SystemRoot***\system32\drwtsn32.exe** in the Run dialog box. In the Options area, deselect the Create Crash Dump File check box. See Chapter 2, "Troubleshooting Setup."

Will my applications work in Windows 2000 Professional? Based upon sales statistics from third-party sources, Microsoft tested the most popular applications with Windows 2000 Professional. Indeed, most of them work properly, as my own experiences testing popular applications with the operating system have proven. Less-popular applications and applications that use operating system-specific features might not work properly, however. If in doubt, check the independent software vendor's Web site for more information about upgrading the application. Alternatively, check Microsoft's site, http://www.microsoft.com/windows, for information about the compatibility of your software and to see whether Microsoft has certified it.

What's the difference between an application, service, and device driver? An *application* is a program that you as a user use to perform a specific task. Tasks include creating documents and browsing the Internet. *Services* are programs that Windows 2000 Professional runs as part of the operating system. Services provide, well, . . . services that the operating system requires. Examples include the event log, disk manager, network client, and installation services. *Device drivers* are the links between the operating system and the devices you install on the computer. Each device driver knows how to communicate directly with a device, causing it to function as you'd expect. For more information about applications, see Chapter 5, "Installing Applications." For more information about services, see Chapter 8, "Managing the Computer." For more information about device drivers, see Chapter 3, "Configuring Hardware."

Networking Questions

Is Windows 2000 Professional good for home networking? Windows 2000 Professional is not suitable as an operating system for use at home unless you're a technically savvy user. Novice users without administrative support will end up frustrated with the very features that make Windows 2000 Professional an ideal business operating system. If you're technically savvy, however, you'll like features like such as automatic IP addressing and Internet Connection Sharing that make setting up a home network easy. For more information, see Chapter 12, "Networking Your Computer."

How is Windows 2000 Professional better for business networking than other Windows? Windows 2000 Professional offers more advanced networking and security features than any previous version of Windows. Network configuration is almost automatic if you're connecting to a Microsoft network. Features such as new authentication protocols and new tunneling protocols make it a highly secure operating system. Finally, connecting to a network that's managed by Windows 2000 Server adds capabilities, such as Group Policy, Active Directory, and Distributed File System, which make it one of the most network-manageable operating systems on the market. For more information about all these features, see Chapter 12, "Networking Your Computer," and Chapter 11, "Securing Your Computer."

Is the logon process any different in Windows 2000 from other Windows processes? Yes. Windows 2000 Professional loads policies the same way that earlier versions of Windows load policies. Also, Windows 2000 Professional supports new authentication protocols that make single sign-on possible.

Administration Questions

How do I defragment my disks like I did in Windows 98? Windows 2000 Professional includes a utility, Disk Defragmenter, which you can use to defragment your disks. Although Windows 98 did include a similar utility, Windows NT Workstation 4.0 did not. For more information about Disk Defragmenter, see Chapter 7, "Managing Disks and Files."

How can I tell which users have accessed what files?   Windows 2000 Professional is a secure operating system, as you learn in Chapter 11, "Securing Your Computer." Part of security is the capability to audit access to any object, including files and folders. Auditing is a three-step process. The first step is to enable the audit policy in Group Policy. The second step is to enable auditing for specific files and folders. The last step is to check the security log to see which users accessed the files and folders you're auditing. Chapter 11 shows you how to do these tasks.

Can I encrypt files so that nobody else can read them?   Yes! A new feature in Windows 2000 Professional is Encrypting File System (EFS). Using EFS, you encrypt individual files or entire folders. Without proper credentials, nobody else can break into your computer and read your files. For more information about EFS, see Chapter 7, "Managing Disks and Files."

What's the best way to protect my computer from viruses?   First, use anti-virus utilities designed for Windows 2000 Professional. Check with any of the anti-virus vendors that Microsoft recommends: http://support.microsoft. com/support/kb/articles/Q49/5/00.ASP. Importantly, don't make logging on as Administrator a regular habit. Use your normal user account because many viruses are opportunistic and require administrative access to the computer in order to do their damage.

I share a computer with other users; how I can control how much disk space they use?   Use disk quotas to limit the amount of disk space that each user sharing a computer can share. You must have administrative rights to set disk quotas, which you presumably have if you're the primary owner of the computer. For more information about using disk quotas, see Chapter 7, "Managing Disks and Files."

How do I compress my disk so that I have more free disk space?   Windows 2000 Professional does not support DriveSpace or DoubleSpace disk compression as Windows 98 does. It has an even more elegant solution. You can compress individual folders, individual files, or entire disks. Disk compression is a feature that's built into the NTFS file system, too, so it's not an afterthought. You learn about more disk compression in Chapter 7, "Managing Disks and Files."

I can't find Registry Checker; where is it in Windows 2000 Professional?   No such utility exists in Windows 2000 Professional. If you want to back up the registry, use Microsoft Windows Backup to back up System State Data or create an Emergency Repair Disk. No utility is yet available to scan the registry for errors. You learn more about using Windows Backup in Chapter 8, "Managing the Computer."

What do I do when Windows 2000 Professional tells me I don't have enough rights?   This is a common frustration for users who do not understand the way security works in Windows 2000 Professional. You can't install many applications or devices with normal user rights. Nor can you change many settings. You can log off and log back on as Administrator to take care of the problem. Alternatively, you can run the utility or the setup program as a different user— a feature called Secondary Logon and more commonly called Run As. To learn more about this feature, see Chapter 11, "Securing Your Computer."

Which is the best file system for me to use: NTFS or FAT?   NTFS is the best file system to use, except in a few circumstances. If you're using Windows 2000 Professional in a dual-boot configuration with an operating system that can't read NTFS volumes, stick with FAT. If you must have access to the disks by starting the computer with an MS-DOS disk, stick with FAT. Otherwise, the benefits of NTFS far outweigh FAT.

User Interface

What are the big new features in the user interface?   This is a good question and one I hear all the time. My favorites include the new capabilities of Windows Explorer, better search features, the new Open With menu, and a more pervasive use of history lists. No single feature is a huge addition to Windows because they're all tiny enhancements that by themselves seem insignificant. Taken together, however, they make Windows 2000 Professional much easier to use than any other version of Windows. For more information about the new user interface features and how to personalize them, see Chapter 4, "Personalizing Windows."

Windows Explorer's right pane is too small; what can I do?   Windows 2000 Professional displays more information than other versions of Windows do in the right pane of Windows Explorer. On smaller screens (or if you're like me and prefer to keep Windows Explorer small), you can use classic folders. On the Tools menu, click Folder Options and then select Use Windows classic folders. Alternatively, you can close the Folders pane by clicking Folders on the toolbar. Next time you need to see the Folders pane, click Folders again.

The accessibility features don't help me; where can I find more advance utilities?   Even though Windows 2000 Professional's accessibility features are innovative and useful for many people, Microsoft designed these features for people's basic needs. You can find more advanced accessibility features by looking for referrals at `http://www.microsoft.com/accessibility`.

Can I create default settings for new users who log on to the computer?
Yes, because users' settings are in their user profile folders. Log in as any user and
then customize the computer as you require. Then, log off and log on as
Administrator and copy the profile folder of the user you configured to the Default
User profile folder. For more information about this technique, see Chapter 8,
"Managing the Computer."

What's the difference between Briefcase and Offline Folders?   In order to
take files with you using Briefcase, you must copy them to a Briefcase. When
you return to the office, you synchronize the Briefcase after connecting to the
network. Briefcase is mainly a manual process that requires a lot of user intervention. Offline Folders is more of an automatic process that can in fact happen with
no user intervention at all, thanks to Active Directory and Group Policy. Also, with
Offline Folders, the files and folders you're taking with you appear in Windows
Explorer in the same locations. You don't have to copy them to another folder
such as a Briefcase. The result is that offline access to network files is much more
intuitive. For more information about using Offline Folders, see Chapter 13,
"Using Mobile Computers."

Index

A

C

I

M

Q-R

S

Windows 2000 Answers

Selected Windows 2000 Titles from New Riders Publishing

Updated edition of New Riders' best-selling *Inside Windows NT 4 Server*. Taking the author-driven, no-nonsense approach we pioneered with our Windows NT *Landmark* books, New Riders proudly offers something unique for Windows 2000 administrators—an interesting and discriminating book on Windows 2000 Server, written by someone in the trenches who can anticipate your situation and provide answers you can trust.

ISBN: 1-56205-929-7

ISBN: 0-7357-0869-X

Architected to be the most navigable, useful, and value-packed reference for Windows 2000, this book uses a creative "telescoping" design that you can adapt to your style of learning. Written by Steven Tate, key Windows 2000 partner and developer of Microsoft's W2K Training Program, it's a concise, focused, quick reference for Windows 2000.

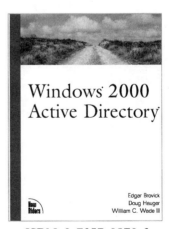

Windows 2000 Active Directory is just one of several new Windows 2000 titles from New Riders' acclaimed *Landmark* series. Focused advice on planning, implementing, and managing the Active Directory in your business.

ISBN: 0-7357-0870-3

Advanced Information on Networking Technologies

New Riders Books Offer Advice and Experience

LANDMARK

Rethinking Computer Books

We know how important it is to have access to detailed, solutions-oriented information on core technologies. *Landmark* books contain the essential information you need to solve technical problems. Written by experts and subjected to rigorous peer and technical reviews, our *Landmark* books are hard-core resources for practitioners like you.

ESSENTIAL REFERENCE

Smart, Like You

The *Essential Reference* series from New Riders provides answers when you know what you want to do but need to know how to do it. Each title skips extraneous material and assumes a strong base of knowledge. These are indispensable books for the practitioner who wants to find specific features of a technology quickly and efficiently. Avoiding fluff and basic material, these books present solutions in an innovative, clean format—and at a great value.

MCSE CERTIFICATION

Engineered for Test Success

New Riders offers a complete line of test preparation materials to help you achieve your certification. With books like the *MCSE Training Guide*, *TestPrep*, and *Fast Track*, and software like the acclaimed *MCSE Complete* and the revolutionary *ExamGear*, New Riders offers comprehensive products built by experienced professionals who have passed the exams and instructed hundreds of candidates.

Books for Networking Professionals

Windows NT Titles

Windows NT TCP/IP
By Karanjit Siyan
1st Edition
480 pages, $29.99
ISBN: 1-56205-887-8

If you're still looking for good documentation on Microsoft TCP/IP, then look no further—this is your book. Windows NT TCP/IP cuts through the complexities and provides the most informative and complete reference book on Windows-based TCP/IP. Concepts essential to TCP/IP administration are explained thoroughly and then are related to the practical use of Microsoft TCP/IP in a real-world networking environment. The book begins by covering TCP/IP architecture and advanced installation and configuration issues, then moves on to routing with TCP/IP, DHCP Management, and WINS/DNS Name Resolution.

Windows NT DNS
By Michael Masterson, Herman L. Knief, Scott Vinick, and Eric Roul
1st Edition
340 pages, $29.99
ISBN: 1-56205-943-2

Have you ever opened a Windows NT book looking for detailed information about DNS only to discover that it doesn't even begin to scratch the surface? DNS is probably one of the most complicated subjects for NT administrators, and there are few books on the market that address it in detail. This book answers your most

complex DNS questions, focusing on the implementation of the Domain Name Service within Windows NT, treating it thoroughly from the viewpoint of an experienced Windows NT professional. Many detailed, real-world examples illustrate further the understanding of the material throughout. The book covers the details of how DNS functions within NT, then explores specific interactions with critical network components. Finally, proven procedures to design and set up DNS are demonstrated. You'll also find coverage of related topics, such as maintenance, security, and troubleshooting.

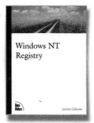

Windows NT Registry
By Sandra Osborne
1st Edition
550 pages, $29.99
ISBN: 1-56205-941-6

The NT Registry can be a very powerful tool for those capable of using it wisely. Unfortunately, there is little information regarding the NT Registry due to Microsoft's insistence that their source code be kept secret. If you're looking to optimize your use of the Registry, you're usually forced to search the Web for bits of information. This book is your resource. It covers critical issues and settings used for configuring network protocols, including NWLink, PTP, TCP/IP, and DHCP. This book approaches the material from a unique point of view, discussing the problems related to a particular component and then discussing settings, which are the actual changes necessary for implementing robust solutions.

Windows NT Performance
Monitoring Benchmarking and Tuning
By Mark Edmead and Paul Hinsberg
1st Edition
288 pages, $29.99
ISBN: 1-56205-942-4

Performance monitoring is a little like pre-ventive medicine for the administrator: No one enjoys a checkup, but it's a good thing to do on a regular basis. This book helps you focus on the critical aspects of improving the performance of your NT system, showing you how to monitor the system, implement benchmarking, and tune your network. The book is organized by resource components, which makes it easy to use as a reference tool.

Windows NT Terminal Server and Citrix MetaFrame
By Ted Harwood
1st Edition
416 pages, $29.99
ISBN: 1-56205-944-0

It's no surprise that most administration headaches revolve around integration with other networks and clients. This book addresses these types of real-world issues on a case-by-case basis, giving tools and advice on solving each problem. The author also offers the real nuts and bolts of thin client administration on multiple systems, covering relevant issues such as installation, configuration, network connection, management, and application distribution.

Windows NT Power Toolkit
By Stu Sjouwerman and Ed Tittel
1st Edition
900 pages, $49.99
ISBN: 0-7357-0922-X

This book covers the analysis, tuning, optimization, automation, enhancement, maintenance, and troubleshooting of Windows NT Server 4.0 and Windows NT Workstation 4.0. In most cases, the two operating systems overlap completely and will be discussed together; in other cases, where the two systems diverge, each platform will be covered separately. This advanced title comprises a task-oriented treatment of the Windows NT 4 environ-ment, including both Windows NT Server 4.0 and Windows NT Workstation 4.0. Thus, this book is aimed squarely at power users, to guide them to painless, effective use of Windows NT both inside and outside the workplace. By concentrat-ing on the use of operating system tools and utilities, Resource Kit elements, and selected third-party tuning, analysis, opti-mization, and productivity tools, this book will show its readers how to carry out everyday and advanced tasks.

Windows NT Network Management: Reducing Total Cost of Ownership
By Anil Desai
1st Edition
400 pages, $34.99
ISBN: 1-56205-946-7

Administering a Windows NT network is like trying to herd cats—an impossible task characterized by constant motion, exhausting labor, and lots of hairballs. Author Anil Desai knows all about it; he's a consulting engineer for Sprint Paranet who specializes in

Windows NT implementation, integration, and management. So we asked him to put together a concise manual of the best practices, a book of tools and ideas that other administrators can turn to again and again in managing their own NT networks.

Planning for Windows 2000
By Eric K. Cone, Jon Boggs, and Sergio Perez
1st Edition
400 pages, $29.99
ISBN: 0-73570-048-6

Windows 2000 is poised to be one of the largest and most important software releases of the next decade, and you are charged with planning, testing, and deploying it in your enterprise. Are you ready? With this book, you will be. *Planning for Windows 2000* lets you know what the upgrade hurdles will be, informs you how to clear them, guides you through effective Active Directory design, and presents you with detailed rollout procedures. Eric K. Cone, Jon Boggs, and Sergio Perez give you the benefit of their extensive experiences as Windows 2000 Rapid Deployment Program members, sharing problems and solutions they've encountered on the job.

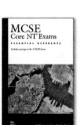

MCSE Core NT Exams Essential Reference
By Matthew Shepker
1st Edition
256 pages, $19.99
ISBN: 0-7357-0006-0

You're sitting in the first session of your Networking Essentials class, the instructor starts talking about RAS, and you have no idea what that means. You think about raising your hand to ask, but you reconsider—you'd feel foolish asking a question in front of all these people. You turn to your handy *MCSE Core NT Exams Essential Reference* and find a quick summary on Remote Access Services. Question answered. It's a couple months later, and you're taking your Networking Essentials exam the next day. You're reviewing practice tests and keep forgetting the maximum lengths for the various commonly used cable types. Once again, you turn to the *MCSE Core NT Exams Essential Reference* and find a table on cables, including all the characteristics you need to memorize in order to pass the test.

BackOffice Titles

Implementing Exchange Server
By Doug Hauger, Marywynne Leon, and William C. Wade III
1st Edition
400 pages, $29.99
ISBN: 1-56205-931-9

If you're interested in connectivity and maintenance issues for Exchange Server, this book is for you. Exchange's power lies in its capability to be connected to multiple email subsystems to create a "universal email backbone." It's not unusual to have several different and complex systems all connected via email gateways, including Lotus Notes or cc:Mail, Microsoft Mail, legacy mainframe systems, and Internet mail. This book covers all of the problems and issues associated with getting an integrated system running smoothly and addresses troubleshooting and diagnosis of email problems with an eye toward prevention and best practices.

Exchange System Administration

By Janice K. Howd
1st Edition
400 pages, $34.99
ISBN: 0-7357-0081-8

Okay, you've got your Exchange Server installed and connected; now what? Email administration is one of the most critical networking jobs, and Exchange can be particularly troublesome in large, heterogeneous environments. Janice Howd, a noted consultant and teacher with over a decade of email administration experience, has put together this advanced, concise handbook for daily, periodic, and emergency administration. With in-depth coverage of topics like managing disk resources, replication, and disaster recovery, this is the one reference book every Exchange administrator needs.

SQL Server System Administration

By Sean Baird, Chris Miller, et al.
1st Edition
352 pages, $29.99
ISBN: 1-56205-955-6

How often does your SQL Server go down during the day when everyone wants to access the data? Do you spend most of your time being a "report monkey" for your coworkers and bosses? *SQL Server System Administration* helps you keep data consistently available to your users. This book omits introductory information. The authors don't spend time explaining queries and how they work. Instead, they focus on the information you can't get anywhere else, like how to choose the correct replication topology and achieve high availability of information.

Internet Information Services Administration

By Kelli Adam, et. al.
1st Edition Winter 2000
300 pages, $29.99
ISBN: 0-7357-0022-2

Are the new Internet technologies in Internet Information Server giving you headaches? Does protecting security on the Web take up all of your time? Then this is the book for you. With hands-on configuration training, advanced study of the new protocols in IIS, and detailed instructions on authenticating users with the new Certificate Server and implementing and managing the new e-commerce features, *Internet Information Server Administration* gives you the real-life solutions you need. This definitive resource also prepares you for the release of Windows 2000 by giving you detailed advice on working with Microsoft Management Console, which was first used by IIS.

SMS 2 Administration

By Michael Lubanski and Darshan Doshi
1st Edition Winter 2000
350 pages, $39.99
ISBN: 0-7357-0082-6

Microsoft's new version of its Systems Management Server (SMS) is starting to turn heads. Although complex, it allows administrators to lower their total cost of ownership and more efficiently manage clients, applications, and support operations. So if your organization is using or implementing SMS, you'll need some expert advice. Darshan Doshi and Michael Lubanski can help you get the most bang for your buck, with insight, expert tips, and real-world examples. Darshan and

Michael are consultants specializing in SMS, having worked with Microsoft on one of the most complex SMS rollouts in the world, involving 32 countries, 15 languages, and thousands of clients.

UNIX/Linux Titles

Solaris Essential Reference
By John Mulligan
1st Edition Spring 1999
350 pages, $19.99
ISBN: 0-7357-0023-0

Looking for the fastest, easiest way to find the Solaris command you need? Need a few pointers on shell scripting? How about advanced administration tips and sound, practical expertise on security issues? Are you looking for trustworthy information about available third-party software packages that will enhance your operating system? Author John Mulligan—creator of the popular Unofficial Guide to Solaris Web site (sun.icsnet.com)—delivers all that and more in one attractive, easy-to-use reference book. With clear and concise instructions on how to perform important administration and management tasks and key information on powerful commands and advanced topics, *Solaris Essential Reference* is the book you need when you know what you want to do and only need to know how.

Linux System Administration
By M Carling, et. al.
1st Edition Summer 1999
450 pages, $29.99
ISBN: 1-56205-934-3

As an administrator, you probably feel that most of your time and energy is spent in endless firefighting. If your network has become a fragile quilt of temporary patches and work-arounds, this book is for you. For example, have you had trouble sending or receiving email lately? Are you looking for a way to keep your network running smoothly with enhanced performance? Are your users always hankering for more storage, more services, and more speed? *Linux System Administration* advises you on the many intricacies of maintaining a secure, stable system. In this definitive work, the author addresses all the issues related to system administration, from adding users and managing file permissions, to Internet services and Web hosting, to recovery planning and security. This book fulfills the need for expert advice that will ensure a trouble-free Linux environment.

GTK+/Gnome Application Development
By Havoc Pennington
1st Edition
492 pages, $39.99
ISBN: 0-7357-0078-8

This title is for the reader who is conversant with the C programming language and UNIX/Linux development. It provides detailed and solution-oriented information designed to meet the needs of programmers and application developers using the GTK+/Gnome libraries. Coverage complements existing GTK+/Gnome documentation, going into more depth on pivotal issues such as uncovering the GTK+ object system, working with the event loop, managing the Gdk substrate, writing custom widgets, and mastering GnomeCanvas.

Developing Linux Applications with GTK+ and GDK
By Eric Harlow
1st Edition
400 pages, $34.99
ISBN: 0-7357-0214-7

We all know that Linux is one of the most powerful and solid operating systems in existence. And as the success of Linux grows, there is an increasing interest in developing applications with graphical user interfaces that take advantage of the power of Linux. In this book, software developer Eric Harlow gives you an indispensable development handbook focusing on the GTK+ toolkit. More than an overview of the elements of application or GUI design, this is a hands-on book that delves deeply into the technology. With in-depth material on the various GUI programming tools and loads of examples, this book's unique focus will give you the information you need to design and launch professional-quality applications.

Linux Essential Reference
By Ed Petron
1st Edition Winter 2000
400 pages, $24.95
ISBN: 0-7357-0852-5

This book is all about getting things done as quickly and efficiently as possible by providing a structured organization to the plethora of available Linux information. We can sum it up in one word—value. This book has it all: concise instructions

on how to perform key administration tasks, advanced information on configuration, shell scripting; hardware management, systems management, data tasks, automation, and tons of other useful information. All of this coupled with an unique navigational structure and a great price. This book truly provides groundbreaking information for the growing community of advanced Linux professionals.

Lotus Notes and Domino Titles

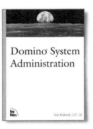

Domino System Administration
By Rob Kirkland
1st Edition
880 pages, $49.99
ISBN: 1-56205-948-3

Your boss has just announced that you will be upgrading to the newest version of Notes and Domino when it ships. As a Premium Lotus Business Partner, Lotus has offered a substantial price break to keep your company away from Microsoft's Exchange Server. How are you supposed to get this new system installed, configured, and rolled out to all your end users? You understand how Lotus Notes works—you've been administering it for years. What you need is a concise, practical explanation of the new features and how to make some of the advanced stuff work smoothly. You need answers and solutions from someone like you, who has worked with the product for years and understands what you need to know. *Domino System Administration* is the answer—the first book on Domino that attacks the technology at the professional level, with practical, hands-on assistance to get Domino running in your organization.

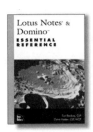

Lotus Notes and Domino Essential Reference

By Dave Hatter
and Tim Bankes
1st Edition
500 pages, $45.00
ISBN: 0-7357-0007-9

You're in a bind because you've been asked to design and program a new database in Notes for an important client that will keep track of and itemize a myriad of inventory and shipping data. The client wants a user-friendly interface without sacrificing speed or functionality. You are experienced (and could develop this application in your sleep) but feel that you need to take your talents to the next level. You need something to facilitate your creative and technical abilities, something to perfect your programming skills. The answer is waiting for you: *Lotus Notes and Domino Essential Reference*. It's compact and simply designed. It's loaded with information. All of the objects, classes, functions, and methods are listed. It shows you the object hierarchy and the relationship between each one. It's perfect for you. Problem solved.

Networking Titles

Cisco Router Configuration & Troubleshooting

By Mark Tripod
1st Edition
300 pages, $34.99
ISBN: 0-7357-0024-9

Want the real story on making your Cisco routers run like a dream? Why not pick up a copy of *Cisco Router Configuration & Troubleshooting* and see what Pablo Espinosa and Mark Tripod have to say? They're the

folks responsible for making some of the largest sites on the Net scream, like Amazon.com, Hotmail, USAToday, Geocities, and Sony. In this book, they provide advanced configuration issues, sprinkled with advice and preferred practices. You won't see a general overview on TCP/IP. They talk about more meaty issues, like security, monitoring, traffic management, and more. In the troubleshooting section, the authors provide a unique methodology and lots of sample problems to illustrate. By providing real-world insight and examples instead of rehashing Cisco's documentation, Pablo and Mark give network administrators information they can start using today.

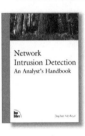

Network Intrusion Detection: An Analyst's Handbook

By Stephen Northcutt
1st Edition
360 pages, $39.99
ISBN: 0-7357-0868-1

Get answers and solutions from someone who has been in the trenches. Author Stephen Northcutt, original developer of the Shadow intrusion detection system and former Director of the United States Navy's Information System Security Office at the Naval Security Warfare Center, gives his expertise to intrusion detection specialists, security analysts, and consultants responsible for setting up and maintaining an effective defense against network security attacks.

Understanding Data Communications, Sixth Edition
By Gilbert Held
6th Edition
500 pages, $39.99
ISBN: 0-7357-0036-2

Updated from the highly successful
Fifth Edition, this book explains how
data communications systems and their
various hardware and software components work. Not an entry-level book,
it approaches the material in textbook
format, addressing the complex issues
involved in internetworking today.
A great reference book for the
experienced networking professional,
this offering was written by the noted
networking authority Gilbert Held.

Other Books By New Riders

Riders We Want to Know What You Think

To better serve you, we would like your opinion on the content and quality of this book. Please complete this card and mail it to us or fax it to 317-581-4663.

Name _____

Address _____

City_____State_____Zip _____

Phone _____

Email Address _____

Occupation _____

Operating system(s) that you use _____

What influenced your purchase of this book?
- ❑ Recommendation
- ❑ Table of Contents
- ❑ Magazine Review
- ❑ New Riders' Reputation
- ❑ Cover Design
- ❑ Index
- ❑ Advertisement
- ❑ Author Name

How would you rate the contents of this book?
- ❑ Excellent
- ❑ Good
- ❑ Below Average
- ❑ Very Good
- ❑ Fair
- ❑ Poor

How do you plan to use this book?
- ❑ Quick Reference
- ❑ Classroom
- ❑ Self-Training
- ❑ Other

What do you like most about this book?
Check all that apply.
- ❑ Content
- ❑ Accuracy
- ❑ Listings
- ❑ Index
- ❑ Price
- ❑ Writing Style
- ❑ Examples
- ❑ Design
- ❑ Page Count
- ❑ Illustrations

What do you like least about this book?
Check all that apply.
- ❑ Content
- ❑ Accuracy
- ❑ Listings
- ❑ Index
- ❑ Price
- ❑ Writing Style
- ❑ Examples
- ❑ Design
- ❑ Page Count
- ❑ Illustrations

What would be a useful follow-up book to this one for you?_____

Where did you purchase this book? _____
_____

Can you name a similar book that you like better than this one, or one that is as good? Why?
_____
_____

How many New Riders books do you own? _____

What are your favorite computer books?_____
_____

What other titles would you like to see us develop? _____
_____

Any comments for us? _____
_____
_____
_____

Windows 2000 Professional 0-7357-0950-5

www.newriders.com   •   Fax   317-581-4663

Fold here and tape to mail

Place
Stamp
Here

New Riders Publishing
201 W. 103rd St.
Indianapolis, IN 46290

New Riders How to Contact Us

Visit Our Web Site

`www.newriders.com`

On our Web site you'll find information about our other books, authors, tables of contents, indexes, and book errata.

Email Us

Contact us at this address:

`nrfeedback@newriders.com`

- If you have comments or questions about this book
- To report errors that you have found in this book
- If you have a book proposal to submit or are interested in writing for New Riders
- If you would like to have an author kit sent to you
- If you are an expert in a computer topic or technology and are interested in being a technical editor who reviews manuscripts for technical accuracy

`nrfeedback@newriders.com`

- To find a distributor in your area, please contact our international department at this address.

`nrmedia@newriders.com`

- For instructors from educational institutions who wish to preview New Riders books for classroom use. Email should include your name, title, school, department, address, phone number, office days/hours, text in use, and enrollment in the body of your text, along with your request for desk/examination copies and/or additional information.

Write to Us

New Riders Publishing

201 W. 103rd St.

Indianapolis, IN 46290-1097

Call Us

Toll-free (800) 571-5840 + 9 +4511

If outside U.S. (317) 581-3500. Ask for New Riders.

Fax Us

(317) 581-4663